ACRES
OF
OAK

ACRES
OF
OAK

A PASTOR RETHINKS CHURCH
IN THE
21ST CENTURY

RICHARD R. KURRASCH

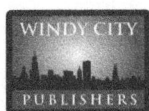

WINDY CITY
PUBLISHERS

ACRES OF OAK
A PASTOR RETHINKS CHURCH IN THE 21ST CENTURY

Scripture quotations are from the Revised Standard Version of the Bible, copyright © 1946, 1952, and 1971
National Council of the Churches of Christ in the United States of America.
Used by permission. All rights reserved worldwide.

Please contact publisher for permission to make copies of any part of this work.

Windy City Publishers
www.windycitypublishers.com

Printed in the United States of America

ISBN:
978-1-953294-34-0

Library of Congress Control Number:
2022922983

WINDY CITY PUBLISHERS
CHICAGO

Dedicated to

Ann Marie Kurrasch

A very modern Sarah who laughed
when the Universe said to go,
journeying with her peripatetic Abraham
to the undisclosed places anyway,
there to thrive.

CONTENTS

FOREWORD

THESE PAGES CHRONICLE A LIFETIME of pastoral service in and to the church. Its seeds were planted in my childhood, which I gratefully acknowledge in the opening chapter, but the story itself begins in 1968 when, my wife of two weeks at my side, I started seminary, and it concludes more than fifty years later on a song of thanksgiving and gratitude...and with a lingering question that has haunted me from the beginning.

The song of thanksgiving has its roots in my good fortune of having been born a Boomer. Through nothing more than the happenstance of birth, the Boomer generation (1946–1964) enjoyed a period of unparalleled prosperity and opportunity, at least for White Americans. In every respect, ours has been a privileged generation and inevitably, as the leading edge of that generation gradually passes its mantle to those coming behind, we take stock of our legacy. Never easy or especially welcome, self-assessment requires just the right reference point, the standard against which we might measure how we have done. Given our inheritance, compared to what—or to whom—do we take stock of our stewardship?

Living all these years with the church, the words and ways of Jesus are the inescapable lens through which the assessment begins and typically stalls for me. An imposing standard, I find that it looms even larger at the journey's end. For good reason, most of us choose not to run our lives through the template of Jesus' own life, but we who do sign on cannot entirely avoid asking how we look under his gaze. In the words of an upcoming chapter, both individually and corporately has *our mission* matched *his message*? Coupled with a remarkable gift in social capital we received from our own elders, what will those whose elders we have now become say about the gift we in turn pass on to them?

Such questions acknowledge that faith has consequences, what I call the "Now What?" or the "So What?" of faith. But how far do we need to take our faith; how seriously do we need to live it? This radical thought, that faith emerges as faithfulness, was first awakened in me as an undergraduate at the university and has stayed with me unresolved for more than half a century.

Some might register surprise that the church can awaken thoughts of any kind, or at least of the interesting kind. As some say of flying airplanes (hours of boredom punctuated with moments of sheer terror), I have found life in the church sometimes tedious and occasionally quite dismaying, but faith communities do also have their moments, aiming high and giving voice and witness to what is noble about the human odyssey. Along the way, its vicissitudes notwithstanding, an intangible quality emerges that makes its people, well, *different*…a very radical thought I dare to tackle at the end.

Because it opens a variety of doors into what we euphemistically call the human condition, wherein we find both a reason for hope and a cause for despair, ministry is hard work, but setting the challenges aside, because we speak at least *about* God, if not at times *for* God and when the situation demands it *to* God, ministry is first and foremost a privilege of the highest order. It takes courage to pick up that mantle and humility (our only protection against the arrogance of imagining one can even speak about, for, and to God in the first place) to continue. Admittedly, sometimes the whole enterprise feels rather pointless, like standing on the shore and shouting into the howling wind expecting to be heard…and heeded, and such moments for me do find their way into the pages that follow, but I trust the larger gift, the privilege of ministry, puts them in their proper perspective.

As will quickly become evident, I grew up and spent the major portion of my ministry as a Congregationalist. I have journeyed elsewhere in the Protestant family and am grateful at journey's end for the Christian Church (Disciples of Christ) where I very comfortably have my standing, but as the twig is bent, so is the tree inclined, and my "bent" toward my Congregational heritage remains dominant. That particularity—some might say that *peculiarity*—needs some explanation because it lies at the heart of my understanding of the church and its ministry, and I include that explanation here rather than scatter it throughout what follows lest it unnecessarily clutter the narrative. Having seen it once, interested readers will know where to find the allusion again if interested.

It almost—*almost*—goes without saying that churches fight and split for any number of reasons, like the person of Jesus (divine-human-both?), the authority of the Bible (*the* Book or *a* book?), the nature of salvation (see "person of Jesus"), and the purpose of the church (see all the above). The role of women, gender, and sexual orientation when it comes to ordination, and the availability of contraceptives and abortion are all guaranteed to start a church fight somewhere. Does theocracy pose a threat or an opportunity; is there too much or too little religion in politics; is there too much or too little politics in religion; is a "Christian Democrat" or a "Christian Republican" an oxymoron or a redundancy—the list and its answers are nearly endless, as the plethora of denominations and sects testify.

Pictured as a tree, these theological arguments and ecclesiastical schisms have created a distressing number of branches into which the church has divided over the centuries. In the hands of his followers, the seamless robe of Christ (John 19.23) has not fared well, and most serious theologies would consider this a scandal within the church and a source of confusion to the wider community. While not ignoring the Roman Catholic and Orthodox ruptures, the plethora of Protestant churches themselves suggests the 16th century Protestant Reformation started something it never finished, perhaps never could finish, pointing instead to an ongoing Protestant Re-formation.

Addressing the many incarnations into which the one church of Christ has morphed and capitalizing on where we might cooperate across doctrinal differences is the domain of ecumenism, and for much of the 20th century, ecumenism, or the Ecumenical Movement as it was called, promoted organic mergers. In 1957, one such merger created the United Church of Christ (UCC) from two denominational bodies, the General Council of the Congregational Christian Churches and the Evangelical and Reformed (E&R) Church. Actually, four historic communions—the Congregational National Council and the Christian General Convention having organized in 1931 as the General Council and the Evangelical Church and the Reformed Church having merged as the E&R Church—became one (organic) church (the UCC). For good reason does the UCC see itself metaphorically as a rope with four strands woven together, the whole different from and greater than any of its parts. Today, the UCC is one of the larger as well as one of the most theologically and socially liberal mainline Protestant denominations in America.

In one sense, the General Council of the Congregational Christian Churches was not a church at all but an umbrella and a bureaucracy which maintained an ecclesiastical structure and provided resources and services to its member churches. Under its aegis, for example, and a system of Conferences and Associations, ministers were trained, standards for ordination and other forms of professional recognition were developed and administered, and a pension system was maintained. The General Council developed mission programs and Sunday School curricula, promoted interchurch-ecumenical relationships, and administered the denomination's overall witness (evangelical and social).

The General Council certainly looked like a church and acted like a church, but unlike the Evangelical and Reformed Church (a single entity with many congregations that came into the new denomination as a single entity), the General Council had no churches to bring to the union. It had patrons (members), but the patrons (churches) practiced the Congregational tradition of local church autonomy. Dating to New England Puritanism, and beyond that to England, they took Jesus quite literally where he says that when the two or three gather together in his name, he is there as well (Matt. 18.20). The implications are profound, for where he and his people gather, there is the church as well, complete and sufficient unto itself and in need of no earthly mediator or overarching umbrella to legitimize its existence, define its doctrine, prescribe its mission or purpose, or dictate its practices. The local church is free and autonomous, though not independent. This latter distinction is critical for autonomous, local churches are obligated to be in fellowship with other autonomous, local churches. In this context, an independent Congregational church is an oxymoron.

This may sound like the kind of ecclesiastical minutia that along with White Christian nationalism drives people out of churches, but it bears on the narrative that follows because in the period leading up to the 1957 creation of the United Church of Christ, the General Council found itself in something of a dilemma: yes, it was ready to join the new denomination, but what about the churches? After all, local, autonomous Congregational churches were bound together by the covenantal bonds of fellowship, and they could only follow their national denominational entity into the new denomination if and when the members of the local church voted to do so. Now, as a matter of fact, in the end a large majority of local Congregational churches did vote to align with the new body...but not all. Reportedly, as many as 1,000 churches from the "old" denomination (the General Council) chose not to join the "new" denomination (the UCC). In some cases, the issue was so contentious at the local level that the congregation voted not to vote at all rather than take a vote and risk splitting the church, although many of those churches and their ministers would maintain a working relationship with the UCC (particularly when the church called a minister or a minister sought a new position).

A large share of those that voted not to join the new denomination tended to gravitate in one of two directions. A group of theologically conservative churches formed the Conservative Congregational Christian Conference (the "4-Cs") which continues to this day with a rigid Evangelical creed. Anticipating a successful merger, other churches formed in 1955 the National Association of Congregational Christian Churches (NACCC or "NA" for short). At its peak, it numbered some 500 member churches. My home church, the Congregational Church of the Messiah in Los Angeles, was one such member.

The merger was for many a battle bitterly fought and when the smoke cleared, long-standing relationships were often among the casualties, so those votes to reject the UCC could only have been taken in response to a deeply felt issue. That issue was the question of how the new church would be governed. At the time, many feared that the new denomination would centralize power in a Presbyterian polity and so exercise authority over the local churches and the clergy. The mere prospect of an ecclesiastical bureaucracy doing the work properly belonging to the local church so violated the legacy of New England Congregationalism (the icons of which are the Pilgrims, though the Puritans gave the movement its definitive shape) that many chose schism over acquiescence when it came to their faith community.

In retrospect, the fears of a centralized ecclesiastical bureaucracy directing the local church from "headquarters" never materialized. In fact, it has been noted that the real beneficiaries in the merger were the Evangelical and Reformed congregations that gained a measure of local church autonomy not previously available. The Conferences and Associations do have rather stringent requirements for the preparation, recognition, and ordination of ministers and the employment process generally, as does the Christian Church (Disciples of Christ) by the way, and admittedly, this does give Committees on Ministry at the Conference level the prerogatives of the Gatekeeper, the power of which clergy ignore to their peril. Whether this step subsequently constitutes a veiled and more subtle form of headquarters pulling the strings or merely illustrates covenantal theology in action (Congregational polity linking autonomous churches together in the spirit of the free affection of fellowship) is a matter of perspective. I can only say that I have worked with UCC ministers and churches my entire career and I have not detected any serious diminishment in the prerogatives of a Congregational polity for local churches in the UCC.

This is not to say, of course, that the merger creating the United Church of Christ was inconsequential, the only difference between NA and UCC congregations being the name on the door. Obviously, it gave birth to a new denomination under which the vast majority of the churches and most of the human and economic resources and such instrumentalities as schools, campgrounds, and mission programs gathered. Recalling the metaphor of the rope, these resources provided the fuel, the raw material, with which the four historical traditions would weave themselves together, creating a single entity, an entirely new and different entity.

As with any merger, though, something is gained and something is lost. As noted, from the perspective of the UCC, much was gained, indeed, but on the other side, for those who fought a bitter and losing battle, the focus fell not on what four historical traditions might create together but on what might be left behind along the way. For them, it was not just a form of church governance (congregational, local church autonomy and its corollary, the fellowship of the churches) that was at issue. By itself, such a parochial emphasis on mere polity would have been unworthy of the intellectual and theological depth they brought to the table. Rather, they saw slipping from their grasp something far more nuanced, a vigorous, intellectually demanding, and personally challenging engagement with Protestant Christianity that was the legacy of New England Puritanism and modern theological liberalism.

Those who fought this battle, clergy and laity alike, came largely from the generation immediately senior to mine, but they reflect a cultural setting and especially a form of education that seem much older. Urbane and erudite, they were the beneficiaries of three hundred years of the Enlightenment and were fully steeped in its history, philosophy, and literature. They appreciated the distinction between covenantal commitment and creedal conformity as the animating principle of congregational life. They trusted that the result would leave its inevitable and appropriate imprint on the social order. Nuanced, sophisticated, intellectually viable, and built upon a free church foundation that placed its attendant demands and responsibilities on the local congregation, it was indeed a "church without bishops in a land without kings." How might such a theology of church fare in a new, organic, potentially authoritarian structure (or at least the perceived possibility for a centralized authoritarian structure)? This was their inevitable question, and their doubts fueled their opposition to finding out.

In truth, such a church (intellectually and theologically liberal in the best sense of the term) might have "slipped away" with or without the merger. Over the last half-century, one can hardly say that it did so well in the National Association, and had the General Council continued, we might well have found a similar outcome as has prevailed in all the mainline denominations. Having done so well for two decades following World War II, these denominations have experienced long-term decline ever since, and there is no reason to presume that the member churches of the General Council and its related Conferences and Associations would have fared any better.

Unlike those of the generation senior to mine, I never bore any animosity toward the United Church of Christ. Perhaps my elders had just lost too much, for the new denomination gathered not just friends and colleagues unto itself but also career opportunities and the array of resources noted above, the colleges and seminaries and church camps and pension plans—in short, everything but those initial 1,000 or so churches, many of which eventually found their way there anyway.

That sting, while understood mentally, was not felt in quite the same way emotionally as my generation came along. I always enjoyed good relationships with UCC clergy and their churches; we worked together in community ministerial associations and projects; and I especially appreciated the prophetic voice by which the UCC regularly called our attention to issues of social justice in the public square. True, that voice may have come from denominational structures and not the local churches for whom such pronouncements were often irritating, frequently divisive, and certainly not binding, but it was there in the public arena nonetheless.

As the evangelical churches and their conservative social agenda gained increasing media prominence in the latter quarter of the 20th century and especially as the right wing of the Republican Party coopted the Evangelical and Fundamentalist churches for its political purposes, the lonely voice of the United Church of Christ crying in the wilderness became all the more critical. There were others, of course (notably, the Episcopal Church), and a handful of national figures spoke courageously from flagship pulpits, but for a down-in-the-trenches, faithful prophetic witness over time, credit goes to the UCC.

Alas, during this same period, the National Association actually took deliberate steps to stifle, if not silence, the prophetic voice at its Annual Meetings and through its governing structures and publications and their spokespersons. In all fairness, this stemmed in part from a zealous adherence to a rigid form of Congregational polity which recognized the absolute authority of the local church. No person or agency external to the "two or three" gathered in

Jesus' Name had or could pretend to assume the prerogative of speaking for the churches on any matter of faith and practice. Drawing conclusions about religious dogma and its implications for society's sins resided with individual churches and members.

Fair enough, but even if resolutions asking the assembly to express its voice on social justice issues could and would not be brought to the floor of an Annual Meeting, there was nothing to prohibit the assembly from *discussing* such issues—nothing, that is, except that it never happened. Lost was the subtle distinction between speaking *for* the churches and speaking *to* the churches. Unfortunately, the church's silence is itself a form of speech that, failing to question why things are or to lift up a vision of what might be, indirectly voices support for the status quo. That may well be the work of the local church but without the encouragement of the fellowship at large, the local congregation may not find its voice and so lose a critical element of its vocation. Thinking that the Annual Meeting was a family reunion, not a political brawl, we tended to forget that the "autonomy of the local church" was only half of the Congregational mantra and that what followed was equally important and binding...the "fellowship of the churches" where mutual care, counsel, and even admonition properly belonged.

For politically and socially liberal ministers serving politically (and often socially) conservative congregations, this took considerable finesse. In later years, a few diehards formed the Washington Gladden Society, named for a Congregationalist and one of the earliest and most important leaders of the so-called Social Gospel Movement (prominent from about 1870-1920), but by then a creeping ossification was working its way through the NA's structure, sucking the much needed oxygen of renewal out of the air, and so while offering a helpful corrective, the Washington Gladden Society never played much of a role in NA affairs, and it certainly had no significant impact on defining or helping to define a purpose for a denominational structure in a rapidly changing cultural context. A means to an end, Congregational polity was uniquely positioned to respond to such a social climate; it might easily have channeled into the life of our wider fellowship the creative energy of a restless generation (the Boomers), intent on making a difference in the body politic (believing that it could make a difference until their own ossification set in) but unfortunately, the polity became an end in itself, the NA its defender and protector lest the tendency of denominational centralization continue its relentless encroachment.

As the end of the century approached, the NA found itself in something of an existential crisis. The fervor of the merger battle had given the fledgling fellowship its purpose, but subsequent generations of clergy had come into leadership positions not having lived that battle. Its energy having begun to dissipate, the need for an evolving purpose took on greater and greater urgency: what would fill the void—or more to the point, what would be permitted to fill the void?

At the national level, the executive leaders and the elected members of the Association's governing structure began to wrestle with an answer to that question and over a period of five years their pooled creativity developed a plan to restructure the national fellowship. The idea was to identify and direct resources to shared goals, but the plan was subsequently dismissed as a "sociological solution to a theological problem" (an insult to the scores of clergy and lay leaders who had worked on this project). Even a proposed agency to recognize ministerial standing (and its termination where necessary) was repudiated at the national level on the grounds that it violated the prerogatives of the local church. This had the effect of leaving the local church at the mercy of clergy against whom serious allegations of malfeasance had been leveled and not resolved as well as candidates presenting themselves to search committees from other traditions not properly vetted. It's one thing to defend local church autonomy from creeping ecclesiastical bureaucracies, but not to recognize at the same time the role of such structures to serve the covenantal obligations of autonomous churches in fellowship with one another is by another name a dereliction of duty.

For thirty years, I served churches affiliated with the National Association and during that period, I had the opportunity to serve in a variety of leadership positions at the NA level as well, including a four-year term on its Executive

Committee (1992-96). My term overlapped with most of the five-year process to restructure our national Fellowship and that monumental effort had resulted in a proposal that would come to the floor at the 1996 Annual Meeting; as chair of the Executive Committee that year, it was my responsibility to present the proposal to the delegates and moderate the discussion before the delegates would vote on its fate. In the end, they voted to reject it.

At the time, I wrote a rather detailed post-mortem on that vote—now, a quarter-century later, it scarcely seems to matter. Some said that in later years elements of the proposal were adopted, so not all was lost, but I must acknowledge that having witnessed firsthand so much hard work so cavalierly dismissed took much of the remaining wind out of my NA sails, and a few years later I left the fellowship altogether for, of all things, a United Methodist Church on Maui.

Back on the Mainland and finding myself in a rather dubious, not to mention precarious, position vis-à-vis a National Association church (that episode gets its own chapter), I learned that Thomas Wolfe was right, you really can't go home again. Having dallied with the Methodists didn't help but if there was reason to leave in the first place, there was hardly reason to expect its reversal upon my return. The Greek philosopher Heraclitus observed twenty-five centuries ago that "no man ever steps in the same river twice, for it's not the same river and he's not the same man." In other words, things change: I was different; the NA was different. With time, differences do not necessarily magnify, but the river had flowed on and stepping into those waters once again, I did not find the makings of a new homecoming. Like a certain prodigal must have discovered, one leaves home for the far country to his or her peril (Luke 15.11–32).

At the same time, some things—or at least one thing—had not changed: that I remained very much a Congregationalist, for then as now, I still believe in the integrity of the laity, the authority of the congregation, and the completeness of the two or three under God. Only as a Congregationalist did I learn to cherish the genius of covenant, to value the power of more truth and light, to recognize the place for—and the danger of—councils and creeds, and to appreciate the distinction between fellowship and denomination. As a Congregationalist, I experienced the glory of the ministry, the allure of freedom, the necessity of responsibility, and the importance of mission.

All this, of course, is hardly an end in itself but a means to an end. Like the experiment first instilled in our Hebrew forebears, the people of God called church serve a higher purpose, a principled calling: to bring "light to the nations" (Isaiah 42.6; John 8.12) as disclosed in the person of Jesus. Very quickly would a community gather around him, a people living into his words and ways, Heralds and Sign Bearers pointing to nothing less than a new age.

Certainly when it comes to the people called church, Jesus deserves better than what he gets, but the noble experiment called church persists nonetheless. Ever the challenge, hearing—and responding to—the challenge. May the people called church seize that summons, for never in the history of the human saga has there been a time when the whole of creation has so needed the church at its best. It has been my privilege to see such a church in the people with whom I have lived as their pastor. Had they had a better pastor, think what we might have done!

Richard R. Kurrasch
Arroyo Grande, California
January 20, 2022

ACKNOWLEDGMENTS

EXCEPT WHERE NOTED, MY EXTENSIVE use of the Bible draws from the Revised Standard Version (RSV). Biblical scholarship and an enhanced library of biblical manuscripts resulted in what is generally recognized as a superior, if not currently the single best, English translation of the Bible, the New Revised Standard Version (NRSV). Since its publication in 1989, I used the NRSV almost exclusively in my pastoral work, but when it came to my memoir, I returned to the version of my early years. Perhaps we all prefer the translation that first shaped our spiritual journey, the language so familiar and comfortable…if not comforting. Perhaps similar feelings explain why so many families would ask me to read from the venerable King James version when selecting passages for funerals and other special occasions. I distinguish translations of the Bible from its many popular paraphrases which, while easier to the ear, lack the rigor of good scholarship and frequently carry the theological bias of their creator. These certainly have a place in Bible studies and for illustrative purposes in sermons where context and meaning can be examined in some detail, but spiritual formation is serious business and needs and deserves the best available tools.

Readers may discern my deep appreciation for Clarence Jordan and his remarkable witness as told in the Koinonia Farm Experiment. His biblical scholarship takes shape as the *Cotton Patch Version* of various, though not all, books of the New Testament (a project cut short by his untimely death). I asked Koinonia Farm for permission to use the Cotton Patch text which was freely given. Along with proper citation of the books, they asked only that if opportunity presented itself, I might mention that Koinonia Farm is still around today and include the website, koinoniafarm.org.

I routinely included what I called "thought pieces" in the Sunday bulletin. These were short quotations that presumably had something to do with the theme of the approaching worship hour but even if not obvious, they also helped focus the worshiper's attention (as Paul advised, Col. 3.2) on the "things that are above" and the various ingredients that nurture the pilgrim's lifelong journey to that end. If these quotations had anything in common it was a shared worthiness for the household refrigerator..."thought pieces" for the week. Over the years, I accumulated quite a collection from a variety of sources (religious and secular), including current books and articles and not infrequently, though quite freely, from colleagues' newsletter columns and perhaps a stray sermon that made the rounds. In keeping with the tradition, from that collection I picked some favorites to head each chapter.

Among the many privileges I have enjoyed in my life is sharing the journey with a gifted musician and composer, and in the still unfolding drama of our life together I include three of Ann Marie's pieces. They may be heard at her website, myheartsongmusic.com/acres-of-oak/.

I am indebted to and gladly acknowledge the responses I received from the very first readers of what was then a very different memoir, Carol and Jerry Walton, both UCC ministers, and from editor Ann Aubrey Hanson whose counsel proved pivotal long before it was ready for editing. The Cuesta College Central Coast Writer's Conference brought together a host of invaluable and experienced leaders to assist authors in writing and publishing their works through which I met and consulted with Literary Strategist Zoe Quinton whose insights were especially timely and helpful.

In its context, I cite my Doctor of Ministry Professional Project, "Crisis of Spirit: Implications from Schleiermacher for the Revitalization of the Local Church," listing specifically some of the theologians to whom I was and remain indebted as I pursued my doctoral degree and developed the thesis of my project, and I would include here my deep appreciation for three Claremont School of Theology faculty members from this period, Dr. Jack C. Verheyden, Dr. John B. Cobb, Jr., and Dr. Mary Elizabeth Moore, in whose classrooms I would gladly sit again.

I have the deepest gratitude and respect for Windy City Publishers, Lise Marinelli, President, WCP; Dawn McGarrahan Wiebe, Project Manager; and Ruth Beach, Editor. Their expertise, counsel, and patience were invaluable.

Aesthetica Society designed and developed over its several iterations the unique and striking cover.

CHAPTER I

IN THE BEGINNING
AND HOW IT BEGAN

"We're not human beings capable of spiritual experience.
In actuality we are spiritual beings having a human experience."

~PIERRE TEILHARD DE CHARDIN[1]

"It takes three things to attain a sense of significant being:
God, a Soul, and a Moment."

~RABBI ABRAHAM HESCHEL
in a speech to the first White House Conference on Aging in 1961

"It was a common saying among the Puritans,
'Brown bread and the Gospel is good fare.'"

~MATHEW HENRY
Commentary on Isaiah

ONE FINE SPRING DAY IN 1971, Ann and I boarded a plane at Chicago's
O'Hare Airport and, with a brief stop in Omaha, headed for Rapid City, South
Dakota, where we would be met by two members of the Search Committee
from Plymouth Congregational Christian Church in Chadron, Nebraska.
Before nightfall, we would have been introduced to a South Dakota Perfume
Factory, Rocky Mountain Oysters, and my future parishioners.

---

1. Popularly attributed to Pierre Teilhard de Chardin but variously attributed to Wayne Dyer,
Stephen Covey, Georges Gurdjieff, and even Anonymous (which could number in the hundreds if
paraphrases of the famous dictum are included). To whomever or wherever proper credit belongs,
the author is grateful for the perspective and, as here, has typically followed the popular choice.

1

I have often pondered which was the more astonishing, that Ann and I should find ourselves in the Nebraska panhandle or that I should find myself in the position of having parishioners at all, for by most any measure, I was an unlikely candidate for a church career. It's not that church was foreign to my family. Quite the contrary: in the same way that we went to school during the week, so did our family go to church on Sunday—so did everyone I knew—but while I developed an early interest in the liberal Protestant theology that defined the Congregational church of my youth, I cannot say that I had any interest in the church as such.

I had not even gone to church camp as a kid. I never thought much about what I had missed until I started hearing my colleagues share stories about their church camp experiences—definitive, transformative moments, it seemed to me, an outsider listening in—almost as if something of a prerequisite. I had gone to YMCA camp and worked for a day camp, but I don't remember church camp even discussed at church or home.

I might even have flunked Confirmation class except for a kind and gracious Sunday school teacher. We were to memorize the two Great Commandments and I had the idea down—something about loving God and then turning it around and loving our neighbors—but there were some qualifiers that had to do with how to love God and a footnote that brought our own selves into the mix. When the final exam came around, I got lost in those details, but she passed me anyway, and I became a full-fledged voting member of the Congregational Church of the Messiah, newly relocated from its former Los Angeles neighborhood to the burgeoning suburb of Westchester.

Maybe she felt a stronger connection with the church would do me some good. After all, Elvis had appeared on the scene by then and the future looked a little shaky and she would have remembered a certain Sunday morning when I was a member of her Third Grade Sunday school class (all boys, as if that mattered), and one day she walked through the door just in time to see her son and me escaping through the window. I remember neither the deed nor its consequences, but it must have made an impression on her because some forty years later, she reminded me of my flight for freedom, and while I would not want to press the point too far—at eight, crawling through an open window may mean nothing more than crawling through an open window—the event does have the character of a metaphor, for like the Sirens of Greek mythology luring sailors to shipwreck and death with enchanting music and seductive voices, the possibility of escaping the church's clutches did occasionally have a certain appeal.

She need not have worried, for soon thereafter, I asked my parents if I could skip Sunday school and remain in the sanctuary with them for the entire worship hour and listen to the sermon. Imagine that—a teenager wanting to listen to a tightly packed, cogently argued, and intellectually demanding discourse, all peppered with references to a supporting cast of philosophers and scientists. Certainly a big part of the reason a pastoral thread weaves its way through virtually the entirety of my adult life has to do with what I found attractive in the church as a youth—that the church asked big and important questions and dared to look far and wide for answers. The existential questions of life's meaning and purpose, why we are here and what happens next, what constitutes the good life and whether it matters how we live, what do we owe one another, if anything, why do we suffer and inflict the same on one another, where is God in the midst of all this and does God matter anyway—the usual conundrums, and what does faith have to say about any of it: I liked that. Little wonder that the church represented for me an intellectual and philosophical exercise of the mind and not a passionate, emotional expression of the heart. (Little wonder, I suppose, that I never heard about summer church camp in that erudite environment.)

In later years I would attempt to moderate, though with limited success, that false dichotomy in the spiritual quest, for religion does need both intellectual integrity and emotional passion to give it coherence and make it effective in this increasingly post-modern, globalized, and pluralistic world. Overly intellectualized, religion becomes dull and sterile, the stuff of books never read. At the same time, overly effusive, religion easily succumbs to fanaticism, the stuff that divides the human family into warring tribes, often with tragic consequences for individuals, congregations, and whole communities generally, and all three of the world's Abrahamic faiths struggle with its destructive impulses inadequately channeled.

All that seemed perfectly normal as the 1950s gave way to what would be a very different decade. Home-school-church were all of one piece for me, religion a comfortable part of the whole. True, we had a neighbor whose religion was a little "peculiar" in so far as rumor had it that he read his Bible on a regular basis. His son was one of my best friends and we played Little League Baseball together. He also had a daughter of whom I took frequent notice, but with a Bible-reading father nearby, I kept my glances to myself...and my Bible closed until seminary suggested otherwise. My intellectually respectable approach to the Protestant faith of my youth made room for the Bible too, but in church where it belonged and on Sunday when our minister announced his text for the morning's discourse.

I was born in 1946, one of the first of the Baby Boomers. My parents belonged to what the renown journalist Tom Brokaw called the Greatest Generation, those who had survived the Depression and won the war. Their generation emerged from the first half of the 20th century having endured years of privation and the scourge of world war and in the second half they helped to create and *share in* (emphasis added, so different from the appalling economic inequality that reigns today) a level of prosperity that in turn created and shaped the American middle class; among the institutions they planted in their neighborhoods were strong churches and good public school systems.

For mainline Protestantism,[2] the most vigorous period was the twenty years following World War II, and in those years these denominations could not build churches fast enough. By the mid-1960s, church attendance had peaked for most of them and there began a decline that started out slowly enough, but by the early years of the new century had reached crisis proportions. Many of the Boomer generation (those born between 1946 and 1964), for whom large,

---

2. More commonly known as the Mainline Church, the culturally defining 20th century Protestant denominations include (in their generic form) Congregational, Disciples of Christ, Episcopal, Lutheran, Methodist, and Presbyterian and Reformed congregations. Mergers and schisms have created a plethora of denominational names, some of which quite intentionally stand outside the "mainline" cluster, but they number about a dozen large, established, recognized church bodies.

dedicated Sunday school space was built, started dropping out of organized religion as soon as they left home; their children picked up the pace; and by the turn of the 21st century, American culture was well along the way to producing a second generation having no notion of church.

Had I been born as little as five years earlier or perhaps ten years later (the Trailing Edge Boomers of 1956–64), I might well have dismissed the church myself as anything other than the place that raised interesting philosophical and theological questions; certainly it would not have beckoned as a career. In 1964, I graduated from high school. That fall, I started my undergraduate work and had nothing more in mind than a vague notion of becoming a teacher and living on a boat in Southern California, a compelling version of a Beach Boys, endless California summer stretching into the indefinite future.

That good vision of the good life came about only because my family transplanted itself from the Midwest to Southern California. My parents were raised along the St. Croix Valley, one on the Wisconsin side and one on the Minnesota side. (The St. Croix River and surrounding countryside is one of the most scenic regions in the United States. I have visited it often and not infrequently longed to settle there.) With another world war on the horizon, my dad joined the Navy. He was aboard his ship in Pearl Harbor on December 7, 1941, and for nearly four years, the Pacific was his home.

After the war, he and my mother moved to Watertown, South Dakota, where my sister and I were born. It has been said that South Dakota's number one export was people, which certainly applied to us because in 1954, without a job in hand, my parents sold their home and most of their possessions, loaded the rest in a U-Haul trailer, hooked the trailer to a 1948 Plymouth, and moved our family to the Los Angeles suburb of Westchester.

I've often thought about that move: no job, no address, two children in the back seat (I was 8, my sister was 6). My career has involved several moves, some with children in the back seat, but except for one painful episode (and by then, our children were grown), I always had a job and an address at our next destination. Having survived the Depression and the war, my parents apparently thought the lack of a job was of little consequence in and of itself, and looking back at the dawn of what would prove to be a period of unprecedented American prosperity for middle-class families, one might conveniently conclude that their instincts were well-grounded, but I have a mental image of looking out the back window of our car and watching the canvas covering our trailer flapping in the breeze as we meandered down a two-lane highway to a new life in a new land. As an eight-year-old, what did I know? Children have no choice but to trust the adults in their world, but I know now that what they did in the summer of 1954 took backbone and courage and I honor them both for that.

It was a tough decision in another sense as well, for in those days, cutting ties geographically was tantamount to cutting ties permanently. With instantaneous internet communication, cheap phone service (our complaints notwithstanding, it is cheap), and a relatively inexpensive air and ground transportation network, geography is not nearly the impediment it once was in maintaining significant relationships, but all this is of recent origin. At that time, leaving the Upper Midwest for Los Angeles carried a pretty hefty price tag precisely because the electronic bridges did not exist and other bridges (like abundant, affordable, routine airplane transportation) were not widely available or utilized. Long distance phone calls were reserved for Christmas and birthdays—or communicating bad news—not staying in touch. The occasional summer vacation "back home" might help with rehearsing family folklore and remembering one's tribal stories, but it was no substitute for growing up and growing old in a community where family and friends lived in geographic proximity with one another.

The harsh reality was that packing up and heading West put families on different paths and over time those histories take us further and further apart. In the beginning, that may not especially matter, or seem to matter, but with time, I have come to realize that I have relatives who are and ever will be essentially strangers to me, as I am to them, and while I would never have had my parents revisit their decision to leave South Dakota for Los Angeles, the reality is that our decisions are always a mixed bag of consequences.

Of course, the flip side of what we leave behind is what we gain in the exchange, and at least at that time, California carried a certain mystic that was not unlike a religion. Like a city on a hill, the Golden State beckoned pilgrims to the new Promised Land with its glorious weather, its unlimited possibilities, and especially its prized freedom. Release from the prying eyes of nosy neighbors and families and emancipation from the stifling social mores and attitudes of small-town America appealed to many people, certainly to those who made the journey. They tasted firsthand the transformative California aura with its new ideas and relaxed attitudes and expanding horizons and as with religion generally, their "new birth" provided a more fertile field in which to cultivate their lives than would have been the case had they remained in the old world. As my dad said some years later, he didn't want my sister and me to grow up with the small-town mentality that had defined his and my mother's growing up years and that similarly prevailed in South Dakota at that time.

Like all immigrant peoples, they brought the "old world" culture and religion with them and as the 1950s gave way to the 1960s, and with the next generation coming of age, the marriage of old and new worlds often generated more heat than light. Certainly the new-world, California version appealed to many, but others often found it appalling (if not dangerous). Chicago's famed columnist Mike Royko, for example, once suggested that a fence be constructed around our fair state as a means of protecting the rest of the country from the debilitating influences of a sun-drenched culture.

Years later, Ann and I would move our family from California to the Detroit suburb of Royal Oak, and unlike the First Congregational Church that had just called me as its senior minister, the First Presbyterian Church had instructed its search committee not to consider any resumes from California applicants for the position of their senior minister. No sun-drenched, free spirits espousing the religion of California would compromise their pulpit, no way. Heeding both the spirit and the letter of their instruction, that church's next minister came from the opposite end of the country...just to be safe, I guess.

Whatever it might be called, however some might feel about it, coastal California was the life (we did not speak of "lifestyle" in those days) to which I aspired. The thought of going to seminary after my 1964 high school graduation was as unthinkable to me then as it would be shocking to my family and friends three years later, and yet, that is precisely what I did: I graduated from the Riverside campus of the University of California in the Spring 1968 and that fall started my seminary studies.

From the ethereal "religion" of California to the real-life, really lived religion of a Nebraska panhandle church is quite a leap, something approaching a cataclysmic shift in my personal space-time continuum even. That a call to ministry could even begin to stir and gain traction in my Beach Boys, California Dreaming enchantment and that I would discern its contours outlining a very different future is itself a wonder to behold, like standing on the edge of the Grand Canyon for the very first time.

Something like connecting the dots, it begins with coming to California in the first place but I begin with the simple phenomenon, the sheer happenstance, not to mention the good fortune, of coming of age in the '60s.

A notorious decade, the '60s, and violent. I started high school during President Kennedy's first year in office and graduated six months after he was assassinated. The assassinations of Martin Luther King, Jr. and Robert Kennedy were keynote addresses surrounding my graduation from the university. Shortly after I graduated from seminary and entered the real world of parish life, the Oglala Sioux and the FBI were shooting it out on the Pine Ridge Indian Reservation in South Dakota, and what was left of the spirit of the decade was soon to give up the ghost in what would prove to be President Nixon's personal Waterloo. Ever-present in the nation's consciousness and conversation, of course, was Vietnam, a foreign policy and military disaster that claimed some 58,000 American lives and an estimated 2–3 million Vietnamese.

But the violence and turmoil of those years was not defined by guns and bullets alone, for new-found freedoms from traditional cultural restraints released everyone from what had passed as "normal" behavior, and excesses of all kinds abounded. Some of it was of no great consequence except that it irritated normal people, things like long hair and an aversion to regular bathing, but much of it was serious. Beginning with alcohol, the widespread use of drugs proved to be and continues to be a plague upon our society. I limited my experimentation to beer. Certainly mind-expanding drugs (like LSD) had its proponents and marijuana its users, but I avoided the former as unsafe and the latter lest I got caught.

More generally, the 1960s challenged traditional morals and social and family values at all levels. I doubt we were ever an "Ozzie and Harriet," "Leave It to Beaver" culture where only "Father Knows Best," but popular radio and television programs of the post-World War II years certainly portrayed that mythology. Certainly, we wanted to believe in the simpler, more wholesome Norman Rockwell world, but a scant twenty years after the end of World War II, a new generation was beginning to notice that not all was well with the body politic.

Like the tip of an iceberg, the '60s stand out because they concentrated American attention on the unresolved, unseen, long-ignored and ever-simmering issues of war and peace, racism, and sexism. Environmental concerns were beginning to emerge in this time as well, although it would take Al Gore forcing the country to face "an inconvenient truth" in the 21st century to understand what was already at stake at the midpoint of the 20th century. Young men burned their draft cards and young women their bras, but these were but the visible signs of an invisible unrest demanding attention.

My generation responded, not because we were uniquely equipped with the mental and moral apparatus denied to humankind to that point but because we had both the luxury of time and the luxury of widespread, post-war prosperity to extend our adolescence from high school through undergraduate and (for many of us) graduate education. Whether we found it or took it, because we had the time and the financing, we certainly enjoyed the luxury of intellectual freedom. We were in the volatile place at the opportune time, and I continue to maintain a half-century later that the excesses notwithstanding, our response was a necessary and worthy catalyst for the ever-unfolding experiment that is American democracy, a catalyst in even greater demand today as we contend with the forces of populist nationalism.

I recognize, too, how hard this must have been on the generation that endured the Depression and won World War II. I think of my own parents: my father was 10 years old when the Great Depression started, just 22 and on a ship in Pearl Harbor at the start of World War II, and 26 when finally free to get on with his life. My mother was 5 years old at the start of the Depression and 22 when the two of them picked up their lives after the war and settled in South Dakota. Both were in their 30s when the family moved to Los Angeles. Ten years later they had moved into a new Orange County subdivision and were sending me to the University of California. Everything their generation went without my generation had, and then some, and there we were, their children, giving birth to a drug culture, the counterculture, and the Generation Gap.

People think of the '60s and picture Hippies, but of course, not all of us were Hippies. We may have "questioned authority" but we did not all "drop out" (certainly not those who would then be subject to the draft). We may have believed in peace and love, but not all of us descended on San Francisco in 1967 for the Summer of Love. We may have liked the music, but not all of us made the pilgrimage to Woodstock in 1969 to hear it.

The point is that quite apart from the visible and iconic, if not excessive, expressions that have since defined the mythology of the period, I find that I was as much a child of the '60s in my sixties and seventies as I was a child of the '60s in my teens and twenties. I did not march on Washington with Dr. Martin Luther King Jr. in 1963 when I was 17 years old, and I was not in Selma two years after that, but 45 years after the tragic shot was fired in Memphis, I still remember exactly where I was when America lost its prophet. I did not hear Peter, Paul, and Mary at the Lincoln Memorial in Washington, DC, as they moved the throngs with the music that shaped my generation, but Ann and I never missed hearing those and the other songs of the Movement when their summer tour brought them to metropolitan Detroit 30 years later—a religious experience in its own right.

In other words, the '60s were not just about an alternative to the '50s; more especially did they first awaken in me an awareness of the ethical or moral dimension that is built into the fabric of creation and so the foundation of human community as well. I cannot imagine never having heard of such in the church of my childhood and early teens, but only as an undergraduate attending the First Congregational Church, United Church of Christ, in Riverside, did the idea of social justice begin to register in my intellectual development.

Undoubtedly, much of the credit goes to the minister at the time, the Reverend Ernest Heeren. He was a pulpiteer of the old school who, with a fearless passion, addressed the intersection of religion and society…and still kept his job (as I would marvel over the years). It was a new message. To this point, I had thought of religion as essentially the personal, mostly private, encounter between God and one's own self. Faith was not so much an affair of the heart as of the mind, an intellectual exercise. Applications to the world were certainly implied, but drawing those conclusions were one's own responsibility, not that of the church, particularly when those applications touched upon social, political, and economic issues.

Not so with Ernie Heeren. He was of a stocky build as I recall and he once told of walking through the church office wearing a T-shirt and smoking a cigar, a visage of their pastor that apparently sent some of his older female parishioners' hearts aflutter. He professed not to understand why but of course he understood perfectly: even in the church—finally in the church, certainly in my experience of the church—change was in the air.

I did not know what to call it at the time, but in connecting a Gospel which I had not heard with the tumultuous world in which I lived, the fiery, passionate, outspoken, cigar-smoking minister of the Riverside congregation introduced me to that great gift from our Hebrew forebears, the prophetic voice. I shall have much more to say about that later, but an appreciative word is clearly in order here because attending this church during my formative undergraduate years served as something like an extended come-to-Jesus moment, a moment of truth with regard to the significance of faith. As I said, church was always a part of my family's life, and it never occurred to me that it would not have a role to play in my self-understanding, but making room in my life for the church and giving my life to the church reflect two vastly different concepts of the nature and purpose of the church, if not religion itself. The bridge from the former to the latter is the call whose seeds were most definitely nurtured by the times (the '60s) and the place (the undergraduate years at the University of California at Riverside).

But a time and a place do not a call make—it takes something more direct, more personal, less ambiguous. As the saying goes, many a preacher has been called to the ministry from the back of a plow, and with their belief in the priesthood of all believers, Protestants have always understood that each of us already has a ministry in and through the church. Elton Trueblood says it best, "If you are a Christian, you are a minister." In that respect, one need not have a special "calling" to the ministry to be a minister.

Far from toiling behind a plow, I remember taking an undergraduate course in Russian literature and actually receiving credit for sitting under a tree in the warm California sun reading Tolstoy and Dostoyevsky. Imagine, getting "paid" for reading great books. Had I not stumbled into the Riverside church, unquestionably a contributing factor in my call to the ministry, I might have spent my ministry as a public-school English teacher. A perfectly fine life it seemed to me (still does, actually). Like my high school English teacher, a foxy lady who drove a Studebaker Hawk in the days before the Mustang and Camaro, I would have instilled a deep appreciation for the proper placement of the comma and good literature, grading papers while sitting on the deck of my boat anchored at Newport Beach (as the mythology goes). I have no regrets (usually) for my choice, but it is a peculiar business (typically), claiming (in all humility) to speak for God.

Sometimes the seeming randomness of events can have the most far-reaching consequences. Why this should surprise us is itself surprising but maybe we need the luxury of time and the perspective it offers to recognize our interconnectedness not just with one another but with the entire creation. We may think of them as seemingly random—or at least inconsequential—events unrelated to much of anything else of great consequence, but out of countless such moments is a life lived.

In any event, one day one of my university roommates (a Baptist) and I had a religious discussion. I have no memory of why or how the topic surfaced, but the question on the table was all the peoples and all their civilizations who had existed before the time of Christ and so had no opportunity to hear and respond to his saving word and work. (We might have had Romans 10 in mind but short of some confirming evidence, such sophistication seems a little suspect to me.) At any rate, if salvation depended somehow on one having had some kind of encounter with the Savior, it looked pretty grim for the masses who had the misfortune to live before the Savior appeared with the gracious offer that would deliver them to a better place.

Not being able to resolve the dilemma ourselves, we appealed to a higher authority for some insight: namely, our respective pastors. At this point, I knew two ministers, Dr. Harry Butman of the Congregational Church of the Messiah in Westchester and Dr. Walter Vernon of the First Congregational Church of Anaheim. My parents had moved from Westchester to the City of Orange in Orange County and transferred their membership from the former to the latter. Both men were and would continue to be enormously important as I began to develop my own understanding of the church and its ministry. Sadly, tragically, forty years later we would have a falling out, a breach never repaired while we three were alive and now beyond repair since I alone remain.

That history a lifetime distant, we each wrote a letter to our respective pastors outlining our dilemma, and very quickly as I recall, I received a response. Time has erased both the letter from my files and any memory of its contents from my mind, and the resolution of the original dilemma for me would have to linger until some time later when I discovered what not even theological liberals seemed to entertain: the biblical warrant for universal salvation.

In an interconnected, relational universe, a seemingly random, or at least an apparently inconsequential event (like writing a letter, say) will necessarily connect to other seemingly random, at the time, apparently inconsequential events, and so here, for along with the letter came an invitation from my minister who offered to drive to Riverside and take me to lunch, which he did, and in the course of that lunch he asked, "Have you ever thought about the ministry?"

That was easy to answer: no! And in case there was any doubt, definitely no! Maybe there was so much else to think about. I enjoyed my focus in the Social Sciences and the Humanities and in retrospect I might rather have worked for an undergraduate degree in Philosophy (had I had the mettle at the time to pursue it). Because of my university experience, I have been a fierce advocate of that tragically endangered species, the Liberal Arts education (how will we ever achieve the more just society without the tools that make us more just and quite possibly human in the first place?). Racial justice, Vietnam, a certain co-ed… it turned out there was plenty to think about, including the church, apparently (I did write a letter, after all, and attended a university church to listen to its prophet nearly every week), but that I might play a part in the church and its ministry? Well, No.

To this day, I cannot say what prompted that question, or even taking the time to drive from Anaheim to Riverside to take me to lunch. When I was home for a weekend, I would attend Sunday services, but otherwise I took no part in the life of the Anaheim church. Yet, there he was, and the question lingered long after he left.

Well over a year later, it all came to a head, a resolution. I had a summer job at Douglas Aircraft Company working the swing shift as a Sheet Metal Burr. It was a terrible job (that earned me enough money to cover all my educational expenses the following school year—except dormitory expenses which my parents paid—and graduate debt-free, so I cannot complain too loudly), but it was hot and dirty and ever-so-boring, sitting in front of a high speed drill hour after hour removing the rough edge—the burr—from aluminum parts for DC-8 and DC-9 airplanes. Those planes are pretty much long gone from commercial service in the developed world today but for years, whenever I walked into one of those planes, I wondered if it bore some of my handiwork. How I wanted to sit in the left-hand seat in the cockpit.

One night, typically hot, ever so boring, my mind wandering about the universe, I turned to the question that I had examined from so many angles for so many months, never quite deciding one way or the other how to answer it, until I did, and as I did, hot and sweaty and covered in aluminum shards, I felt a sense of calm and peace, a benediction as it were. I had never heard of such persons, but when later I learned how John Wesley felt "his heart strangely warmed" in the reading of Luther's Preface to the Epistle to the Romans or Martin Luther's "Here I stand, I can do no other," refusing to recant his convictions when his church demanded such of him, that moment in an aircraft factory would once again come alive. It was the summer before my senior year.

I have wrestled from time to time with my call to ministry and I make no apologies for doing so. Quite the contrary, just as the Bible opens with a picture of God brooding over the stewpot of creation following the Big Bang, so might we mere mortals brood over the shape and meaning of our calling, possibly even its validity, lest we become complacent in our work and, dulled in spirit, lose our cutting edge. Besides, if you're doing your job, you will probably find yourself in some degree of warm-to-warming-to-hot-to-scalding water (and if not, the question is, why not), and in such moments, my brooding mind typically turns to Jeremiah.

We know Jeremiah as the weeping prophet because of his frequent complaints which he sent directly to the Source. "Lord," he whined, "you deceived me and I was deceived" (Jer. 17.7). Pretty strong language, but if Jeremiah could raise his laments and allegations heavenward and still find himself standing at the end of the day, I figured I could get away with it too. Fortunately, though, my laments needed only to reach outward as far as my wife, thereby sparing myself the Lord's rebuke...or worse.

For his part, Jeremiah probably expected something more in keeping with the comforting bedside manner of a good Shepherd, but he might have done well to remember the Lord's response from an earlier encounter (Jer. 12.5):

> If you have raced with men on foot, and they have wearied you,
>> how will you compete with horses?
> And if in a safe land you fall down,
>> how will you do in the jungle of the Jordan?

But I digress, for in both safe lands and sticky jungles, I have not wandered alone. For more than fifty years, in fact, Ann and I have wandered both terrains together. We met at UCR and for a long time saw each other because we both lived in the same dorm and ate in the same cafeteria and socialized with the same small group of friends. Men and women could occupy the same building, a big deal in those days, although they were sequestered in separate wings. It wasn't exactly living together, more like being at home where one part of the house crackled with some mysterious life force that was daunting to the males of the species.

Eventually, I detected that same mystery radiating in her life force, but by then I had announced my interest in going to seminary, and so our upcoming shared journey in ministry did not exactly come as a surprise. In those days most ministers were men and so their spouses were women (this was true of gay ministers as well, not a few of whom brought wives with them to the parsonage in order to get to a church at all). Not that we knew what she was getting into as the "Minister's Wife," but at least the title did not come flying out of left field and into her world sometime after the wedding when it was too late to run away without running away from the marriage as well.

She was not particularly prepared for the role. I recall the president of the seminary (a man) gathering the wives of the graduating students together for a conversation about life in the parsonage, but Ann never said much about it despite my probing. Either the discussion was not helpful or the help it offered was not particularly to her liking (I suspect the latter). In any event, with so many women now serving as the church's lead pastor, the "minister's spouse" may well be a husband (or maybe not), and I think men have a much easier (though not necessarily easy) time as the Minister's Husband than do women as the Minister's Wife.

Some women really do take to the role, in effect serving as the unintended—and unpaid—associate pastor, but in my experience few ministers' wives willingly and gladly accept *that* job, and Ann definitely did not! I'll have more to say about that at later points in this story but for the moment it will suffice to say that while she was good for the church, the church was not always good for her. I often wondered how often that might apply to other ministers' wives simply by virtue of the time demands and scheduling constraints placed upon the minister...scarcely ever a completely free weekend, always on call (even when parishioners respect off-hours for all but essential calls to the house, as I enjoyed), the necessity of sharing the minister with the "church family" who has less in turn to give to the home family. Such dynamics can and do (and did) weigh on a spouse, a marriage, and a family.

What matters most, though, is not how the minister's wife does (or does not) get along in the church but how she and her husband get along at home with (and in spite of) the church ever nearby. Not that I need reminding (usually), but looking at photos of myself from that period, the seminary years and our first church in Nebraska, I am reminded nonetheless how fortunate I have been these many years to have my wife by my side: for I scarcely recognize that skinny, bookish-looking kid staring back at me. I can't imagine the likes of him alone in a church, of all things—but then that was not the case, for his lady is there, too.

Though not quite a proper English lady, English blood does course through her veins, tempered with forebears from Holland and, it turns out, possibly that part of Australia where they sent the felons, all peppered (according to family folklore) with some Tennessee Cherokee influences. As I would learn, staring back at me in those photos is a woman of unusual capacity to forge new chapters in her own life and put up with mine and raise two stellar children (as we would see).

Along with a call, life inside the church requires a high degree of tolerance for ambiguity and a good sense of humor. The former, the capacity to live with the unfinished nature of the work, has its genesis in the many ways we miss Jesus, his words and ways. The gap between promise and reality, between the goal where we live abundantly, justly, and peacefully as intended in the beginning and the hints and the bits and pieces of the promise we taste now and again, never seems to narrow, much less close.

This is not to overlook the significant progress humankind has made over the eons. We live longer (many of us), and better (more of us), but (pardon the understatement) evidence abounds to the point that we humans have a ways to go in embracing the future to which Jesus points. After all this time, might we not have expected humankind to have advanced somewhat in its spiritual sensitivities?

That assumes, of course, first that we understand what Jesus is talking about and then that we want to do something about it—or better, that we want to do something about *him*. As to the first, understanding Jesus seems to have plagued his people from the very beginning. Even the first disciples, the inner circle of followers, often missed the point of Jesus' teachings, and when things went badly in Jerusalem and the religious and political authorities conspired to rid themselves of this threat to *their* well-being, the men Jesus picked to lead the church considered their own well-being and their good intentions notwithstanding, they fled the scene lest they suffer a similar fate.

So today: we who call ourselves disciples still stumble along the path of faith and faithfulness, listening but not hearing, looking but not seeing, musing but not grasping. Very convenient, in a way, as if he were speaking in a language we just cannot understand and so justifiably give up even trying. One definition of Jesus, though, suggests just the opposite, that Jesus is God speaking a language we *can* understand, and the theological nuances and endless controversies regarding the Person of Jesus notwithstanding, getting a handle on the gist of his public ministry is not all that difficult. (I have often said that the part of the Jesus story, and the biblical drama generally, that bothers me is not what I don't understand but what is only too clear.)

Maybe at issue, then, is not that understanding Jesus is so hard but rather that he is first and foremost so *different* and that starting down his path invites his followers to be so different as well—so different, in fact, that joining the Jesus Movement is enough to make his people aliens in their own land. Maybe that explains our conundrum whenever Jesus enters the picture, how we welcome on the one hand the compelling impulse of his invitation and at the same time resist the implications of the very impulse we welcome. His is a Way to be walked, but at the cost of becoming an alien. Little wonder we crawl through that Sunday school window, tripping over our own mishmash of responses—our Yes, No, and Maybe—sometimes all uttered at the same time!

The idea of disciples as aliens only begins to take actual shape in relation to the surrounding culture in which Jesus' followers find themselves. Certainly an apt metaphor for discipleship in our time, the theologians Stanley Hauerwas and William Willimon introduced the notion to me in their book, *Resident Aliens: Life in the Christian Colony* (1989), where they describe the impact of a shifting cultural milieu upon the church. Unlike colliding tectonic plates deep beneath the earth's surface, this collision occurred very much above ground and in full view of the citizens of Greenville, South Carolina. On a certain

Sunday evening in 1963, the Fox Theater opened in defiance of the state's blue laws and seven members of the Methodist Youth Fellowship entered the front door of their church, stayed long enough to be seen, and then slipped out the back door to join John Wayne at the Fox. The message was clear: if the church will have succeeding generations of Christians, the church will have to take sole responsibility for faith formation, for not even in evangelical, Bible-Belt South Carolina will the Fox Theater lend a hand by remaining closed on Sunday.

The point is that at one time, growing up American was tantamount to growing up Christian, or better, to grow up American was to grow up *culturally* Christian, the social fabric of the surrounding community itself preserving some semblance of the language and stories of the biblical drama. Here we distinguish cultural from biblical Christianity because a cultural faith asks nothing by way of confession or commitment and makes no pretense regarding depth, coherence, and discipline as one would expect of biblical Christianity.

In any event, thanks to the blue laws, neither shopping nor youth sports nor anything else interfered with religious activities on Sunday and by common consent, Wednesday "church nights" were often sacrosanct as well. With nothing else to do and social expectations supporting such things, people went to church. Those who refused to cooperate voluntarily on Sunday morning might still get their religion elsewhere, osmosis-style, perhaps at the annual *Christmas* program in the public schools or by the reminder of the approaching *Easter* vacation on the school calendar. Prayers for divine guidance at city council meetings and safety on the field during sporting events or the Ten Commandments emblazoned in marble in front of the courthouse connected some kind of *Christian* religious awareness with the cultural conditioning of children and their families. Blurring the distinction between church and state in effect conscripted the latter as an agent of the former and helped reinforce its own traditions in the consciousness of the people. Of course, growing up American was tantamount to growing up Christian. Our 18th century Deist founders may have separated church (religion) and state in *principle* but in *practice*, by 1963, the church had given its definitive shape to Greenville, South Carolina…and beyond.

Not anymore, not since the Methodists and the Fox Theater conspired to undo the convenient symbiotic relationship that had placed some of the burden of discipleship on the wider community. As the saying goes, too soon we grow old—too late we grow smart, and only when we had grown decidedly older and finally noticed that the second generation following the rogue Methodists of Greenville had failed to show up in church did we begin to grow somewhat smarter, at least in the dawning awareness that the Fox Theater was but a mere symptom of a much larger tectonic shift in the dominant culture: the secular emancipation of humanity from God.

Who knew that a cadre of youth escaping from their Methodist Youth Fellowship to see a movie would prove so consequential, but like the Tempter in the Garden (something about an Apple), in bringing John Wayne to the big screen on Sunday evening, the theater ever so subtly introduced the seed of a new idea into the community. Of course, it came as an invitation…have you thought about the joys and possibilities of your secular emancipation?

Well, they probably did not think of it in quite those terms, but they might as well have, for the choice was ever so clear: the Sabbath for those who like the Sabbath and something a little further afield for those who want something a little further afield. The Fox Theater did not so much challenge the Sabbath (as practiced, we hasten to add, which may or may not have had much to do with the Fourth Commandment as intended) as ignore it; indifference, the ultimate dismissal, was the order of the day.

Perhaps there was another underlying message, a more subtle and in some measure a more anxious message, certainly a more serious message, that the wider community, theater and church alike, had not perceived and so could not articulate. For in promoting the secular emancipation of the community from its religious strictures the Fox Theater had dared to suggest that maybe, just maybe, God could be pushed a little further away from the life of the community as well. As with the First Temptation, the Tempter (dressed as a movie house) did not question God's existence. The metaphysical question—Does God exist?—is a perfectly fine and worthy question for those given to metaphysical musings, but even in 1963, deep in the Bible belt, normal people wanted to have a different conversation and the Fox Theater seized the opportunity to change that conversation: not does God exist metaphysically but does God matter existentially even if God does exist metaphysically.

With a thud, the ball landed in the church's court. If you will, if you even *can*, please explain yourself, dear pastor: the Fox Theater having removed God *functionally* from the world, how now can the Methodist Youth Fellowship possibly compete...and why should it even try? John Wayne at the Fox vs. God and cookies in the church social hall: no contest there—and not just for youth.

Many words ago, I said that in addition to a call, ministers need a high degree of tolerance for ambiguity and an abiding sense of humor. I close this chapter with what has become over the years a melting pot of all three.

My response to Greenville over the years was to bring John Wayne into the church on a regular basis—in the pulpit, as part of study groups, when opportunities presented themselves in board and committee meetings, in working with staff—so that the secular and the sacred might share in the same conversation...or at least make the attempt.

One such attempt occurred during Lent, a serious season for serious reflection on the deeper contours of the spiritual journey upon which a resurrection people have traveled. Instead of John Wayne, the Fox Theater (dressed in the guise of the church's minister) featured Clint Eastwood and his film, *Unforgiven*, a powerful film that I include on my personal list of the best of the genre of old-fashioned morality plays otherwise known as Westerns.[3] It offered much grist for conversation of the religious kind, and several of us were fully engaged in considering the age-old problem of evil and the seeming inevitability of violence on the one hand and on the other the quite different message and model offered by Jesus. It was good Lenten, getting-ready-for-Easter fare.

---

3. Others on the A-list include, *High Noon, Shane, Pale Rider, The Shootist, True Grit* (both the 1969 original with John Wayne and the 2010 remake with Jeff Bridges, a slight edge going to the latter), and *Open Range*. With their larger purpose in mind, *Cheyenne Autumn* (addressing the mistreatment of Native Americans historically and in film) and *Django Unchained* (perhaps the first film to tackle the scourge of American slavery) certainly belong on this list as well. I once asked my congregation to add their favorites, the results showing a great deal of interest in the genre and generating a long list of candidates for best Western.

Meanwhile, down the hall, unbeknownst to me, one of the women's groups, a strong and important fellowship group which included some of the strongest and most devoted members of the church and key members of the leadership core, the very leaders on whom both the members and I depended...*that* women's group was holding a lingerie party.

Lingerie in the parlor vs. God and guns in the library: apparently, not much of a contest, either.

At the time, I was not feeling terribly charitable toward the choice a goodly number of my members had made, but with time comes perspective, and with time I came to appreciate how lingerie fantasies in the parlor had undoubtedly made their way from the church to the homes of my parishioners, there to have enjoyed greater effect than my dour musings on the problem of evil and the use of the gun by our violent race.

It helps, too, that I can enjoy the tale as if for the first time from the comfort of my retirement where I no longer have to deal with such things, and really, what else is there to do but enjoy the humor and move on? Of course, I was initially angry (this was Lent, after all); then I was embarrassed, more for me than them ("What...during Lent?" I heard my colleagues say, eyebrows raised, self-righteously grateful that it was *me*, not *them*); finally, a gracious moment and the reminder that as children of God, Someone loves unconditionally. At the end of the day, are not grace and humor merely different sides of the same coin?

Not that I had any choice in the approaching tsunami, but as a rule I support our secular emancipation. It frees humankind from all manner of narrow, prejudicial, and destructive orthodoxies, the religious sort among the most odious, and while secularism has a *tendency* to remove God *functionally* from the world, final credit or blame for the consequences lies not with the nefarious Fox Theater and its legion of conspirators but rather with human beings who once liberated *from* God must then choose what to do *about* God, if anything.

Apparently, freedom *from* God does not necessarily mean that one is thereby done *with* God, for no sooner does the Fox Theater pull us away from the times and places for such considerations than who should turn up but Jesus with his haunting observation that we humans do not live by bread (read: "the Fox Theater" or "sexy lingerie") *alone* (Matt. 4.4, emphasis added). Certainly each has a place, but apparently there is something more to human being that secularism does not and cannot address. Psychoanalyst Carl Jung put it this way (*Collected Works* 11, ¶ 509, 1932):

> Among all my patients in the second half of life—that is to say over thirty-five—there has not been one whose problem in the last resort was not that of finding a religious outlook on life. It is safe to say that every one of them fell ill because he had lost what the living religions of every age have given their followers, and none of them has been really healed who did not regain his religious outlook. This of course has nothing whatever to do with a particular creed or member-ship of a church.

Whatever its form, that "religious outlook" apparently serves a very partic-ular purpose (*Modern Man in Search of a Soul*, 1933):

> About a third of my cases are suffering from no clinically definable neurosis, but from the senselessness and emptiness of their lives. This can be described as the general neurosis of our time.

In other words, secularism may well come along as a great liberator, freeing us *from* all manner of social, political, and religious dogmas, but it does not necessarily tell us what we are free *for*, what we are to do and to be and to become, whether our lives have purpose and our efforts meaning, or how we identify that which is worthy of human being. A secular outlook alone cannot equip us to distinguish right and wrong, discern the contours of justice, or rec-ognize the difference between mere knowledge and genuine wisdom. Unless what we understand as life is just the happenstance of physics and chemistry, raising these age-old questions blends the best of religion and philosophy, lit-erature and the arts, rational thought and creative imagination—the essence of the sacred and the secular. Ironically, but necessarily, human beings are driven to escape the limitations of a secular mindset and embrace the very realm from which the secular world had set us free.[4]

The question, of course, is how to combine the promise of both spheres, the secular and the sacred. Maybe necessity will force a convergence, the deficiencies of a secular process that has removed God *functionally* from the world becoming so obvious—and intolerable—that a new spirituality will be born. One can only hope, and soon, for while humankind continues to fiddle, our only planet slowly burns, inching closer and closer to that 2° C threshold (some more recently have set the maximum at 1.5° C) beyond which climate change may spin totally out of control. Some place their bet on science and technology coming through in time, human ingenuity and the free market rescuing the damsel in distress; others speak of an evolving spiritual consciousness taming, if not completely transforming, self-centered, competitive interests, secured by the gun, a sustainable human community emerging in time, before the end.

A secular savior on the one hand—the peaceable kingdom on the other, all by the end of the century: either way, a long roll of the dice.

What will it take to capture our attention sufficiently so as to motivate the action that will save us finally, for with abundant signs and portents flickering on the horizon, humankind is rather like my parishioner who had undergone emergency heart surgery and was in Intensive Care when I walked in his hospital room. Before my even saying hello and making sure he knew who I was, he looked at me and said, "I don't need you, yet." If by "needing me" he had in mind something like my delivering the Protestant version of Last Rites, he was quite correct—in fact, he needed neither of us, yet, neither the minister ushering another soul into the Great Beyond nor the undertaker waiting in the hallway. Someday, yes, but not *this* day, for on *this* day, the best of science and

---

4. I should note that behind my reflections in this section lies some extensive research fully documented in my Doctor of Ministry Project, *The Crisis of Spirit: Implications from Schleiermacher for the Revitalization of the Local Church*, University Microfilms International, Ann Arbor, MI, 1987. In addition to Schleiermacher himself and several theological treatises on his seminal work, I should at least mention Raimundo Pannikar, *Blessed Simplicity*, and Wolfhart Pannenberg, *Christian Spirituality*, as major contributors to the discussion on secularism, but there are others writing on an incredibly important subject not only for the future direction of religion in the Western world but the future of Western culture itself.

technology had quite literally given him a new lease on life and he recovered and went home to live again.

I learned early not to plan funeral services for people who did not need them—one day, yes, but maybe not *this* day or even next week and quite possibly not even next year—but in the meantime, until such time as the church and its minister are needed, what is each to do? There must be something, if only grappling with the timeless existential questions of life, like, why is there something instead of nothing and given the "something," does it have a purpose and a destiny beyond the present moment? Weighty questions, indeed, and fortunately distractions abound around us to draw our attention elsewhere. Day to day, we live as if the whole enterprise and each one of us will go on forever, all the while knowing full well that it—and we—will not. In the meantime, each day has enough trouble of its own, as Jesus himself reminds us (Matt. 6.34, *Cotton Patch*)…mouths to feed, diapers to change, jobs to keep. An occasional crisis, or even the minor bump in the road, gives us reason to pause and consider "things" (the nature and purpose of the sacred, say, and how the sacred may intersect the secular…were we to let it), but the moment passes or we recover and life moves on. Before we know it, a life is lived, and then it's time to call the church whose minister will summon God from the margins to which a secular society has *functionally* consigned such things.

Life goes on…until, of course, it doesn't, at which point we ask larger, ultimate questions for which an advanced but essentially secular society is not fully equipped to answer, but what if we brought God into the conversation before it was time to call for the undertaker as well? What difference might it make to the journey itself?

In just such a question is a ministry born, like *our* ministry, seminary behind us and the Nebraska Panhandle before us. It was 1971—I was just 25, Ann was almost 24.

CHAPTER 2

A MISSION TO
MATCH THE MESSAGE

"The Church exists by mission just as fire exists by burning.
Where there is no mission there is no Church;
and where there is neither Church nor mission,
there is no faith."

~EMIL BRUNNER
Swiss theologian, in *The Word and the World* (1931)

EQUALLY AS ASTONISHING AS HAVING parishioners was finding them in Chadron, Nebraska, our new home and first church. Located in the northwestern corner of the state, one hundred miles south of Rapid City, South Dakota, Chadron stands at the transition from the vast expanse of the Great Plains to the east and the first hint of the Rocky Mountains to the west. As we quickly learned, this was cattle country and those who raised cattle were ranchers, not to be confused with farmers who raised crops. With the area's higher elevation, shorter growing season, and limited rain, the ranchers would plant a little winter wheat and mow a lot of alfalfa, but the real crop of Nebraska's Panhandle was some of the best grassland in the world.

Chadron remains today a small town of about 6,000; when in session, Chadron State College adds 3,000 students to the population; taken together, Dawes County, of which Chadron serves as the county seat, is home to fewer than 10,000 people. A vast countryside, sparsely settled.

Many people find such environments unnerving, even oppressive. To them, the emptiness of America's Great Plains and even the vast expanse of the Rocky Mountain West (apart from a crowded park or resort) is something to fly over or get through as quickly as possible. Initially, travelers may look around and find little to attract their attention. (I remember looking at the landscape from the airplane as it approached the Rapid City airport and feeling a strange kinship.) They will pronounce the countryside dull, the native culture lacking, and so press on to what feels like a more interesting and compelling destination, but underneath this surface appraisal there may well stir a more primal apprehension having to do with reminders of human mortality and the limitations of human power. It is but a very short hop from there to an uninvited confrontation with the mystery of life itself, if not the whole cosmos. The vast landscape means that the sea really is so big and my boat is inescapably so small, which only seems to confirm my own insignificance. Even if there is a God in heaven, does this God care about or even notice me? We call this wilderness spirituality, and it can be very disconcerting.

Little wonder, then, that most of us choose the city where we feel existentially safe, or at least comfortable. We are the products of a modern, urban society, and we find security in tall buildings acting as sentinels against the chaos and the barbarians lurking without. Within its protective walls, we have created comparatively stable social systems that channel goods and services our way. Taken together, we cannot help but notice that our creative and intellectual capacity, coupled to an applied technological prowess, give us god-like power to shape the world around us to suit our every whim—and even destroy it if we so choose (the looming choice so far when it comes to the climate crisis). When pressed, we may acknowledge a Creator, but in the day-to-day management of our social, political, and economic affairs, we hardly need and so seldom defer to this Higher Being. We know that life on this planet is fragile and ultimately temporary, but in the city we can live as if it will go on forever.

These days, of course, the internet connects people anywhere on the globe at any time, mitigating any psychological and emotional distress brought about by geographical separation from our urban props, but in 1971, we had access to a handful of radio stations and a single television station. Cable TV was available, but claiming poverty, we opted for the limited offerings of a satellite station from Rapid City that cobbled its daily programming from the offerings of two networks. Our phone (landline only, obviously), connected us with the outside world, but even then, long-distance calls were pretty much restricted to holidays and emergencies. To fly anywhere, one first took the 13-seat commuter flight to Denver or drove to Rapid City. For serious shopping, a day's outing to "Rapid" (as we locals referred to the nearest metropolis with a population of 50,000 or so) was the destination of choice.

No trip to Rapid was complete without a detour to the "Faces" (aka Mount Rushmore) and an excursion through Custer State Park. Both belonged to South Dakota, but the state line was almost a happenstance of history, for "out there," in the vast expanse of the Nebraska Panhandle, Rapid and its nearby Faces belonged as much to us Cornhuskers as it did to the residents of the Coyote State. Part of the felt ownership had to do with a shared identity with the West, with Wyoming and the Dakotas and the Rockies and a place where ranches were measured in thousands and tens of thousands of acres. I never knew if the local folks were serious, but at the time, discussion was underway to take the Panhandle out of Nebraska and link up with Wyoming. Nebraska's capital at Lincoln, nearly 500 miles away in the more densely settled Midwest, never gave them any attention anyway, and so, nestled in their own Pine Ridge, the Black Hills with its Faces a mere 100 miles north, inevitably the people would look West, where they belonged. Nothing came of it but the prospect has always symbolized for me that our new home was not just "a thousand cattle on a thousand hills" (to paraphrase the Psalmist—Psalm 50.10) but a way of life unique unto itself.

A good number of my parishioners were ranchers and they all lived the hard-working, rugged, every-stool-standing-on-its-own-legs individualism that defined the mythology of the Old West. Many of them had a twice-daily commute over dusty, gravel county roads to get their kids to school. I would call on one family who lived so far off the county road that if there was water in the creek, somebody would have to meet me in a four-wheel-drive truck and take me the rest of the way to their home because my shiny red 1969 Ford Torino GT fastback with its 351 cubic inch V-8 engine and a fake hood scoop was useless for such travel. We went on roundups and brandings and saw from whence came the Rocky Mountain Oysters that were barbecued and served to us hours after arriving in the Cornhusker state. We learned about calving and putting up hay and could only imagine how they managed to make the business side of their operations work.

We celebrate the rugged, no-nonsense, salt-of-the-earth pioneers who settled the West, and its folklore lives today in the people who still respond to the siren call of the Great Plains and western gateway to the towering mountains beyond, even if it is only while looking down from 35,000 feet or sailing down the highway in air-conditioned land yachts.

At the same time, life on the plains is hard and its harsh, unforgiving landscape has seemingly left a certain hardness on the cultural landscape as well. I don't know if the stories are true or apocryphal, but either way they offer access to the mentality of the community, for according to local folklore, mere childbirth offered no necessary excuse from personal responsibility for tending to one's obligations: a mother might have her baby in the morning but she was expected to be back in the field by afternoon. (It must be apocryphal...unless it isn't.) Faltering along the way might carry unforgiving penalties, and because inevitably we all falter along the way, scrambling to keep pace and make a place under such circumstances often surfaces as anger and bitterness, harsh tongues, remembered slights, and unforgiving judgments.

Even so, I have always maintained a certain fondness for the people and the place, so much so in fact, that on one trip through the Black Hills years later we actually looked at potential retirement property in the area. Nothing came of that, but for a moment at least, it flashed on our radar screens.

An adventure it was, our new home, but we did not come to our new home for the sake of an adventure alone. We came because the people of Plymouth Congregational Christian Church had called me to be their minister. Plymouth had its genesis in the merger controversy that gave birth to the United Church of Christ. I refer to this chapter of ecclesiastical history and its significance for me personally in the Forward and so will not elaborate further on it here other than to encourage the reader to keep in mind that when fighting erupts, trauma soon follows, and the memory of the battle and its scars will remain with the combatants long after the smoke has cleared. This is true of ecclesiastical conflict no less than the conflict that sets families and communities, tribes and clans, and whole nations against each other. The merger question may seem like a small skirmish in the grand sweep of the church's history of skirmishes, and not even a blip on the world's radar, except to those invested in its outcome. For them, the cause takes center stage, the conflict its unwanted but inevitable companion. Eventually, the battle ends and one side wins and the other loses (actually one side just loses less and so *seems* to win). The winners go one way and, unable or unwilling to accept the outcome, the vanquished go the other.

Such was certainly the case for the people of Plymouth Church. Their former church, the First Congregational Church, had studied the merger question and its members voted to affiliate with the new denomination, the United Church of Christ—or a majority had, anyway, but not all. Those not willing to accept the church's new direction subsequently left their church and founded Plymouth, a member church of the National Association of Congregational Christian Churches (NACCC or NA for short). I arrived about eight years following their departure.

Understandably, feelings were still running deep. Regardless the circumstances, much had been lost—a building, yes, but more than brick and stone, their memory of and history with an entire faith community and its multitude of relationships as represented by a building. It was not unlike a death in the family and so like a death in the family, the members carried their grief along with considerable anger and hurt with them to their new location. Eventually, families will pick up their lives and move on, but the wounds linger and fester for years. Like whole nations, so within families, battles may end, but wars have a way of going on and on and for this church family, their war not over, these wounds lingered and festered.

The situation called for healing and conflict resolution. There was just one minor problem: I had never studied the healing of schismatic churches and had never even heard of conflict resolution. In those days, it was just not part of my (or any?) seminary curriculum. I suppose at some intellectual level, we seminarians had some primitive awareness that churches and church people do fight, like Martin Luther and the Roman Church in the history books. "Here I stand," he had said so heroically at the dawn of the Protestant Reformation—some fights apparently needing to be fought, it seems, though the rift still tears at the once-seamless robe of Christ.

Of course, it is one thing to read about a battle in the history books half a millennium after the fact and quite another to experience a battle so fresh that it might have happened just yesterday. Yes, life does go on (they say); of course, it will be different now (they add); but eventually a new path will open (they hope).

But is it the work for a neophyte, the messy cauldron of a church fight? Unlike, say, the United Methodist Church, churches of our faith and order do not send ministers to labor in a particular corner of the vineyard. Local churches call their ministers who in turn make a decision, yes or no, in their response to the call, and under that system, I obviously said yes, but it was a tough place to begin, no question about that. Not just baptism but baptism by fire. Not for nothing, I suppose, have I always appreciated Isaiah: "And I heard the voice of the Lord saying, 'Whom shall I send, and who will go for us?' Then I said, 'Here am I! Send me'" (Isa. 6.8). I don't remember hearing voices, that of the Lord or anyone else, but I did feel an inner nudge that translated to a call, and so off we went (an "Isaiah moment" with others to follow).

Cementing our mutual venture, pastor and people, a few months later, on Halloween of all things, October 31, 1971, I was ordained a minister according to historical Congregational practice. Let the journey begin!

The big question, of course, was journey to where, to what end?! It turned out that dealing with the residual fallout from the church fight was only part of the answer, and the easier part at that. The larger and more difficult challenge was answering the question of the purpose or mission of the church. What are we to do...and why?

For a time, the answer focused on planting a new church committed to the principles of historic Congregationalism and its emphasis on local church autonomy. In other words, the new church adopted a form of polity (or church governance) as its distinguishing characteristic, its preservation and extension a defining mission. Uniquely among Chadron's churches, Plymouth would stand as a beacon to the Free Church tradition with roots dating to Puritan New England.

As someone who grew up in and would later serve such churches, I have to say that Plymouth's instincts are well-grounded here. A four-hundred-year-old tradition has served the American Protestant church honorably and, not incidentally, has left an indelible mark on America's experiment in democracy. In serving Congregational churches, I have recognized its opportunities for clergy and laity alike and have taken great care to see that both the church and I have exercised its inherent responsibilities faithfully.

At the same time, as one who honors the tradition, I also recognize that we have often confused means and ends, where the polity is a means to an end greater than itself. In other words, a church's polity or how it structures and governs itself is not in and of itself a mission or a purpose at all but a tool, a means, that facilitates that larger purpose we call its mission. By itself, it can never capture—or at least cannot long hold—the attention of a people, including those who love the Congregational Way. In the *other* Congregational Bible, *History of American Congregationalism*, authors Gaius Glenn Atkins and Frederick Fagley make this point clear:

> The church in New England was not an end in itself but existed for what was considered to be community well-being. It followed that the fellowship of the churches did not exist for the promotion of denominational prestige but did have for its mission the cure of injustice and the lifting of the level of the whole of life.

Ever the challenge: keeping the church focused on "community well-being" and not itself, a means to "lifting of the level of the whole of life." In that same vein, I have always appreciated how Albert Camus put it in addressing a group of Dominicans in 1948 (emphasis added):

What the world expects of Christians is that Christians should speak out, loud and clear and that they should voice their condemnation in such a way that never a doubt, never the slightest doubt, could rise in the heart of the simplest man. That they should get away from abstraction and confront the blood-stained face history has taken on today. The grouping we need is a grouping of people resolved to *speak out clearly and to pay up personally.*[5]

In a word, not *how* you make decisions, but *what* those decisions are and *why* they matter, such does the world ask of us.

This was a real dilemma for Plymouth. A sizeable group (the membership eventually peaked at about 100) had left their former church, purchased a very adequate corner lot in town, and completed the first phase of what was intended to be a larger building program. At that point the number of churches in town had increased by one, one more Protestant church in a town not particularly given to attending church. Quite apart from the people who believed in and supported it, what would capture the attention of the wider community, stimulating the spiritual consciousness of the people and in general furthering the purpose of the church in the world?

This is so much easier to describe years later! At the time, out there on the Nebraska plains, such thoughts had not taken form in my understanding of ministry, but looking back I wonder why we (seemingly why the churches together) had not given more attention to the plight of Native Americans and the living conditions on the Pine Ridge Indian Reservation located just north of the South Dakota-Nebraska state line, some 50 miles away by car. A tragic and shameful chapter, the treatment of native peoples by the first European migrants and subsequent Americans: no wonder many today look at Columbus Day as the beginning of the genocide of indigenous peoples that continues in some form to the present.

---

5. Many citations, this from Volume XX, No. 14, MANAS Reprint April 5, 1967. From his book, *Resistance, Rebellion and Death*, essays and other writings Camus selected as representing "the primary concerns of his life."

An American genocide? I must have slept through class the day my high school history curriculum touched upon that topic. Or maybe that message could not compete with the cultural mythology that while various peoples (our Native Americans, Canada's First Nations) may have settled the land, John Wayne conquered it. Manifest Destiny (the 19th century view that the United States could, and was destined to, stretch from coast to coast) seemed to have helped, pushing settlers further and further westward; indigenous tribes that were "in the way" were…relocated. Not all of them, of course, but only the ones not otherwise dispatched.

Fairly quickly, and with complete disregard for their humanity and culture, the pioneers and the governmental structures, agencies, and armies that followed brought a new order to the landscape and by the end of the 19th century, the die was cast. Perhaps in Hollywood westerns but otherwise lost in the American narrative are the definitive battles: the Battle of Little Bighorn, 1876; the Cheyenne outbreak from Fort Robinson, 1879; and the Wounded Knee Massacre, 1890.

Lost, too, is awareness of and so interest in the reservations. Much like racial segregation in the South and economic segregation everywhere, reservations isolate and ghettoize native peoples yet today. Without adequate education and access to job training and the employment marketplace, reservations will continue to cripple creativity, stifle hope, and breed personal despair and social breakdown.

One day, Ann and I took the long way to Rapid City and drove through the Pine Ridge Indian Reservation. We clearly did not belong, two white faces staring out the windows of our shiny red car, voyeurs really, the Dawes County "69" on the Nebraska license plates locating us in Chadron, the town that pulls in the welcome mat when the monthly government checks arrive on the reservation. The poverty, our neglect, and a century of broken promises all took shape before our eyes. It was terrifically uncomfortable, and we never did it again.

The question is, getting real, what could we do? How might churches bridge racial, cultural, and economic injustice and a history of broken promises?

What brought all that into focus was the Wounded Knee incident. On February 27, 1973, some 200 Oglala Lakota and followers of the American Indian Movement occupied the town of Wounded Knee, South Dakota, on the Pine Ridge Indian Reservation, site of the Wounded Knee Massacre of 1890. In part, the issue was internal, having to do with tribal politics and allegations of corruption by tribal leadership, but protesters also confronted the U. S. Government over its failures to honor treaties with Indian people and demanded negotiations be reopened.

The occupation lasted 71 days, and garnered national attention and sympathy from the American public as issues of long-standing injustice related to Native Americans became part of the national conversation, at least for awhile. More locally, though, the issue was security, for along with the national attention came participants with no direct connection to the reservation—a potentially bad combination with the potential for trouble both on and off the reservation. One of my strong lay leaders was himself deputized and posted along with other volunteers at the entrances to town…just to be safe. Maybe it worked, for of the wounded in various shootings (including thirteen protesters and two government agents), none was local, although at least one of the Wounded Knee casualties was taken to our local hospital, guarded by members of the local posse.

Violence would persist on the reservation for several years, but on May 8, the immediate crisis, the siege itself, ended. The government resumed control of the disputed area and things returned to whatever had passed for normalcy, that is, to a state of equilibrium within a system that had momentarily been rendered unbalanced. It was a predictable case not of justice delivered but power administered and in a way, how could it be otherwise? Initially, someone picks up a megaphone; in the interlude, people seem to listen; and 71 days later it all boils down to a show of force and which side has the more bullets. Of course, the siege ended and things returned to "normal"—they always do.

Wounded Knee provided for me an early case study of the church's mission and purpose in the world. At issue was not so much the *theory* of mission, what God *intended* for the church, but what it takes for the church to deploy its members and other resources to fulfill that purpose. Or as Camus put it, just what does "speaking out clearly and paying up personally" look like here, in this place and at this time?

To bring it a little closer to home, what does speaking out clearly and paying up personally look like with regard to, say, Wayne Blind Man? Wayne Blind Man, so named because he had lost the sight in one of his eyes, was an Ogallala Sioux from the reservation who periodically found his way to the parsonage in Chadron. His countenance notwithstanding, Wayne was essentially harmless. He represented a problem, though, by virtue of standing on my front porch, and he was certainly problematical because Jesus taught us how he routinely showed up in the guise of such persons (Matt. 25.31-46).

What to do? What he (Wayne? Jesus?) wanted, of course, was money, not very much (if necessary, he would cut the grass to earn it), and charity demanded some kind of a response, but everybody knew the result of even modest charity. In later years, they would come, the endless is-the-pastor-in parade of street people, and in later years, as drugs became increasingly problematical, we would drop the "essentially harmless" modifier and lock the church door because we just didn't know. Wayne Blind Man was a problem but his successors often displayed an unpredictable intensity born of desperation not just for the next fix but as victims of the torn fabric of society's dysfunctional and collapsing social contract.

The question with which I ever wrestled beginning with the day we drove through the Pine Ridge Indian Reservation was just how seriously or how far to take the church's work in the world. Wayne Blind Man scared Ann and I have to say that while I was not afraid of him, I did not like the idea of his knocking on the parsonage door when I was at the church…harmless though he was, of course. Theory is one thing (speak out clearly and pay up personally) until it's time to speak out and pay up.

So instead, we look at more practical ways to make a difference in the world: fundraisers so the kids can go to camp; walk-a-thons to feed the hungry for a few days; cast-off rummage for the already-marginalized; leftovers from the pledge drive to support the mission budget; the inevitable appeals following the latest natural calamity. The old saying reminds us that when we give a man a fish, we feed him for a day, but when we teach a man to fish we feed him for a lifetime. All well and good, of course, but giving a man a fish is still a good thing, yes?

On the other hand, I once asked a friend, an avowed Marxist, to contribute to an upcoming Walk for the Hungry in my community. He did, but only with great reluctance because he saw his act as enabling unjust behavior on society's part and putting off the inevitable revolution that would free the oppressed from the systems that oppress them. Only when the masses are truly hungry, he said (no fish to be found for anyone, anywhere, anytime soon), will the proletariat achieve its due measure of all things needful for a satisfactory life.

Try preaching that on Sunday morning and see how quickly that lands you unemployed!

Is there an alternative, a midpoint between taking on social systems, inherently resistant to change, and ignoring the problem altogether? Is it enough to apply Band-Aids to festering wounds, treating symptoms while ignoring the underlying infections? Ideally, yes, unjust systems and unfair structures (Paul's principalities and powers, Eph. 6.12; Rom. 8.38) do require the church to direct its corporate energy and passion for justice to the amelioration of underlying causes and not just the treatment of superficial symptoms, the cost notwithstanding. The guiding principle here is that how we *actually* treat others is a testimony to how we *really* feel about God.

Yet, in the mundane practicalities of everyday life, the church is going to schedule still another rummage sale so the already-marginalized can clothe their families. It will host another hunger walk so Wayne Blind Man might eat another day. Better to give the already-marginalized their full humanity and to teach Wayne self-reliance, but in the meantime, until then, we are reminded that taken together, our churches have done a lot of good work—no one would deny that. The time, talent, and treasure of individuals and their congregations have combined to touch any number of the world's deep hungers. As has been said of the Quakers, so could the same be said of broad swaths of congregational life, that their influence greatly exceeds their numbers.

Lest we become self-satisfied and, worse, self-righteous, the church needs to dream dreams and see visions (echoes of Joel 2.28 and hints of the distant Pentecost to follow) worthy of its calling. Where does it begin? By living prophetically into God's future, and that is so hard to do. The lesson from Wounded Knee is only too clear on that point. For 71 days, the spotlight shone on the grievances of a people who trace the beginnings of their genocide to 1492, and that nothing changed in the end merely shifts the spotlight from their lament to our choices, or more to the point, the consequences of our failure so to choose the Way of the Christ.

With so much to do by way of mission, and my fondness for the Nebraska Panhandle notwithstanding, the fact is that I did not stay long at Plymouth, something less than two years. The seeds for my departure could already be anticipated even before my arrival—will a city boy be happy so far removed from a city? I essentially grew up in Los Angeles, and the opportunities of the secular city and the mentality that went along with it were second nature to me. I missed that.

It sounds a little specious even to me, but I did not have enough to do. In those days, we said a 250-member church warranted a full-time pastoral position; Plymouth had less than 100 resident members. I could have counted my blessings, looked at the many opportunities for ministry and personal reading and study, pursued any number of other ways of doing ministry and being church, but the fact of the matter is I did not do any of that. I had a narrow view of my job and from that narrow perspective, I was very much underemployed.

And underpaid. The pretense of a full-time position did not include a commensurate salary. Even a decade after its founding, this was still a mission church. The budget had denominational support and the people supported the church as best they could, but we were barely limping along from month to month, a family of three by then. There was nothing set aside for benefits and we only maintained a modest health insurance policy because I had a Discretionary Fund at my disposal which, at my discretion, I used to pay the premiums—not quite kosher but nobody seemed to notice.

Today, Ann and I both acknowledge a fourth factor, more personal and certainly more subjective than the others, not so much named as felt. It had to do with the very serious complications that followed the delivery of our son, Peter George. His birth was decidedly fathers-wait-outside old-school, and it followed a long twenty-five hours of labor but a day or two later, I did my part and delivered a new mother and our child to our home.

All was seemingly well until Ann started hemorrhaging and probably only survived because we lived across the street from the hospital and I was able to get her there immediately. The problem was that the doctor had performed an episiotomy and somehow cut her uterine artery. The details are excruciating to recall even from this distant point and are really not necessary for the narrative—the fact itself speaks for itself. Had that happened today, and perhaps had it happened even then in a more medically sophisticated environment—had we been more astute ourselves for that matter—the incident would have been investigated, if not by the hospital itself and some licensing board, then at the initiative of a lawyer, perhaps our lawyer, but nobody spoke to us about such things. After all, the patient survived and while the doctor very soon thereafter left town to join a practice in another state, nothing more was ever said.

Except that plenty was said, not just up front and out loud. Ann had lost a lot of blood and had multiple transfusions as a result. A new mother who had nearly died…let me just say the recovery did not fit the mold of that apocryphal story about having your baby in the morning and being back at work in the afternoon (certainly apocryphal…unless it wasn't). Fortunately, Ann's parents were retired and could drop everything and come to Chadron. I don't know what we would have done without them.

The settled opinion in the church was that the recovery was taking much more time than necessary and that the minister's wife needed to pull herself together and get on with things. The harsh, unforgiving landscape had given texture to the surrounding culture that surfaced in the attitudes of the people, not all of them, certainly, but the judgmental voice was unmistakable.

At our age, we no longer need to worry about dying young, but that night in a moment of horror we saw the fragility of life nipping at our heels. How close was Ann to becoming a maternal statistic, a tragic casualty, and me a single father at 25? Except for our immediate family, we basically weathered the trauma alone. Ann's parents had come in the immediate crisis and when she could not get the traction on her recovery by herself, she took Peter and flew to them in California. I joined them a few weeks later for my vacation and we came back together ready for a new year.

I cannot say that our experience in that time played a decisive role in our leaving when we did, but neither can I say it didn't. We put up a good front in our public personas, but as they say, you just never know what goes on behind closed doors.

In any event, I was approached with another opportunity. Actually, it took two attempts—the first time I declined, but the search committee asked that we take a second look, which I did, and a few months later, we found ourselves moving to Mukwonago, Wisconsin, and the First Congregational Church. It was jumping from the frying pan and into the fire.

My second pastorate, like the first, took me to a church that had suffered a serious fight and subsequent split. Almost a year to the day prior to my arrival, the church had voted by a margin of seven to withdraw from the United Church of Christ and align with the National Association of Congregational Christian Churches. At the time of the vote, the church claimed some 400 members; following the vote, the minister and 65 members on the "losing" side (again, the side that lost more) resigned immediately and formed the Mukwonago United Church of Christ, their number eventually increasing to 100 or so. The "winning" side (the side that lost less) kept the building and property and the larger share of members (the church's profile sent to prospective pastoral candidates listed 325 members) and retained the institutional history and memory and the inevitable weight of its traditions and baggage. Neither church, though, escaped the effects of a bruising battle and broken relationships that pitted friends and even families against one another.

I have always felt that the Mukwonago church fight need not have resulted in the church splitting; that had the internal conflict been handled differently, had cooler heads exercised a little finesse, people might have hung together and weathered the storm. That's not to minimize the significance of the subject over which the members fought which in this case was twofold: as in Chadron, a sizeable number of members were unhappy with the United Church of Christ, but their discontent was not limited to the more academic question of the merger itself, for now social issues were taking center stage. The walls dividing (shielding) congregations of all stripes and denominations from their dominant culture had eroded and volatile issues inflaming the secular community—Vietnam and civil rights and racism—had the same impact on the religious community.

Still, give credit where credit is due: from the pulpit and educational platforms, in its governance and decision-making, and through social justice committees or other structural avenues for extending its witness into the world, many local churches did not bury their heads in the sand when it came to the national conversation; but at the same time, it was like pouring gasoline on a fire, and the national offices of major denominations provided the fuel in the form of pronouncements destined to collide with the more conservative social and political leanings of many of the people in the pews. This was especially true for member churches of the United Church of Christ, traditionally one of the most (some say traditionally *the* most) liberal of America's Protestant denominations.

In that respect, give credit to the Mukwonago church specifically! They may have been fighting but the fight at least identified a people who cared and who invested their considerable energy in the moment and toward the future! Maybe that energy could have been directed to more constructive ends—maybe not... who can say all these years later, but whereas the Mukwonago folks finally did implode with a Bang, at least they did not fade into the sunset with a Whimper (to borrow rather freely from T.S. Eliot's poem, "The Hollow Men"). In that period, churches and church people took to the streets to protest the War in Vietnam. Thirty years later, not even the so-called "forever wars" in the Middle East could rouse the church from its ecclesiastical stupor. So, yes, give credit where credit is due: the fallout notwithstanding, restraint and finesse in short supply, subsequent answers indeterminate, at least the people on both sides rose to the challenge of a question worth facing.

Protection from the fallout was available and the heated discussion that divided the members momentarily might not have divided them permanently had they paused to affirm the covenantal foundation of their life together and to consider the significance of two prepositions. Seemingly forgotten was a very subtle nuance of their polity (how they govern themselves), that where the members are connected by voluntary covenant and not authoritative structure, pronouncements from the national body are never binding anyway. The national body does not speak *for* the church but *to* the church. That does not necessarily make the national body any less irritating, but it might just free the local church to have a necessary conversation without the shadow of "headquarters" pronouncing the outcome of the conversation in advance.

In addition, the Mukwonago church was not destined to crash and burn on the pyre of Vietnam because somewhere in their journey together, the members had developed the capacity to entertain these delicate conversations about social issues. This is no small matter and bears repeating: these people could actually have these conversations! Why do I say this: because in the immediate aftermath of a cataclysmic contest surrounding a social issue, Vietnam, the remaining members had to regroup and appoint new leadership, including members of a search committee. That committee in turn had to prepare their church's profile, the document that introduces the church to prospective candidates for the position of minister, and attach to that document a list of five requisites for the next minister. Of the five, one specified a candidate "who does not get *too* involved in social issues" (emphasis added) which I interpret to mean not that the subject is taboo but that it requires a modicum of pastoral sensitivity both in how it is expressed by the minister as well as how it is received and processed by the membership. Remarkably, the embers still smoldering from the heat of battle, the committee might have ignored the subject altogether—or worse, they might have pronounced social justice issues taboo in any form—but instead they acknowledged the inevitability and even the necessity of these conversations and so they left the door open to the next time they appear, hopefully in a form that does not result in such dire consequences. A remarkable and underappreciated statement.

Remarkable and underappreciated...and suggestive? Maybe it was not just Vietnam and other big-ticket items that troubled the church. As noted, the civil rights and antiwar movements loomed very large in the body politic and quickly found their way into religious bodies as well, and the ongoing social revolution from the tumultuous '60s continued reshaping the values and life-styles of the surrounding cultural landscape, but most churches managed to maneuver a changing landscape without melting down, and the more I listened, the more it became apparent that personality conflicts between certain members and with the minister also added their own irritating friction—so much so in fact that I eventually began to wonder if the church had not split for a lack of good manners.

Good manners seldom reduce to a book of etiquette alone. Polite society also recognizes appropriate behavior that needs no specific rule because, as everyone knows, it is just not done, like lighting a cigarette during the sermon, say, or serving cocktails from the Communion table. You don't find rules about such behavior for the simple reason that no rule is required—those things are just not done—and yet as I listened to the stories, what I called gratuitous irritation did its share to fuel the fire as well. This was aptly illustrated by the person who reportedly removed his shoes and socks and proceeded to trim his toenails during a meeting. People may fight over social issues, but common courtesy and accepted standards of decorum say they will do so with their shoes on. Clearly, the discussion got out of hand.

Whatever the final mix of factors pushing the conflict, the conflict finally arrived at the moment of decision and a vote was taken, the majority supporting the motion to withdraw from the UCC by a margin of seven—for all intents and purposes, a virtual tie. With a vote so close as to represent a stalemate, an outside observer—a conference executive, say, or a trained mediator—might have suggested that the members pause and think things over, maybe even give the covenant a chance to work, but such was not the case and however slight the margin, the majority carried the day and the course was set. The church lost upwards of one-third of its members; the aftermath quite literally divided families, some leaving to form the new congregation and others staying with the continuing congregation, and as in Chadron, it left hostility, distrust, broken relationships, and deep scars in its wake for a generation.

A nasty business, a schism.

One other principle that might have saved the church from the cataclysm bears mentioning: the church does not exist for the sake of the members but rather the members for the sake of the church and its purpose in the world. In practice, this means that church members need to ask not what *they want* by way of program and services from the church but what does *God ask* of them by way of extending the church's witness and work into the world. In the four Servant Songs of Isaiah (Isa. 42.1–4, 49.1–6, 50.4–11, and especially 52.13–53.12), our Hebrew forebears remind us that the faith community appears in the world in the role of the Servant, even the Suffering Servant. A resurrection people, we know that as with the Master, so with the disciple, the path to Easter may lead first by way of the cross. I will return to this theme momentarily.

In any event, I was just 27 when we moved to Mukwonago and for the second time, I found myself struggling with how to resolve serious conflict, but this was also a time of major change for our family. Mukwonago is situated about thirty miles southwest of Milwaukee, close enough to a major city to enjoy the benefits of an urban environment and far enough removed to enjoy the benefits of a rural farming community in the initial throes of suburbanization. With its gently rolling hills and pastoral ambiance, we liked it very much. The church had built a beautiful and spacious parsonage across the parking lot from the church and our family of four lived there very comfortably.

We three became four with the birth of our daughter Deborah Marie in February 1974, almost a year after our having arrived. As reported by her mother, the birth was smooth, just four and one-half hours of labor, and this time, I was present in the delivery room. We had taken the Lamaze birth classes but outside of holding her hand and being in every way the expectant father, I cannot remember actually doing anything helpful. We were thankful for the doctor and the hospital and our daughter.

This joyous event was followed by the loss of three family members in two-and-one-half years. Our daughter was born on Lincoln's birthday and Ann's mother died three months later, a few days before Mother's Day, of complications following gall bladder surgery. She was 65 and prior to going into the hospital, she had uncharacteristically straightened up her house, taking care of piles of papers and collections of notes, as if she knew she was not coming back.

Later that fall, two days before her son's sixth birthday, my sister died of a toxic mix of drugs and alcohol. Her name was Georgia (we called her Gigi) and she was 27 and divorced. She was also a pediatric nurse and certainly knew better, but the coroner ruled her death accidental. A single mother: is there any harder path to follow in these benighted times? I have held her former husband partly responsible for failing to meet his obligations to his son (so with all errant, MIA fathers). In latter years, though, as symptoms mounted, the head injury he had suffered in Vietnam was probably more serious than anyone thought, another casualty of a misbegotten war afflicting wife and son, and I have tried with modest success to be, if not more charitable, at least more understanding.

My sister had named Ann and me as guardians of her son, Bill, in her will and we immediately tried to adopt him, but his paternal grandparents filed a counter motion with the court and ultimately prevailed on the grounds that further disruptions in Bill's living arrangements (there had been some extra-familial caregiving in his recent past and he was currently with his grandparents in California) were not in the best interests of the child. We were living in Wisconsin but had retained a California attorney and made a trip to California to meet with the social worker on whose recommendation the court would rely, and quite frankly, we were dumbfounded that the court would ignore the expressed wishes of both the deceased mother and a willing, capable, and intact family—he would have been the older "brother" to our two children, his cousins.

I have harbored my suspicions ever since, groundless in terms of substantiation, that by design or happenstance, something occurred along the way to derail the process—a casual remark was made, an allegation went unchallenged, the vetting process was compromised by inexperience or cut short in the interest of efficiency...who can say? Our attorney recommended that we not appeal the decision and we accepted his recommendation and the court's decision, but the ramifications of the path not taken and the consequences of its inherent losses obviously continue to the present day.

Parents, of course, are not supposed to bury their children. It's not natural; in the proper order of things, we live our three score years and ten, fourscore if we're lucky (Psalm 90.10), and our children give us a proper funeral, but six months after losing his daughter, my father was diagnosed with prostate cancer and eighteen months later (two years and a few days after her tragic loss, two days before what would have been her 29th birthday, and on the 35th anniversary of the Japanese attack on Pearl Harbor, which he experienced on board his ship), he died. He was 57, I was 30.

Is it mere coincidence that these three losses occurred around what to each one was a significant date, a holiday or anniversary of some sort? Except in the case of a deliberate act of suicide, we do not generally think that we actually choose the time and manner of our exit from this earthly sojourn, but we learn early enough in life that although life is hard, something drives us forward anyway, even in the face of overwhelming obstacles and towering challenges—some unfinished agenda, a compelling purpose, a reason to live...until the work is done, the purpose is satisfied, and the reason no longer applies, at which point maybe we call it a day, and who is to say that we do not pick the day or the season or the anniversary that marks our departure from the earthly sojourn.

As individuals, a mission can spell the difference between merely existing—going through the motions of everyday life—and truly living, tasting life abundantly, meaningfully, joyously. I once had a parishioner, for example, whose sole purpose in life was caring for her daughter, who had Down syndrome. Eventually, the daughter died and within a matter of weeks, the mother died as well. Neither in planning her funeral with her immediate family nor in remembering her life with her church family, no mention of suicide ever surfaced. Caregiving is hard work and even when based on the love of a parent for a child, the physical demands and the emotional stress do take their toll on the body.

A perfectly reasonable explanation, that her body just wore out, but at the same time is it so outlandish to imagine that, even if subconsciously, my parishioner might have felt that her purpose had been fulfilled and that she could see no other relationship(s), no other purpose, mission, or cause taking its place. This was even though she had other happily married children and grandchildren who understandably felt insulted that she did not find them sufficiently worthy to give her a sense of purpose and a continuing reason to live.

We all reach those inflection points where, having finished one particularly significant chapter in our lives, especially if tumultuous and painful, we then either do or do not muster the will to begin the next? I have contemplated that question so often in relation to my dad's life. He and my sister were estranged at the time of her death. Its root causes unaddressed, their reconciliation now beyond reach, he remarked to Ann not long before he died (she only told me of this conversation many years later) that he was tired of living and wanted to be with Gi. Yes, he had cancer and it eventually spread to his back with excruciating pain; yes, he exploited all available medical treatments that in time failed in their purpose; and yet, in addressing both the diagnosis of the disease and its progression, can we rule out the role the elusive will to live might have played, if only subconsciously, in his life's trajectory? So with any of us.

Life is hard (as if we need reminding!), but to borrow from Don Quixote de La Mancha, indignant that he lives in a world where "evil brings profit and virtue none at all" and so takes up the life of knight-errant, what matter the challenges, for "a knight must not complain of his wounds, though his bowels be dropping out." Or his health generally, for that matter, for "what is illness to the body of a knight-errant? What matter wounds? For each time he falls, he shall rise again, and woe to the wicked"—the "monstrous giant of infamous repute," perhaps a windmill, its arms flailing about, the picture of injustice in its many forms and just as pointless to attack…except that one must.[6]

To be possessed of such a mission!

6. From the musical, *Man of La Mancha*, by Dale Wasserman, the immensely popular (if not more accessible) entry to one of the greatest novels of all time, the seminal *The Ingenious Gentleman, Don Quixote de La Mancha* by Miguel De Cervantes Saavedra.

What holds true for individuals holds true for churches as well. Churches need to be possessed by a mission. Not just any mission, but a mission worthy of the message entrusted to the church. That search for a mission to match the message weaves itself through these two churches and would continue to hound me throughout my pastoral work, for the church is not so possessed… and seems perfectly content to have it so.

We cannot say that the church lacks a framework for mission; a theory that translates to practice. The two Great Commandments spell that out clearly enough, to love God with all we are as persons and to extend to neighbors and self (and, I add these days, the creation) the same regard. We need to remember, though, that mission and purpose change with changing circumstances and so whatever form the mission took before their respective battles, that battle dramatically changed the circumstances of not two but four churches (a continuing congregation and a new church in each of the two communities discussed here), and each one needs to assess immediately its next steps—its new mission, if you will.

It takes a lot of energy to refocus on a new path into a different future. In Chadron's case, eight years following their departure from their former church, the members had not really answered the "What Now?" question— or for that matter, had not even seemed to have *asked* it. I described at some length the Native American backdrop, inescapably a looming piece of the cultural landscape, that might have given at least some context for addressing the nature of the church and the purpose of its ministry in that part of the country, but about the only thing the community wanted of its Indians was that they stay on the Reservation. Somewhat more charitably, given the age of the members, even had the spirit been willing, the flesh had given its full measure and then some to the life of the church and its extension into the wider world.

Because it had ended so recently by the time I arrived in Mukwonago, much of the church's energy was directed to the battle itself, its roots, its costs, its casualties. It seems that the immediate aftermath of the fight itself only marked the beginning of its rehearsal, who did what to whom—who is still doing what to whom—who might do what to whom again. The immediate mission of the remaining congregation is to heal, purpose enough at the moment, but it takes a lot of energy to keep the battle going and so easily can focusing excessively on the past rob the people of the resources to embrace the future.

As inevitable and necessary as wading through the history and its associated feelings may be, I was not prepared for the toll it would take on Ann and me. I cannot say I was in any way naïve about the hard work involved and I held before the people the promise of healing and subsequent reconciliation (2 Cor. 5.16-21), but for the first three years the journey to the promised land was largely putting one foot in the front of the other and pressing on. Living with and working through the constant undercurrent of hostility, its atmosphere of distrust, a legacy of broken relationships, and the testimony of festering scars imposed a long, tedious, and arduous process on all of us. I had had a strong dose of all that in Chadron and it continued in Mukwonago, coloring more than its share of my emotional and spiritual landscape for those three years.

The turnaround came during the third year when I took a unit of CPE—Clinical Pastoral Education—with Harvey Berg. Whether the nature of CPE itself or Harvey himself (or both together, the pendulum accenting the latter), the opportunity for a little introspection on the human condition came along at just the right moment, and I had enough good sense to take advantage of it, for the experience taught me the meaning of grace.

Harvey was a Lutheran pastor and ran the Waukesha office of Lutheran Social Services. He had a fine sense of humor and the timing to have succeeded at stand-up comedy had that been his choice. In particular, he had a deep well of ethnic humor from which to draw. He was Norwegian and so could get away with describing a "mixed marriage" in the Northern Wisconsin town of his childhood as the union of a Norwegian and a Swede. As he taught us, humor cuts through history (there's a reason people hate each other) and brings people together...which is, after all, the way of God with humankind, grace at work.

I have always appreciated Victor Borge's quip that "laughter is the shortest distance between two people" and have not infrequently defined grace and laughter as the flip sides of the same coin. God loves us anyway...how can we do less, and where we cannot laugh (another mass shooting, another drunk driver, another payload of bombs, another tragedy demonstrating humanity's inhumanity to its own kind), we weep, as does the gracious God, who loves us anyway; so intimately does God love such as us as to number even the hairs on our heads (Luke 12.7). Essentially, the semester of CPE with Harvey at the helm transformed the idea *of* grace into a feeling *for* grace, the academic definition given a soul as it were. He made it possible to continue the work in Mukwonago for another three years and to pronounce all six years as good.

CPE had an immediate and profound impact on my understanding of pastoral care in the day-to-day work of pastoral ministry, but as Dr. Peggy Way would later teach us, pastoral care has less to do with pastoral ministry as narrowly understood—that is, as limited to professionals with theological training and denominational credentials—and more to do with what she called pastoral persons. In her understanding, pastoral care is another word for the "servant church" and belongs to the pastoral persons who are its members. Sigmund Freud once identified three impossible professions: governing nations, raising families, and doing psychoanalysis. Dr. Way, who taught for many years at Vanderbilt Divinity School, adds a fourth: pastoral ministry, that is, the pastoral ministry of pastoral persons, and she offers poetic imagery to give shape to the high calling. For example, pastoral persons are *Stewards of Narration*, storytellers who listen to the stories of others and find ways *the* Story intersects their stories. As *Existence Clarifiers*, we see the significance of ordinary life and place high valuation on ordinary people whose lives carry depths of meaning. We are *Choreographers of the Human Dance*, seeking to help people learn how to stay together over time. We are *Sculptors* who capture a moment in time. We are *Hosts and Hostesses* who call forth hospitable community.[7]

---

7. In 1983, Dr. Way was the Bible Lecturer for the Annual Meeting of the National Association during which she introduced delegates to these metaphors describing pastoral persons.

A high calling, indeed, not to mention hard work, especially when churches fight and otherwise fall short in living into the words and ways of Jesus. Gentlers and tamers of savage ways; primary interpreters of the nature of human existence; arbiters among persons whose contrary stories just do not collapse together; signposts directing pilgrims through the innumerable tight places of life and the community toward an unknown future with no clear way to get there: Jesus would approve, a way of life that carves a path through the forest with his words and ways. The poetry works much more easily for individuals who see themselves as pastoral persons in the course of their everyday lives than for congregations to extend themselves as pastoral bodies in their corporate life, but it lays the groundwork for that elusive mission equal to the message.

Camus is right: the world needs to hear the church speak out clearly and pay up personally. To that end, the church must speak prophetically, reminding itself and the wider world alike of the divine imperative, the moral demand of "thou shalt" and "thou shalt not" built into the fabric of creation, but then it must also live prophetically, putting the words in action. Understandably, talking such talk and then walking its walk takes courage.

It also takes commitment, and sustaining commitment over time has something to do with feeding the spirit in time. I have already hinted at this but over the years, I would find myself drawn to the wilderness, the fiercer the landscape the better, to sustain my sense of call. Said differently, when it came to finding and maintaining my footing, mere geography mattered. This would not apply to all people to the same extent and certainly not for all people in the same way, but some of us find that the quality of our spirituality specifically and our sense of well-being generally has a direct and intimate connection to our physical surroundings.

We call this the spirituality of place and loosely stated, the idea is that *where* we are geographically has something to do with *who* we become personally. I mentioned an early illustration of this: flying into Rapid City to interview with the search committee in Chadron. Looking at the countryside, I felt right at home, and the drive from Rapid City to Chadron, a mere 100 miles, only confirmed that first impression.

I cannot really explain why but the wilderness has always had a strong attraction to me, especially the desert. It appeals to me, the landscape devoid of all signs of human habitation, in some cases seemingly bleak, harsh and heartless, unforgiving to the unwary and careless. A dirt road and a vehicle with enough clearance to protect the crankcase from an errant rock is the face of seduction.

Our children would confirm that we camped for years in some very unlikely places...on purpose. Private campgrounds sporting recreation rooms looked like aluminum ghettoes to me, and we only stopped in state campgrounds if a national forest setting was unavailable. We might have welcomed a hot shower, but running water generally meant electric hookups which powered transistors and annoying devices that had no place in the wilderness. In later years, Ann and I would drive to certain secret spots in Michigan's Upper Peninsula where you could spend an entire day and not see another living creature. Maybe it had something to do with age—or maybe it had more to do with the decline of civilization as we knew it—but we eventually gave up on camping because the quiet places increasingly fell victim to an encroaching and invasive civilization from which camping had offered its temporary escape.

To appreciate the moment, imagine a place on tourist-heavy Maui off-limits to rental cars and so unknown to most tourists. On the south side of the island, Haleakala, its highest peak rising some 10,000 feet, dwarfs the ant-like bipeds inching their way west from Kaupo. A lava flow from an ancient eruption of the volcano gives the landscape the appearance of what I called the backside of the moon. And with the backside of the moon to one side and the restless sea on the other, the fragility of life and our tenuous hold on existence was exquisitely proclaimed. It was wonderful.

Submerging myself in such places has a way of cleansing my soul, washing away the sins and stains of human civilization (so called and so imagined). I am not frightened by the sea-is-so-big-and-my-boat-is-so-small universe in which our insignificant blue marble seems suspended. After all, a little humility is good for those who in all humility (?) climb into a pulpit week after week to say something about the Creator. The desert Fathers and Mothers knew of what they spoke when they fled the snare of the world (that is to say, the snare of worldly ways) and counseled the same for all would-be pilgrims. Immerse yourself in the fierce landscape, they seemed to say, and see if the indifference of God does not in the end rather lead to God. In the end, this is the gift of the wilderness, that it leads to and so renews one's relationship with the Creator, and so renewed, it is possible to pick up the work once again and continue along the way.

With its much denser population in southeast Wisconsin, the wilderness was more a frame of mind than a geographical setting. But in a pinch, a nearby marsh (especially bleak in the fall) and the easily accessible Kettle Moraine offered their own opportunities of abandonment. At a minimum, the human spirit needs open spaces and quiet places and suffers accordingly when parks are neglected, adequate recreational outlets ignored, and squalor and ugliness dominate the surrounding environment.

If the first three years at Mukwonago comprised the difficult, one-foot-in-front-of-the-other chapter, the second chapter, nearly as long, marked a generally happy, productive period. We did not make much progress on my quest for the holy grail of a mission to compel our commitment. In rejecting the United Church of Christ, the remaining members clearly knew what they did not want in terms of their denominational identity and its mission, but they had not taken the more difficult step of identifying what they did want with their new fellowship—the National Association—and a mission. While outwardly calm, unfinished agenda still festered beneath the surface as the members continued to deal with the aftershocks of the earthquake that split the church. Resolving issues from the past consumes energy not otherwise available for looking ahead.

Along with the church picking up its life and continuing the journey, so did Ann and I have a parallel journey in the wake of having lost three family members in such a short time. Three times did we return from funerals in California with little or no response from the congregation. Midwestern reserve? Longstanding expectation that the parsonage family will take care of itself? A failure on their part to ask? (What, you have to ask?) All these years later, still a puzzle? Some extra time off, a long weekend with the family, some acknowledgment that it's OK to idle for awhile before racing down the road would have sent a nice message.

Life for the First Family carries with it a built-in element of loneliness. For perfectly understandable reasons ministers were cautioned never to have friends in the church, and while this did not necessarily apply to the minister's wife to quite the same degree, it did close off friendships the family as a whole might have had with other church families. Other unwritten but deeply felt expectations definitely attached themselves to her position, though. Not so entertaining then but all these years later, we have to laugh in recalling how at one point the Mukwonago search committee turned its attention to Ann and informed us of the sins of her would-be predecessor: it seems their previous First Lady smoked, swore, eschewed shoes, enjoyed short skirts, and protested. Inappropriate behaviors for the wife of the resident Congregational minister, apparently, and as part of the interviewing process, the committee quizzed her regarding those practices: smoking—no; swearing—in those days, no; bare feet—not in church; short skirts—not in church; protesting—only for cause. History no longer records her precise responses, but she must have slipped by because they called me anyway.

A moment of levity that nonetheless illustrates the downside of the job for which the minister's wife never applies.

Too bad they did not ask what she might bring to the church besides her husband. She might have talked about the summer before my senior year in seminary when I served as the Chaplain at a Pennsylvania State Park. More accurately, I would interject, the summer *we* served, for she led the singing.

A tale in its own right. Ann had taught herself to play the guitar listening to Peter, Paul, and Mary records and she readily adapted the standard hymns from the venerable *Pilgrim Hymnal* to the guitar in time for Sunday services. This was a large park and campers numbered in the hundreds at our services. Thinking it might be fun, we announced a midweek evening hymn sing and once again went to the venerable *Pilgrim Hymnal* (really one of the premier hymnals in the English language), selected a representative corpus from the great body of English hymnody with some Peter, Paul, and Mary and the other standards from the '60s thrown in for good measure, and printed up song sheets. We estimated maybe twenty-five, possibly as many as forty, might show up. Imagine our surprise when two hundred and more gathered around the campfire (as darkness fell, and the back rows of camp chairs disappeared in the forest, it was hard to tell the exact number, but as the summer wore on, it was probably in the range of 400 or so).

Imagine our greater surprise when no one knew the great hymns of English hymnody and seemed never to have heard of Peter, Paul, and Mary. It turned out that we were deep in the Bible Belt and what these good folks sang in their churches was Gospel. I had never heard of Gospel music, my church having left out the necessity of being washed in the blood of the Lamb and such messages in my tender years. Ann's upbringing was not quite so limited and so she had a passing familiarity with their requests, but between that Wednesday and the next, we both learned a lot of really fun Gospel music. The theology posed some dilemmas, but we have never forgotten the sound of several hundred voices joyously celebrating the saving work of Jesus, and even today we will occasionally break out in songs we first learned fifty years ago from our summer sojourn in the Bible Belt. We had a small battery-powered public address system with a handheld microphone, completely useless in an outdoor setting with several hundred enthusiastic voices reaching to the heavens, and I still marvel at the image of a 5'3" blond, an acoustic guitar around her neck, leading the masses, showers of blessings filling the air and everyone anticipating that day when the trumpet shall sound and time will be no more. Amen.

Somehow early in our marriage we managed to buy a grand piano and Ann's gifts as both a pianist and composer have always nurtured my own spiritual life. We would often choose Sunday's hymns together, and if I was lucky she would add a Gospel riff before we were done, always fun. Occasionally, she would write religious music, but from somewhere deep inside her own being she generated melodies and modulations that carried the self to places only accessible by music (and not necessarily "religious" music). It was always a disappointment to both of us that the music departments of our churches essentially ignored her gifts and in one church in particular she quit singing in the choir because she tired of the choirs' complaining about the minister. I suspect being the church's First Lady was a liability to her participating on the same footing with other members, but I always found worshipful moments when she was at her piano.

Be that as it may, in terms of numbers, Prince Gallitzin State Park in the summer of 1970 was our zenith, never again to be matched, and little did we know then the latent creativity that would find expression in a lifetime of composing. Already in Mukwonago, though, Ann's creativity found expression in both original pieces and in arrangements of standards, both performed by a group she founded, the Trinity Singers.

As our sixth year at Mukwonago began to unfold, I felt that pastor and parish were running on cruise control. The worst of the civil war was behind us, continuing skirmishes notwithstanding, and while not a place to dwell too long, pausing for a time on a plateau after a particularly tough upward climb has its rewards.

In that frame of mind, Ann and I drove to the Annual Meeting of the National Association. I went (and frequently we both went) every year to the annual ecclesiastical family reunion. Depending on the location, we often took some vacation time following the meeting. This year, however, the meeting was held in Toledo and with no other plans, we expected to attend the meeting and return home. The assembly always concludes with a banquet but for both the church and for us personally, money was tight and so pleading poverty, we decided not to attend the closing extravaganza that year—no problem.

Then, one of those seemingly insignificant, certainly inconsequential events took place that changed our lives forever. A colleague and his wife, Harry and Mary Graichen, offered their banquet tickets to Ann and me. At one time, Harry was on the staff of Pilgrim Congregational Church in

Pomona and was the founding minister of the Naperville Congregational Church, in a southwestern suburb of Chicago, where I had done my student intern work while in seminary (smaller world still). We had nothing better to do that evening, and the meal was always good, and so without much enthusiasm we accepted their kind offer and to the banquet we went.

The after-dinner speaker that year was Dr. Benton Gaskell of Pilgrim Church, Pomona, and he had us in stitches. In one especially memorable story, Ben recounted how he had slowly disappeared into the grave intended for the deceased as he finished the words of the committal service at the cemetery. Apparently, the ground was soaked and it had started to rain again and everybody ran for cover—everybody, that is, except the parson who stood his ground even though the ground gave way as he raised his hand for the benediction and slowly slipped from view.

Along those same lines, he also shared the time he rode with the funeral director to the cemetery only to look down at his feet and discover that his shoes did not match. How someone could put on two different shoes and not notice until hours later is something I never quite understood, but you can imagine the horror for the person wearing two different shoes, and that Ben was telling the story on himself gave the rest of us permission to relish the humor...and its resolution, for the funeral director got to the cemetery in time to place Ben at the proper spot and wrap his feet in flowers so nobody would notice that the preacher wore two different shoes. Of course, that the preacher did not leave his post until all the mourners had abandoned theirs would have been noticeable, but better that peculiarity make the gossip circuits than word get out that young Mr. Gaskell did not have the wits to dress himself in the morning, poor fellow.

It just so happened that Pilgrim was looking for an Associate Minister. I was not looking to make a change and was even less interested in a staff position than a solo or senior position, but that night I saw a side of ministers and ministry that caused Ann and me to consider the opportunity at Pilgrim Church. We went home, had my profile sent to the church's search committee, and four months later I reported for my first day on my new job.

Eventually, my boss arrived and invited me into his office. By anyone's standards, the large and spacious office was splendid, even lavish. He pointed me toward the chair in which I was to sit while he took his place behind his expansive, substantial executive's desk. I eagerly anticipated his first words, which were these: "Well," he said, "you know what they say…[pause]…that the only thing worse than *being* an associate minister is *having* one."

So began my treasured relationship with Dr. Benton S. Gaskell, Senior Minister of Pilgrim Congregational Church, Pomona, California.

CHAPTER 3

THE OASIS
AND THE FRYING PAN

"A faith which involves no sacrifice turns out in the end to be merely
an excuse for being the sort of person one is."

~T. S. ELIOT

"The Truth to be told…the Way to be walked…the Light to be lit."

~MOTHER TERESA
on Jesus' own question, Who do you say that I am?

PILGRIM CONGREGATIONAL CHURCH PROVED TO be something of an oasis for us, a midpoint between the shambolic aftermath of two churches that had fought and split and another version of the same…on steroids. The oasis metaphor does have something of a drawback in that it suggests a time of rest and a place of refuge, neither of which really applies, but in offering a breather from two conflicted churches and yet another lurking in the wings, Pilgrim gave me time and space and opportunity to expand my ministerial expertise, and so in that respect, Pomona offered a much-appreciated oasis indeed.

And little did I know at the time that Pilgrim would also open the door to an enduring friendship and mentor in Ben Gaskell. Like many of his immediate peers, Dr. Benton Gaskell was very well educated and extremely well read. Articulate and erudite, he also possessed a dry and sometimes piercing sense of humor and in recognition of his razor sharp wit, I happily purloin one of his more cryptic observations in the title of my book. "Acres of oak" was shorthand for the empty pews he could not escape noticing on a Sunday morning in the very large Pilgrim Church sanctuary. It spoke volumes about the changing cultural landscape and its attendant challenges that I catalog in these pages.

He was a rising star in the old denomination in the years following World War II. He served churches both large and small, new and established, and had come to Pilgrim for what would be his last pastorate, but unlike so many of our kind, he seemingly lacked all sense of pretention, hiding his intellectual prowess behind his self-effacing humor. He would call on the phone—this intelligent, educated, cultured, informed minister—and frequently he would identify himself by saying, "This is Old Ben." Old Ben. I knew a host of senior ministers, esteemed leaders of our denomination, men (they were all men in those days) my younger generation never addressed by their first name but only as Dr. So-and-So (they all had doctorates and many had three names). Perhaps of the same craft but certainly not their equal, not a one would I have ever addressed as "Old So-and-So" (lest I be swallowed up by the Pit) and never would one of their esteemed caste have called me saying, "this is Old Whomever," and for good reason: they had earned their formal recognition, and while I took note of what they did and how they did it, I would not call them my mentors.

Pilgrim was one of a growing number of "red brick" churches in those days, a euphemism for the once-large, formerly influential, frequently iconic, and now gradually diminishing, mainline Protestant churches located socially, if not geographically, at the center of a city or town. The community's movers and shakers, families of means, key business leaders, and a large swath of professional people all belonged to such churches. As preposterous as it sounds today, for a long time following World War II, social standing, business contacts, and access to the proper circles made membership in select churches necessary. It would be unfair to say that was the only reason people joined the church—surely, people sought out churches looking for answers to questions religion routinely explores—but woven into the public landscape of the period was a kind of "cultural Christianity" where good people went to good churches and lived good lives, a sanitized Jesus watching from the wings.

"Red Brick" Pilgrim was also centered in a community in demographic transition. Like much of metropolitan Los Angeles, Pomona was experiencing a rapidly expanding Latino population and a correspondingly rapid decline in the "Non-Hispanic White" population (the latter in 2010 was just 12.5% of the total population while "Latino or Hispanic of any race" was 70.5%).

In hindsight, I wondered if the church's leadership had considered bringing a Latino/a minister to the staff in 1978, or at least a staff member conversant in Spanish, but even if some were reading the demographic tea leaves, I never sensed anyone felt the need (or dared) to test those waters. Today, churches have no choice but to engage their wider community whatever its makeup as an alternative to either closing their doors or settling for museum status, but when I arrived on the scene, Pilgrim could still ignore the inherent challenges of demographically induced social and institutional changes, at least in the short-term. This was quite understandable, for Pilgrim was still a large church with enough people and financial and other resources to develop and maintain its traditional ministry and program offerings. Its members were largely middle class and upper middle class, with a smattering of the Old Pomona social aristocracy. They had wide-ranging interests and the education and means to pursue them. In other words, it was an interesting place with interested people who loved the church that had served them and Pomona alike for decades.

But the inevitable cracks had begun to appear in the outward façade as the traditional model for large churches—a combination of great preaching, good music, and quality programming, all serviced by a competent staff—began to lose its effectiveness. By the time I arrived, Pilgrim membership and attendance were both down from the "glory days," and pledge income was no longer sufficient by itself to support current operations. (I was taught that dependence on endowment and other non-pledge income was the original "red flag" that something was wrong.)

The numbers alone, though, did not tell the whole story. Demographics were certainly problematical (more of "them," fewer of "us," the new ethnicity reducing the traditional pool of potential members for "our" kind of church), but the educational wings told the larger, and more important story. Built after

World War II for the Boomers, they were expected to produce next-generation members, but increasingly, instead of wandering from the Sunday School to the Sanctuary, the children wandered out the door, their parents often following.

As a harbinger of a declining customer base, I think of the middle-aged couple that left the church in this time period because the whole thing no longer made any sense to them. They were not at odds with the church's theology and programing or angry with the clergy or other members. They had simply raised their children in the church and with the children grown and on their own, they could not for the life of them find any compelling reason to continue and so they withdrew their membership. Their numbers would become legion over the next few decades.

Like the tip of an iceberg, such anecdotal evidence and its dry and sterile counterpart, raw statistics, do little more than point to trouble lurking beneath the surface, about which there is much to say (essentially, the rest of the book!), but I will simply acknowledge here that while we ("we" here being both professional and lay leadership) could not ignore the tip, neither did we particularly care to dive into those unfamiliar waters. The old build-it-and-they-will-come model of maintaining the life of the church may have been showing its age, but so long as a little oil stopped the squeaking machinery, we applied more oil.

I do not recall actually using the word, but in coming decades, churches (and all other manner of American institutions for that matter) would begin to add a new word to their ecclesiastical dictionaries: innovation. Anyone could oil the hinges and under the guise of the Church Growth Movement, we were all tinkering and oiling and doing whatever was necessary (short of substantial change, of course) to keep the institution humming and everyone happy. Robert Schuller, the founding pastor of the Garden Grove Community Church in Southern California and the backbone of the sprawling television ministry, Hour of Power, was one of the first to suggest that maybe we needed to think a little larger.

Exhibit A was Schuller himself. He began his work in Orange County in 1951 by leading services from the concession stand roof at the local drive-in theater. "Come as you are in the family car," the first of many slogans, took root and resulted 30 years later in the iconic Crystal Cathedral, the $20 million (an enormous sum at the time) glass church that could only have appeared in Orange County, almost within view of Disneyland's Matterhorn Mountain. From his office in the 16-story adjoining Tower of Hope, he could see the unlikely spot which spawned a religious empire.

Although I did attend his "Institute for Successful Church Leadership," I was never a Schuller disciple. His hybrid theology, "Possibility Thinking," was too heavy on you-can-if-you-think-you-can...with-God's-help and too weak on the prophetic voice for my enthusiastic endorsement. He was famous for his quips, many of which echoed the ever-popular self-help movement, the accent falling on *self*. Catchy they are: "inch by inch, anything's a cinch;" "the tassel is always worth the hassle;" "tough times never last, but tough people do;" "turn your scars into stars;" "beginning is half done."

But not exclusively on the self: perhaps the most popular, "Find a Need and Fill It, Find a Hurt and Heal It," drew upon an actual model, Jesus washing the disciples' feet (John 13.1–17)! He taught that any church could succeed if it had unchurched people with needs within commuting distance of its location; whether it actually *would* succeed, however, was a function of putting the needs of the unchurched above the interests and preferences of the members them-selves. In effect, this makes each local church a mission station (one of his most important contributions to contemporary ecclesiastical thought). As such, and in light of overwhelming human need, a church would only fail if it chose to fail, its own selfishness taking precedence over the needs of the neighborhood beyond its own walls. Nothing shallow or superficial there.

My personal favorite, however, is this: never let the problem-solving phase interfere with the decision-making phase. Rather, we are to make the right decisions and then solve the problems because we never have all the problems solved at the beginning and by combining the two phases, the decisions will not be creative, innovative, and inventive. It turns out that the difference between success and failure has nothing to do with opportunities (or the perceived lack thereof) but how one responds to ideas and the decisions one makes in light of them. In sum, a successful, growing church will have clear goals and objectives built on superlative ideas arising out of human problems that call for a solution; such goals are at once exceptional and inspirational as well as practical and effective in the field.

Nice theory, but back home, does it work? On the one hand, it always seems so obvious as to what must be done to serve effectively whether the mission station is one of the countless garden-variety churches populating street corners across the country or a powerhouse like the Crystal Cathedral. Having worked with the principles of Church Renewal-Congregational Revitalization for my entire ministry, I have seen time and again that the problem lies not with the theory but the execution, for between the idea (Find a Need and Fill It, Find a Hurt and Heal It) and its implementation, congregations and their leaders forget that addressing needs and healing hurts after the manner of Jesus washing the disciples' feet puts the Other before the Self. In plain language, the church exists for one reason, to give itself away. Church growth recognizes that fundamental principle. At our best, we do not "grow" the church for its own sake, to get more paying customers in the pews, but to address the needs of those who may come to fill our pews and support our various ministries (and, yes, facilities) with their time, talent, and treasure, but then that intervening variable gets in the way, the stumbling block between envisioning our best and doing our best...the prospect—and more realistically, the likelihood—that something must change. Even for modest proposals, the pressure to remain the same often stalls the desire and even the commitment to transform existing structures (ministries and programs) into something new.

So, back home, with innovation ringing in my ears, what did we do? A large part of my portfolio involved children and youth and their families and among the catalog of responses we made to our changing situation, two in particular centered on Sunday school and youth programming.

Most every church will have a group of people primarily interested in its children and youth and as I quickly learned, the "CE" (Christian education) folks at Pilgrim had long felt neglected by the church's professional leaders. Six months after my arrival, they wanted me to know that in their opinion things had not improved. Their assessment warranted further exploration, and so I scheduled a meeting to look at those things still needing improvement. For my part, and feeling somewhat defensive, I pointed out that the church did in fact provide the church school with a substantial theology and an abundance of ideas. I observed further that the members routinely committed considerable financial resources to the children and youth, including that portion of my salary directed their way by my job description, necessary classroom materials, and the maintenance of classroom and recreational space for their use. They themselves constituted a substantial core of caring leaders—what more could a church offer its children and youth than its own people?

While sincere, or sincere enough as far as it went, my efforts did little to allay feelings of neglect, so I rehearsed with them the circumstances facing the church that accounted for its numerical decline in spite of our best efforts to navigate the uncertain waters of a changing world. Yes, they knew that Pomona was changing demographically but, they said, we still had a sizeable number of children and youth on our Sunday School rolls. Of course, the Evangelical and Charismatic churches were getting all the attention and most of the glory but, they reminded me, we were not an Evangelical or Charismatic church and were not likely to become so, nor were the children and youth of our Sunday school. Obviously, the illusionary world of "Ozzie and Harriet" had long since evaporated (if it had ever existed) but, they observed, the children of our families did not expect to grow up in an "Ozzie and Harriet" world so what were we going to do to equip them to navigate a social climate that was decidedly different from "Ozzie and Harriet," a world that was pluralistic in attitude and values, contradictory in agenda, and not particularly concerned with the fading glory of Christendom.

I don't recall any attorneys in their number, but they had prepared and argued their case very well!

In such a world, they wanted to know, how do we tend to the education of children and youth (and for that matter, adults)? On that critical matter, our Sunday school cadre felt neglected (maybe for cause, I began to suspect—to myself of course). From the second century, Tertullian had reminded the church that "Christians are fashioned, not born" (I hear echoes of Greenville, South

Carolina, and those Methodists who abandoned us for the Fox Theater) but the church had always counted on the wider culture to help out in that regard: *Christmas* programs, *Easter* vacations, Blue Laws, Church Night, the obligatory invocation at civic events were all standard fare. Once that was gone and the church had to fashion the faithful by itself, the church had a problem: not just *what* to do but *how* to do it because now the church had competition when it came to the formation of young hearts and minds, spiritually and otherwise.

No wonder some might have felt neglected by those who supposedly had the answers to such questions. A presiding judge hearing such a complaint would most certainly have found for the plaintiffs (I would have ruled for the plaintiffs): neglected, indeed.

But not abandoned, for we took two actions, the first of which focused on Sunday morning by naming two passionate educators superintendents to work with me in designing and supervising a two-hour Sunday school program, each hour with a different purpose, format, and structure and the two hours together complementing each other. At the time, it met the need. A decade or so later, the situation with regard to church families and Sunday schools would become more complex and so demand a more extensive and more comprehensive solution, but this early response taught a basic lesson: to identify the people with the passion for the mission-ministry under consideration, give them the tools to succeed, and empower and free them to go to work.

And work it did! There was no more talk about neglect, and as for the two superintendents who transformed our Sunday school, they were understandably busy with their program but we found time to celebrate their wedding (to one another) anyway.

The second step we took was to purchase our bus, not a luxurious bus like the Country and Western stars and their bands use when on tour and not even one of their castoffs, but a castoff school bus. Built by Ford with a very thirsty V-8 engine, it bounced and lurched something fierce, but we were visionaries: with talk about oil depletion in the air and prices escalating, we knew it was just a matter of time before people would start abandoning their cars, and we reasoned that the church family might be willing to put up with the discomfort of a hot and noisy school bus in order to do fun things with their other, equally miserable compatriots. Family outings with the church family…a winning recipe for the church if ever there was one.

We were fortunate in that one of the men of the church assumed the task (more like the burden) of the care and maintenance of our bus, and it had to pass a state inspection, so at least it was safe…or so we told ourselves. As a former parishioner used to tell me with disturbing regularity, God takes special care of fools. Maybe so, but to this day, whenever I see a church bus, I give it wide berth.

I actually became one of the drivers, a scary tale all by itself, for my experience was limited to a few maneuvers in the parking lot and a dozen or so turns around the block, and off I went to the Department of Motor Vehicles which, after a ten-minute romp, determined I was worthy of chauffeuring 66 persons around the streets and freeways of California.

One event is worth the telling. Coming back from a trip one pleasant afternoon, we pulled off the road to change drivers. (Like doctors, we would practice as we go.) Quite inadvertently, we stopped directly in front of a sleazy building, which turned out to be an adult bookstore. Our church name, boldly emblazoned on the side, was enough to bring out the owner, obviously alarmed that a group of Christians was about to challenge his service to the wider community, but he had nothing to fear from the Christians for as quickly as he came out, we just as quickly drove away (both saved, as it were).

What was that verse again, something about "go ye into all the world…and so forth?"

We make our approximations and carry on, but really, finding ourselves in front of an adult bookstore (if only to change drivers), was that the best we could do, which is to say, doing nothing? Have Christians nothing pertinent to say when it comes to human sexuality? Was it just serendipity that we changed drivers at that very spot…or the leading of the Holy Spirit? Were we to hone the driving skills of our team of drivers or lead a discussion on what the Seventh Commandment suggests when it comes to human relationships?

I did not connect the dots at the time, but as in Chadron with its proximity to the Pine Ridge Indian Reservation, so in a sleazy corner of the teeming metropolis, the question of mission would continue to perk, matching the mission to the message ever the challenge.

I will ever be grateful to Pilgrim Church itself and its Board of Christian Outreach for nurturing my own developing sense of mission. The church actually tithed on its operating budget at that time and had direct involvement with projects in Mexico that included a school, the Pan American Institute (PAI) in Tijuana. Ann and I still sponsor a student there forty years later. One of our Congregational ministers started the school in the 1960s by rounding up a few old typewriters, plopping them down in someone's patio, and finding someone to teach some young teens how to type. The goal was to give them a marketable skill they could take downtown and get a job. In the 1960s, I graduated from one of the finest public education and university systems in the world. A hundred and fifty miles to the south, separated by an invisible line called a border, existed another universe where teenagers who learned to type might get jobs in poverty-stricken Tijuana.

Talk about different worlds! I had no idea. Apart from driving through the Pine Ridge Indian Reservation in South Dakota, I had never seen the face of poverty up close and personal. The Los Angeles suburb of Westchester was very White, very middle class, and very protected. We were so isolated socially (such people lived not all that far away geographically) that the minister of the church in which I grew up once preached a sermon on what the church would do if a "Negro" walked into the sanctuary one Sunday (he or she would be welcome). The church of my childhood and youth did not exactly plant the seeds of the Social Gospel.

The deficiencies of my upbringing were finally addressed, though, one fine Saturday when a Pilgrim missionary invited me to drive to Tijuana, see the school, and drop off some supplies. Even long after I left the church, I would speak of him and his wife as Pilgrim's missionaries. They were not "missionaries" in the traditional sense of the word, that is, as those sent to do church work abroad, but they did so embody the missionary spirit as a *way of life* as to qualify in my estimation as Pilgrim's missionaries in the best sense of the word. I suppose that at our best, *being* church and *doing* ministry makes missionaries of each of us and when I wonder what that looks like in practice, those folks from Pilgrim come to mind.

They had a special love for Mexico and in addition to the school, they supported an independent medical clinic further down in Baja California. They never fully (or even partially) disclosed their methods and sources, and I finally decided there were some things I just did not need to know, but over time various supplies would accumulate and find their way across the border. One remarkable day, they brought their adopted daughter home from Mexico who today with her American citizenship and the opportunities it provides is living a life that would have forever eluded her grasp.

So, not content just to talk the talk of Christian Outreach, my missionary-parishioner and friend and I drove the 132 miles from Pomona to Tijuana and crossed the border into another, not particularly parallel, universe where I saw the face of poverty up very close and all too personal. It was a profound, life-changing moment, an ever-evolving piece of the ever-evolving puzzle of just what it means for the people of God to be in mission and the need to develop a sense of mission that involved more than improving the skills of the church's bus drivers.

My tenure at Pilgrim would prove to be relatively short-lived as became apparent when Ben announced his retirement. Of course, I knew that day would come sooner or later—in this case, it just arrived sooner than later—and with it came the "Now What?" question for our family.

This posed a real dilemma. Technically, I was eligible to apply for the senior position, but I recognized that staff clergy are seldom promoted to the senior position (the leap from the "junior" to the senior role presents a psychological challenge for the congregation). In addition, a group of Ben's detractors had tried to entice me to their side (a divide-and-conquer strategy that most certainly would have gone badly for everyone), and when I refused to let that happen, they became less enthralled with me as well, a liability for anyone starting in the senior role.

A bigger issue, though, was my own hesitation and subsequent indecision born of doubts on two fronts. On the one hand, I felt ill-prepared to lead a church whose cultural context—that is to say, whose neighborhood—was in social, economic, and demographic transition. At the same time, I also harbored serious doubts that the members would follow me along the path I knew instinctively I would want to pursue.

In the end, my misgivings won out and I chose not to apply for the Senior position. Obviously, we will never know for sure how it might have turned out either way because shortly thereafter, another opportunity came along which I did accept and the question of Pilgrim became moot, although (and not to put too fine a point on it) I would note that no one expressed any disappointment that another church had snatched me away from them.

For many reasons, Pilgrim was good for me. I took advantage of the opportunity to develop some pastoral interests (especially the eternal question of the church's mission, in this case shaped by Pilgrim's urban setting) and the experience I gained from working in a large church and the insights and wisdom I gleaned from my friend and mentor, Old Ben, have served me and my ministry ever since. WWBD?—What Would Ben Do? Not that I always did it, but I never stopped asking.

Returning to California and my serving as Pilgrim's Associate Minister had benefits of particular importance to Ann as well, perhaps the most significant of which was the opportunity to complete her undergraduate Bachelor of Arts degree at Pitzer College, one of the cluster of Claremont Colleges in nearby Claremont. Reflecting her first love and real interest in music, a second Bachelor in Music Education and a Master's Degree in Music Composition would follow in coming years, but even at Pitzer she managed to take a class in orchestrating an original piece she had composed. I always thought it was remarkable that she had taught herself guitar listening to Peter, Paul, and Mary records, but hearing an assembled orchestra play her original music was nothing short of astounding. She had the talent and had she had the encouragement from home and school she might have become a concert pianist, but men dominated the music field, including teaching positions, and her (male) guidance counselors steered her in other directions.

Eventually, she picked up where the original journey had left off but as a full-time wife and mother and part-time student also managing a part-time job. A generation later, our daughter would find the same attitude in a high school math teacher, but taking a cue from her role-model mother and the support of both parents, she refused to let the deficiencies of the culture dictate her future.

Pomona also gave Ann a respite from the role of Minister's Wife. Things had gradually settled down in Mukwonago, but the expectations were still considerable. In Pomona, those expectations had essentially disappeared for her because the Senior Minister's wife, Audrey, had enthusiastically shouldered them for years. It was a welcome breather for her.

How quickly that would now change, for having decided not to pursue the position of Senior Minister at Pilgrim, I was at liberty to consider and finally to accept the position of Minister at Mayflower Congregational Church of San Gabriel, some twenty-five miles west of Pomona. The mixed metaphors aside, if Pilgrim was something of an oasis, my new position was definitely jumping into the frying pan in so far as it came with the same internal conflict that I had experienced in Chadron and Mukwonago, only more so.

Just how bad was the in-fighting in San Gabriel? Not content with only two antagonists, early on I identified four warring parties. The members lined up in various sectors depending on who was in charge at the moment and how they felt about the minister. Among the two of the more important quartet, one group called a meeting of the membership and elected me as the (new) minister while another group held on to the machinery of its governing structure and refused to let the (old) minister resign, in effect calling me to serve in an office not yet vacant!

In short order, adjustments addressed that technicality, but as I would also quickly learn, over the years as the various factions see-sawed for control, the losing faction(s) did not so much leave the church, giving the spoils to the victor, as retire to the backbench, there to wait for opportune moments to strike back. Among the combatants were a few of whom I was actually afraid, not for my life as such but certainly for my welfare and that of my family were they to pull some string or push some button.

Congregationalists from three area Congregational churches founded Mayflower in 1961.[8] Their churches had affiliated with the United Church of Christ, and unwilling to accept their respective church's decision (a quick reminder: each local congregation individually took its own vote on the merger issue, a yes or a no typically the choice, although some voted not to vote at all), the disaffected left and formed the new church. Apparently, it had a place in the wider community because by the end of the decade Mayflower had become a 900-member church. Phenomenal growth, but the numerical measures also reflect that something serious was stirring, for while the church grew rapidly and held steady through the mid-1970s at around 850, by the mid-1980s, membership had plummeted by two-thirds (a loss of some 600 members in ten years).

Finances followed membership, and by the late 1970s the church depended on rental and investment income to cover budget deficits. In just one year, the number of pledging units dropped by one-third from 215 (1975) to 138 (1976). By 1984, just one-third of the operating expenses came from current income (at which point the church had 52 pledging units). Little wonder that just 20 years from its founding, at the time I began my ministry at Mayflower in 1981, I should wonder if the church was still viable.

Taken as a whole, the lifespan of the church featured phenomenal growth, a brief plateau, and a rather spectacular implosion, all in a brief 35 years.

Although I resist the mere notion, the collapse had an aura of inevitability given the confluence of issues that swirled around the people at the time. I count four such factors, each of which contributed to a breakdown in the vital relationship between the church and what I like to call the "neighborhood" if the church is to thrive and in many cases even survive. The term itself, neighborhood, is shorthand for the social and cultural landscape, the wider community and the surrounding context, within which a congregation's mission and purpose take shape...or not. The neighborhood is not so much a matter of geography as a state of mind (or spirit). With television,

8. For the record, Oneonta Congregational, South Pasadena; First Congregational, Pasadena; and Arcadia Congregational, Arcadia.

and certainly the internet and various social media platforms, the concept of neighborhood as a place becomes practically meaningless, but pragmatically speaking, where a church and its members are grounded geographically, the neighborhood may extend as far as the time its members routinely take to drive to work.

In any event, a church—*any* church—must ever monitor what it means to *be* church and *do* ministry within its neighborhood setting. This is difficult enough in relatively calm and stable neighborhoods and it becomes exponentially harder when the social and cultural landscape of the wider community is changing, as was the case in the San Gabriel Valley at the time. Whether because it would not or could not, Mayflower did not seriously address its surrounding social dynamics, and it simply did not have a theological foundation with sufficient depth to raise and wrestle with the necessary missional questions that might have helped to right the ship. The same, of course, might be said of most any of the mainline churches, but in Mayflower's case, the consequences of the growing mismatch between the church and its neighbors were devastating.

Of the four factors, the first was strictly sociological: demographics. Nothing challenged the mainline churches in the San Gabriel Valley (if not the Los Angeles basin generally) like the profound demographic changes taking place in the latter years of the last century and continuing into the present. Not just declining membership figures and financial support but Chinese, Filipino, Korean, Japanese, and Vietnamese immigration should have signaled the need to revisit the defining mission, what it means to *be* church and *do* ministry, in light of tectonic changes in the surrounding culture.

Households in Alhambra, for example, had so many children that the public schools had to go to double shifts. In the extremely affluent community of San Marino, some 44 different languages were represented among the high school students. Chinese immigrants settled in one nearby community in such large numbers that it was not uncommon to hear someone mutter that the last American to leave Monterey Park should please bring the flag. Pained, yes; racist, certainly; encouraging, not very.

Suffice to say, area clergy certainly talked about local immigration among themselves and made ample use of school and governmental resources and agencies to help get a handle on the complexities inherent in cross-cultural relationships, but try as I might, I could not get much traction with my people to build on those discussions or make use of those resources in any meaningful way. Some churches, like the United Methodist Church which had seminary-trained ethnic clergy to deploy and the bishop's authority to place them, added multiple ministries within existing congregations, but most of the rest of us just stood on the sidelines and watched our membership numbers either stagnate or continue to decline. From time to time, one ethnic church or another would ask to rent space in our facilities. A Korean church even asked to join (not rent from but become members of) Mayflower and were denied that opportunity (the first step in taking over, so the argument went). Following suit, rental requests never went anywhere, either.

A second, and closely related, factor was competition: too many churches vying for members at a time when changing demographics in the San Gabriel Valley created a decreasing pool of potential White, middle-class members from which to draw, the traditional source of support for these churches. Some might find the marketing language offensive, but as one lay leader would remark 20 or so years later in similar circumstances, "there just aren't enough White people left to prop up all these White churches." A little crass, perhaps, but still descriptive.

Real estate was not only changing hands (so to speak) but it was also becoming more expensive in San Gabriel and surrounding communities, forcing younger families to settle in more distant suburban and exurban areas. This left an older population and an increasing number of single-generation households in place which further hampered membership development. As will be seen momentarily, the age of the remaining congregation was a key issue in the matter of addressing its challenges.

In sum, and illustrating the impact of demographics on competition, the Pasadena area had seven (so-called) "Congregational" churches within reach of each other (eventually the eighth would come from a Mayflower schism). Encompassing liberal (five) and evangelical (three) theologies and two denominational affiliations (UCC and NA) as well as "independent" status, they were hardly cut from the same cloth, but prospective members either not interested in or otherwise unaware of the nuances regarding denominational affiliation (if any) had choices. Taking into consideration the broad range of other (especially mainline) churches and the varied theological orientations and ecclesiastical expressions of a pluralistic faith community only exacerbated the "marketing" challenge.

The answer to the above, of course, is for the members to tackle the third factor, theology, by which is meant both their faith and their faithfulness, that is to say, both their core beliefs and what they do with it (the "Now What?" or the "So What?" of faith) as individuals and as a faith community. To understand the theological challenge Mayflower faced, though, one must begin with the church that spawned it, the First Congregational Church of Los Angeles. (My later immersion in that church takes a whole chapter to tell all by itself, but its title, "My Dark Night of the Soul," sets the tone in both places.)

In its glory days, the Los Angeles church was the largest Congregational church in the country with some 4,500 members and was known for channeling the religion of Jesus through the strainer of conservative politics and free enterprise capitalism. The upshot was the creation of a system where Christianity so closely resembled capitalism that Jesus was equally at one with Wall Street and Main Street, with a slight edge granted to the former.

In the wake of the Great Depression, American businesses had naturally fallen into disrepute. In an effort to counter the "creeping socialism" of the welfare state and its collectivist mindset, major corporate patrons and business lobbies like the United States Chamber of Commerce enlisted sympathetic clergymen as their champions—chief among them was the minister of the First Congregational Church of Los Angeles, who was instrumental in blending capitalism and Christianity together under the banner of "godly capitalism," the answer to the so-called "pagan stateism" [sic] of the New Deal of President Roosevelt and the chief culprit standing in their way.[9]

Like parent, like child. The new church did indeed carry liberty's torch to the suburbs. For example, its literature clearly stated that the purpose of the new church was to maintain the Pilgrim heritage of freedom which they felt had been compromised by the (perceived) threat of ecclesiastical control in the new denomination and to remain clear of any possible entanglement with the National and World Councils of Churches. So as to leave no room for doubt, the church's covenant specified that members "promise to maintain this Church as an independent Congregational Church, subject to the control of no other ecclesiastical body."

Clearly, the fervent affirmation of local church autonomy (misappropriated as "independence" in the covenant) and fealty to the Pilgrim "fathers" had its roots in the merger battle of the mid-1950s, but there is also a conservative political component at work here as well. Other church documents from that period, for example, stress the desire to hear, finally, if not recover, "God's Word," implying that God's Word had been lost in the ecumenism of the time with its rush to centralized denominational control. Further compromising the "Word of God" was the "Social Gospel," as if the Social Gospel could not possibly have a foundation in that Word.

The language of a "Free and Independent Church" conveniently shielded the members from both the unwanted meddling of denominational bureaucrats

---

9. So argues Kevin Kruse in two articles, "How Corporate America Invented Christian America," *Politico Magazine*, April 16, 2015, and "For God So Loved the 1 Percent," appearing on the Opinion page of the *New York Times*, January 18, 2012. He is also the author of *One Nation Under God: Corporations, Christianity, and the Rise of the Religious Right*. Essentially, he connects the rise of what we call civic religion to the period. I have chosen not to develop further the pivotal role the First Congregational Church played in championing what Kruse described as a "new union of faith and free enterprise"...suffice to say, Christianity was interpreted to warrant the phrase, "godly capitalism." The main point here is that the connection with conservative politics begun in the 1940s and 1950s continued through the John Birch Society in both the Los Angeles congregation and its satellite, Mayflower Church, San Gabriel, a kind of "First Church East."

in local church affairs and the intrusion of a liberal (progressive) agenda associated with national and world ecclesiastical councils; more significantly, perhaps, such language also removed a challenging counterweight to the agenda of conservative politics, the real creed of the new church.

Half a century later, we are incredulous that anyone gave a second thought to the National Council of Churches, the nefarious power of denominational structures, or the political agenda of the Social Gospel but at the time, the struggle was between the Soviet Union and its Communist Conspiracy (of which so-called left-leaning ecclesiastical bureaucracies were seen as hostages) on the one hand and American democracy and free enterprise on the other. The Civil Rights and Voting Rights Acts (1964 and 1965 respectively) were close at hand, recognition that not all was well in the land of the free, and the tragedy that would be Vietnam was underway, but a reactionary mission built on the "Pilgrim fathers" and a "recovered" Word of God (code for a religion of Americanism) did have its appeal as the 1960s unfolded. To repeat, a mere decade after its 1961 founding, Mayflower had become a 900-member church—very impressive…and obviously appealing.

By the early 1980s, though, when I was trying to right the ship in a tumultuous sea, it appeared the message had lost its appeal, at least among the surrounding neighbors, but rather than take the hint and grapple with the founding theological underpinnings, correcting what I would call the inadequacies of the inheritance bequeathed by the parent upon the child and adjusting the mission accordingly (a herculean task, to be sure), a fourth factor reared its head: as if the struggles without were not enough, the members turned inward upon themselves. Whether an unexamined theology or internal conflict finally cast the ship upon the rocks, I cannot say (probably a goodly measure of each)—it scarcely matters at this point. All I know is that unable to quell the internal conflicts, we never really got to the other challenges, demographics, competition, and most significantly, theology and mission.

I mentioned earlier in this chapter that I quickly identified four warring parties. Three had their own ringleader, and the members lined up in the various sectors depending on who was in charge at the moment and how they felt about the minister. Understandably, the place was a network of intrigue and subterfuge. The congregation had a history of circulating petitions and letters and, as the bylaws allowed, voting by proxy. Certain people collected votes like children collecting candy on Halloween, using them as leverage against each other. This was my first exposure to what I will call raw power, but power is channeled through persons, and as I also noted above, I actually came to fear a few of my so-called parishioners and the power they exercised in their corner of the ring. I remember wondering at times if my study was bugged...and conducted some business as if it were.

Everyone, of course, was a potential target for the barrage of insults and dismissive remarks that bounced off the walls, but in my case they carried an added barb because the economic well-being of my family depended on my continued employment. I had no ecclesiastical safety net, certainly no social safety net, to catch me—and us—if the thin veneer of stability were to crumble. In the elaborate game underway, I was clearly out of my league and I knew that at any moment, with the next anonymous phone call or letter with no return address, the other shoe could drop and I could be removed from the scene when it became convenient to do so. All it would take was enough proxy votes by one side to overrule the other side—what a way to live!

I still believe it was unlikely ever to have reached that point (and in any event, my leaving first rendered the matter moot), but the shadow never receded for long which meant that I was ever on guard, defensive, like police officers responding to a domestic dispute and not entirely certain who or what might be lurking down the hall. What I failed to appreciate at the time was what to call it...violence. We often think of violence as physical, but psychological violence is still violence and its impact has both personal and corporate consequences. I sometimes wonder that I survived it at all.

That noise notwithstanding, I plugged along—after all, something had to be done...or attempted. By the time I arrived, the so-called Active Member list had become largely meaningless and based on my subjective appraisal of things, I suggested that we think of ourselves as a 100-member church (maybe a bit more since we averaged mid-60s to mid-70s attendance) with substantial facilities and financial resources with which to work. It was enough to rebuild… providing we could agree on a blueprint for the future.

Ever the question: a blueprint for the future. Other than fleeing the scene, what could possibly be done under such circumstances? To address that question, I conducted a rather detached, objective, head-level analysis of things generally, the fruits of which I spelled out clearly, succinctly, and undiplomatically for the church to see. I did not sugar-coat the cost of the fighting and the ongoing need for healing. I stressed the imperative of clarifying, defining, redefining, and envisioning a mission; I applied newly emerging research on why the mainline Protestant church, its roots in classical liberal theology and a firm hold on middle America, was beginning to struggle on its cultural slide to the margins. I warned against the tendency to commit institutional suicide by becoming something of a private club—the Jesus Club as opposed to the Jesus Movement, as I would in later years phrase it. I repeatedly called upon us to face the demographic changes sweeping through our area and California generally, the gateway for both Asian and Latin American immigration producing nothing less than a social revolution in the Golden State (and, of course, the country as a whole).

Eventually, these thoughts took shape in what I called "Mayflower's Five Choices," a document that was prescient for its time. Essentially, it said that as an alternative to a slow death, major surgery—what we now call Congregational Transformation—was the order of the day. It entailed such necessary steps as coming to grips with mission (what we now call Missional Church) and the possibility of allocating resources to either a new ministry in this place (what we now recognize as a Parallel Church) or relocating and starting over in a different place. Either way, I proposed that we take the time to understand—and appreciate—the surrounding culture as the necessary step to connecting with our neighborhood and I suggested that we could adjust our strategies, *how* we do ministry (guitars anyone?), without compromising our core principles or sacrificing our integrity. In a word, it was all there, everything necessary to succeed.

I even went so far as to consider the theologically sound and ecclesiastically impractical question of reconciliation which Paul had named as a prime ministry of the church (2 Cor. 5.16–21). In Christ, he writes, God has bridged the gap between God and the world ("hugging the world" to God's own self, as the *Cotton Patch* version so descriptively puts it), and has given those aware of their new status (the "new creation") a similar work, God's ambassadors, "hugging the world" and all its creatures to themselves after the manner and in the name of Christ.

Reconciliation, as I made clear in my report, is not merger, not wandering strays returning to the fold where they belong. Reconciliation is a coming together, a meeting in the center by all who have strayed. Reconciliation recognizes that sin and therefore the need for forgiveness fall on all parties equally. So, the question was, can any or all of the various groupings into which the Mayflower body had splintered come together? Can the members overcome their own history, commit to a sustained process of problem-solving, and in Christ envision a new creation, a church whose warring factions become not what they were, not what their church was, but a new and different community altogether?

These options and the series of reports in which I discussed our situation with the members did not appear out of thin air. I read widely in the area of the Church Growth Movement and consulted with trusted colleagues and leaders in the field. The latter included the Yokefellow Institute and the Alban Institute (so insightful was its research on the so-called Age of Christendom, why it was collapsing, and how to cope with and adapt to a new church in the process of being born).

Each option presented its own strengths and liabilities and none gained consensus among the outside groups and persons with whom I consulted. The church's patterns of failure and repetitive conflict, its internal resistance to change, and its absolute rejection of any kind of liaison with an ethnic congregation were all duly noted. One consultant said it was essential to "build bridges" to the Korean Congregationalists who had approached us even though it would take ten years (which we did not have). Another asked how I (we) would go about introducing new dynamics into a passive, maintenance-oriented congregation. Not terribly encouraging!

A dubious enterprise with dim prospects from the outset, the undertaking outlined in "Mayflower's Five Choices" never really got off the ground. In presenting the choices at hand, each with its own promise and peril, I made it clear that the church had reached the end of the line...as had I. The emotional toll, I acknowledged, was too demanding personally, the never-ending round of conflict and tension, always wondering who was next going to do what and to whom and with what consequences. The situation with the world was too desperate, I suggested, to tolerate the luxury of a church fight. You have (not we, but you) one last chance I prophesied, to do something about the thin thread that actually sustains the church. I offered to do what I could to facilitate positive steps the members might want to take, but in the end it was their decision.

In the end, though, even my bluntly stated appraisal failed to move the membership. A planned two-day workshop, led by one of our national executives, to wrestle with and conceivably make some decisions about our circumstances generated so little interest that I had no choice but to modify the workshop into an evening of informal conversation; three months later, I was gone.

Notably, the church did secure the consulting services of Fuller Theological Seminary after I left. Fuller was doing pioneering work in the area of church growth and renewal in those days (and is world-renown for its missional programs today). Fuller's recommendations notwithstanding, the church was unable to reverse its patterns and would close within a decade.

Predictably it would close, I suppose. Why the members would put up with a church under those circumstances was beyond me, and attrition gradually did take its toll, but it must have been exhausting as well as distressing, and by the time the game ended, their energy spent, the remaining members lacked the wherewithal to begin again.

Little did I know that it had not so much ended as stopped, only to be resurrected nearly two decades later in my immersion with its progenitor.

CHAPTER 4

IF THE MISSILES GO UP

"To know the truth partially is to distort the Universe."

"A clash of doctrines is not a disaster; it is an opportunity."

"An attack upon systematic thought is treason to civilization."

"Religion is what the individual does with his own solitariness."

"God is the poet of the world, with tender patience leading
it by his vision of truth, beauty and goodness."

"God in the world is the perpetual vision of the road
which leads to the deeper realities."

~ALFRED NORTH WHITEHEAD
English mathematician and philosopher

A FIRE WILL BURN ONLY as long as combustible fuel remains available, and at times it seemed as if the flames that kept the Mayflower cauldron simmering would blaze forever—at least it felt that way to me during my turbulent six-year tenure. Another decade of effort would follow but would not change the troubled, downward trajectory until the members finally declared an end to the Mayflower experiment.

I have long pondered why we—pastor and parishioners—could not direct the heat to other ends. After all, we had the talent, and at least in the beginning we had the time, and up until the end, they had the resources—but nothing ever seemed to click. It was as if random threads wove themselves throughout a common tapestry, intersecting with and bumping into one another but never really connecting so as to create a common picture. These accidental threads even appeared at the end when the church closed and dispersed its assets, the most shocking feature of which was the decision to give the building (which must have been worth a fortune) to an independent Congregational church with a fundamentalist creed. (To add some perspective, the National Association, presumably representing the historic Congregationalism on which the church had been founded and of which the church was a member, received a token $5,000.) I may have taken issue with certain features of Mayflower's founding creed, and some of the founders themselves had caused me no end of grief, but transferring their legacy to a form of Congregationalism so theologically and culturally removed from their initial vision did them a disservice. They deserved better, and I felt badly for them.

I was not surprised to learn that the church had closed, but the absence of surprise when the end finally did come is not to say that the end was inevitable—predictable, perhaps, but not inescapable. Certainly, before even a rudimentary consensus could begin to develop around a vision for the future, the members would have needed to address immense challenges—chief among them resolving a history of infighting and corralling a stewpot of conflicting feelings—but I never ceased believing in the possibility of a future for the church.

Key word, possibility. Why it looms so large in my thinking and how it might have taken root even in Mayflower's troubled environment is the subject of this chapter, and I place Mayflower front and center at the outset as a prelude of sorts because the church illustrates so clearly a puzzling and unresolved conundrum: that naming the possibilities for proceeding in the present and toward the future will often play little more than a minor role—and sometimes not even that—in shaping the outcome. How can that be?! What happens in the present that we will ignore another path or a different trajectory that has every reasonable prospect of creating a more favorable tomorrow?

What happens, of course, is that acting upon new possibilities for the future introduces in the present not just the inevitability but also the necessity of change…and we resist change both for ourselves as individuals and for our institutions and organizations. At best we change very slowly and even then it will most likely entail some kicking and screaming. We know the drill: procrastinating, we start the process too late; distracted, we stop too soon; in denial, we sometimes do not even begin.

A conundrum: that we take the time to look at the possibilities for renewing, altering the course of, and breathing new life into the very communities (the social groupings) in which we live and move and find our being, and then fall short in delivering in sufficient measure the renewal they so desperately need. Apparently, recognizing the need for and then actually implementing the midcourse corrections operate on different time frames.

We can trace most of our foot-dragging to a matter of *commitment*, the simple willingness to look at the circumstances in which an organization or social group finds itself, weigh the options, and then choose to get involved in a change process…or not, but another factor may intervene from time to time as well: when the mountain is just too big and our boats really are too small and "I will" (or "I won't") becomes "I can't." This is the point where a matter of choice, a Yes or a No, gives way to the question of *capacity* and the sobering assessment regarding our physical, mental, and spiritual ability to adjust a given trajectory (personal and social) in time so as to avoid its predicted consequences.

A sobering thought, indeed: that human evolution might not yet have brought us to the point where we can meet the challenges bearing down upon us this century. I wrestle with competing counsel on this, on the one hand Jesus telling his disciples that they will do what he does—and even more (which is to say, anything)—and on the other hand Paul letting the Romans off the hook (John 14.12 and its larger context in the farewell address to the disciples ever in tension with Romans 7.14-23, pointedly, v. 19). We will have opportunity to look at both texts as this story with its ever-lurking conundrums unfolds.

These musings have swirled around a single word, *possibility*, but the word itself has roots that for me reach deep into the Claremont School of Theology Doctor of Ministry (D.Min.) program in which I enrolled while serving Mayflower. I had earned my Master of Divinity (M.Div.) degree a dozen years earlier from Bethany Theological Seminary, the Graduate School of Religion of the Church of the Brethren. Like other churches in the Anabaptist tradition (the Amish and the Mennonites probably the best known), the Church of the Brethren is a historic peace church, and its members are pacifists and as such they refuse to serve in combat roles in the military. Today's volunteer military does not rule out the threat of conscription and so men must still register with the Selective Service System upon reaching draft age (18), including pacifists. Those who cited religious or moral objections to bearing arms could apply for Conscientious Objector (CO) status, but this did not necessarily excuse them from the draft or serving in some capacity, and in fact many COs did serve in very dangerous combat zones as medics. Options made available through Alternative Service provided other ways to satisfy what was described as their military obligation.

Society does not exactly hold parades for its pacifists, and so I continue to honor both the commitment and the courage represented by a CO classification. As an undergraduate, I had a student deferment and would have been subject to the draft the moment I completed my degree. With the lottery system in place in those years, my "number" (the month and day of my birth) was close enough to the top for me to expect a notice from my draft board, but I followed the university with seminary, and divinity students were also deferred. By the time I graduated from Bethany I was effectively too old to serve (or if not too old, too much trouble as a religious-type to bother with) even though the War in Vietnam would continue another four years.

All that sounds so quaint now, but accepting deferments of any kind meant that someone else fought in place of those who had them. Those in a position to go to college avoided Vietnam and the rest took their chances (some 58,000 not quite so lucky). Convenient, the student deferment, and according to some of my Church of the Brethren friends, immoral as well because cooperating with the Selective Service System made one complicit with the war machine itself even if one removed himself from combat as a CO. I remember well the day the FBI came to our seminary to arrest a fellow student who refused to cooperate with the draft by registering so much as his name.

Typically, the M.Div. is a three-year program (four years for those churches which require a one-year intern experience prior to the senior year and graduation) and along with the four-year undergraduate degree, it served for many years as the basic and minimal educational credential leading to ordained ministry. The D.Min. represented an additional year of work and was designed for ministers approximately at mid-career. While academic, it is a step below the full Doctor of Philosophy (Ph.D.), replacing the original research that becomes a dissertation with a practical application of how the theory and the practice of ministry will intersect in the real world.

People with the Ph.D. anticipate a life of research and teaching at the college, university, and graduate school level. People with the D.Min. continue with their ministry in the church or a related agency, now better equipped for the productive, mature years that lie ahead. Not incidentally, the degree also increases one's marketability! Overall, it proved to be a remarkable turning point in my life and ministry and I have always felt all churches really should make the D.Min. available to their ministers.

In my case as well, the academic discipline also offered some periodic relief from the stresses and strains of the parish by giving me other things with which to wrestle, and high on the list was another conundrum: theodicy or the challenge of justifying the ways of God to humankind and answering the most basic of questions: why are there earthquakes? A nasty business, earthquakes. Presumably, an all-powerful, all-knowing, all-loving God would do something about earthquakes, creating a stable planet, for example, or moving persons out of the way before the ground shook.

More broadly, theodicy asks how we are to speak of the goodness of God in the face of suffering and evil and all the horrible things humans visit upon their own kind (if not all manner of living beings). From dictators with armies to individuals with guns, from the terrorist with a bomb to a drunk driver at the wheel, from innumerable "Final Solutions" to unconscionable "holy wars," from marketing drugs to trafficking persons, for what some do and because the rest tolerate it, how are we to account for the human capacity to hurt one another in a just universe presumably under the watchful eye of a benevolent, omnipotent, and omniscient God? Why do bad things happen to good people and what are we to say when they do?

Consider what every parent fears the most, the police knocking on the door late at night with the worst news possible, a child killed in an automobile accident, the victim of a drunk driver. Where to begin, how to explain, who to hold responsible? It turns out that with her husband at work and unable to find a babysitter, a young mother leaves her infant son at home alone just long enough to drive to an end-of-the-season party for her sports team. She is there just long enough to get very intoxicated before jumping in her car and racing home. On the way, speeding down a main thoroughfare, she runs a red light and slams into a car crossing the intersection with the green light; police estimated she might have been traveling nearly 100 miles per hour, fast enough in any event to cut the car literally in half. Three young college students are killed instantly; the driver dies a short time later at the hospital, leaving four devastated families. One of the kids and his family belonged to my church.

How are we to account for such a senseless tragedy? A few seconds earlier, a matter of seconds later, and the driver would have sailed through the intersection, most likely arriving home if not well, then at least safely. Why could God not "arrange" things so as to avert tragedy, maybe changing the timing of the stop light or delaying the departure of the drunken driver by just one minute (or better, giving one of her teammates the idea of taking the young mother's keys so she could not drive at all)? That's not too much to ask for the sake of three bright, promising kids on the cusp of adulthood.

No, we can't turn God into some kind of monster by saying that God must have wanted those bright lights in heaven, leaving permanent scars on four families and countless friends. Not any better is falling back on the mystery of everything: that for now we see in part but one day all will be clear (1 Cor. 13); that God's ways are not our ways (Isa. 55.8–9); that like the earthly parent, the heavenly Parent is testing us, giving us some room to grow and develop, seeing what we might become; that in the end, we live by faith and await the triumph of love—something to talk about, certainly (at least as an academic exercise), but try telling that to the four families. If someone said that to me under those circumstances, I would have shown them the door. Robert Browning might claim that "God's in His heaven—All's right with the world" ("Pippa's Song"), but we always come back to that which we cannot ignore, that even with God in "His" heaven, clearly not all is right with the world.

Within limits, we must acknowledge that the experience of pain is necessary for survival and in that respect is a gift; the problem, then, is a matter of proportion. For example, physical pain tells us when the bath is too hot and the stove is still hot. Psychologically, pain serves as an "attention-getter," motivating emotionally distressed persons to do something about their disease and stimulating our inner growth and development generally. Spiritually, pain can even function as "God's megaphone" (C. S. Lewis in his book, *The Problem of Pain*), reminding us that something is wrong in this morally fallen world. As philosopher and theologian John Hick observes, the world is not a hedonistic paradise but a "vale of soul-making" (Keats) which prepares people for life in the kingdom of God.

Perhaps so: in limited quantities, suffering might serve a greater good, but in excessive amounts (the drunk driver killing three college students and herself, say, and so visiting lifelong pain on four families and a wider circle of families and friends, expanding ultimately to embrace the whole community), suffering crosses the threshold and becomes disproportional and counterproductive to any good it might have produced (insights, growth, or learning, say) and may achieve only the opposite, immobilizing the person and stifling the otherwise creative impulses and aspirational tendencies that under less intense circumstances might reasonably be expected to benefit persons and the community alike. For some, the problem of pain reaches a point where it creates an impenetrable wall between the person and God.

Instead of a "megaphone" drawing one toward God, the cacophony of pain sends the suffering running away from God, perhaps forever.

The problem of excessive suffering, the tragedies individuals and nations visit upon one another and the world, posed not just a textbook exercise for me but also raised an existential dilemma, for every seven days I had to have something to say about God and the people of God. Increasingly, I found myself wondering if I had anything at all to say about God and the people of God generally if I could not find something to say when confronted by the suffering and tragedy from which none of us is immune specifically. This was not so much a crisis of faith as a crisis of vocation. I needed to find some resolution to the dilemma if I were to continue in parish work.

That resolution came one pleasant afternoon while sitting in class, somewhat slumbering as I recall. The time frame was the Cold War era, and suddenly I heard my teacher say, "If the missiles go up, the missiles will come down." Once fired, he went on to say, they will do what they were designed to do, and then came the clincher: that *not even God can intervene and turn them from their path* (emphasis mine). A moment of insanity, a matter of human or technical failure, a case of misunderstanding and mutual distrust—it hardly matters—for once ignited, they will go up; and if they go up, they will come down; and when they come down cockroaches and crabgrass will inherit what's left of the earth.

In a word, God is all-loving but not all-powerful. It sounds heretical, but central to this understanding of why bad things happen to good people is the idea that God shares power with the creation, most importantly, with human beings, honoring the exercise of our power such that if we push the button and the missiles go up, God will not intervene *because God cannot* intervene and prevent them from coming down.

How are we to understand such a view of God? Are humans absolutely free and does God honor our freedom absolutely? According to the opening of the biblical drama, God created the world and pronounced it "good" (Gen. 1, repeated seven times). From the initial chaotic stew of the Big Bang, a harmonious world emerged, the gift of the loving Creator to the creation. The

First Couple came along, and God told them to enjoy the creation, which not incidentally included the gift of each other's companionship, but within assigned limits: they could name the animals, enjoy its fruit, and tend to their chores (Gen. 2.15) and in so doing, they must respect the harmony of the creation. Maintaining that harmony, however, required that they not aspire to be "like us" (Gen 3.5, 22), that is "like God" (here pictured as surrounded by the heavenly court). Reaching for God-like power would most certainly disrupt the harmony of creation with devastating consequences to follow (dutifully recorded in Gen. 3–11).

Remarkably enough, though, the choice was theirs: "We forbid you from doing so," God says, "but there it is." Hmmmmm…what to do?

Such is the story of human being. We exhibit little interest in living within the assigned limits, boundaries that clearly distinguish the created from the Creator, and instead succumb to the temptations by which we reach beyond our grasp so as to be *like* God (little gods). God-like we are, having built machines that have the capacity to destroy several times over what God has created. Failing to learn our lesson, we are destined to struggle with its consequences, the disharmony that characterizes our relationship with God, one another, one's own self, and the creation itself. Along the way, bad things happen to good people.

An all-powerful God would seemingly bear responsibility for such a world. Start with the world itself: as things stand, the world gives us earthquakes and volcanoes, tornadoes in one place and drought in another. Nasty things, these. Why not wait for a stable planet before introducing the likes of us? While waiting, the world might reach a point where steady rain, reliable harvests, balanced seasons, and water in the right places and in the right amounts would guarantee enough at least of the basics for everybody. And if everybody had enough to provide for themselves and their families, maybe those with less would not have to fight those with more to get at least some. Of course, were God to wait for such a planet, God would still be waiting to introduce the likes of us…and so would we be waiting for our introduction.

Obviously, premature or not, we came into a world that still features earthquakes and volcanoes and all the rest but a world still pronounced good by its Creator, a realm where all its creatures live together in harmonious relationships…except, of course, that in the real world we do not so live. So something is amiss: we do live in a Good world, a world with the capacity to provide for all its creatures living with each other harmoniously, but history does not document that such a world ever existed.

Why not and who is responsible?

Again, I flash back to that day in class when my teacher, renown process theologian John Cobb, woke me from my semi-somnolence and recast the direction of my ministry. He mentioned something about missiles. Some 15,000 nuclear warheads (90% of which belong to the US and Russia) currently exist, although only some 9,600 are in military service so the crabgrass and cockroaches should be safe enough, and we have exercised control of them through the doctrine of Mutually Assured Destruction (MAD) which holds that within minutes of launching the first one, the rest would soon all be airborne and by the end of the day civilization would be history, undoubtedly along with humankind. Of course, it would be utter MADness to pretend otherwise. Presumably, some Pentagon officials entertained the notion of contained, limited, and winnable nuclear engagement, victory to the side quickest on the draw and having the better aim, but a 1985 Joint Soviet-United States Statement on the Summit Meeting in Geneva settled the matter, proclaiming "that a nuclear war cannot be won and must never be fought."

We—our side—might know better, but you could never trust the Communists on such matters, such was I taught as a child by my school in the 1950s—*taught*, mind you. We were taught to accept that these things exist, that there is nothing we can or even should do about them, and that our responsibility accordingly is to prepare for their use by adapting to their consequences. I never heard anyone talk about disarmament in my world, not at home, not at church, and certainly not in school. My school did not teach me to raise questions about social policy, particularly as it related to military matters. My school taught me what to do when the teacher yelled, "Drop!"

The infamous "drop-drills," an unrecognized form of child abuse. Without warning, in the midst of a lesson, the teacher would yell "Drop!" and thirty children would crawl under their little wooden desks, eyes closed (to protect the retina from the burning brightness of the exploding bomb), arms covering the ears (to protect hearing from its deafening roar), and hands clasped behind the head (to protect the body from disintegrating walls and collapsing roofs), all the handiwork of the evil Soviet Union. It never occurred to us that boys and girls in the Soviet Union were being similarly "educated" (i.e., conditioned) to prepare for the handiwork of the evil Americans.

The horror so unthinkable, might the power of God easily just deflect the instruments of destruction into space or disable them so they only land with a thud and not a bang, the love of God thereby saving us from ourselves, the heavenly counterpart of the earthly parent? If only, we say. In God We *Truly* Trust. I suppose it could work that way, the *power* of God and the *love* of God working together to protect the child running into the street not aware of the approaching car. Of course the heavenly Parent will intervene. For parents heavenly and earthly, not to intervene would be monstrous.

So where is God when monstrous things happen? Three young adults killed by a drunk driver—where was God, everyone asked? Students and faculty, victims of gun violence at a school shooting—where was God, pondered a parishioner who would not be in church that Sunday…like God taking a vacation. Another woman, another statistic—where was God when it came time to restrain my assailant, she cries?

Why does God not keep us safe? Perhaps because God invests us with and honors our freedom and could only overrule bad things happening to good people by denying us our agency, what we do of our own volition and the responsibility we bear for its impact in the world—good and bad. Some do argue that God could have created human beings with the illusion of freedom, the façade of agency, when in reality we are puppets on a string. Such manipulation of human being amounts to a violation of love and does neither the

Creator nor the created any favors. The fundamental principle at work in the ongoing drama of creation is the power God shares with us, making us co-creators with God, and with power comes the freedom to choose whether and how to exercise our power in relation to God.

This understanding of the ways of God in relation to humankind stretches our traditional and customary conception of God's power—there is no doubt about that! Of God's love, we may feel secure. Like any loving parent, our all-loving, heavenly Parent would certainly deflect the missiles and save humanity (and the creation generally) from profound suffering and obliteration, but having shared power with a multiplicity of beings with power of their own (especially humans who become co-creators with God as a result), what God *might* do in acting lovingly is limited by what God *can* do in acting power-fully. At some point, parents heavenly and earthly are powerless to intervene on behalf of the child they love. We built those heinous machines—if they go up we have none but ourselves to blame when they come down.

We call this a "process theodicy," that is to say, a response to why bad things happen to good people from the perspective of process theology, and to this point I have placed the accent on the process view that God does not have all the power in the universe. God has great power, but not a monopoly of power. We would say that God has "perfect power," i.e., the greatest power it is conceivable for a being to have, but not all the power (not exactly a tradi-tional theism, to say the least).

In such a universe, God's role is to influence and not control, to persuade but not coerce. God is not the tyrant imposing the divine will upon the cre-ation but rather the "Hound of Heaven,"[10] who envisions new possibilities for the multiplicity of beings and lures all manner of entities, from electrons to humans, to realize new ideals of concreteness (being) made available to them by God. That sounds pretty bizarre, that electrons have an element of choice in what they become and what becomes of them, but we need to bear in mind that

---

10. An autobiographical poem by Francis Thompson in which the poet pictures himself graciously, lovingly, and purposefully pursued by a Hound from Heaven down all the dark corridors of his life, its dead ends and failures duly noted, until at the end, the poet turns and accepts the gift.

persuasive power operates within physical and biological limits or boundaries (God does not lure an ant to write a symphony, for example).

Obviously, if God shares power with other entities and can only persuade or lure those entities to actualize God's ideal aims, the entities may or may not conform, as we humans know only too well. We may say Yes to the divine lure...but we might also say No, and in fact, experience teaches that the "No Vote" is frequently the default setting. The sainted Augustine, responding in a pre-saintly life, once prayed to God, "Lord, save me...but not just yet." Like Paul, we know what God calls us to be and do, and so at our best we delight in what the Apostle calls the "law of God," but well we know that we are not always at our best and so inevitably we are also at war with "another law," the law of sin (think of the ways we "fall short" of God's purposes for our lives) to which we are captive.

Fortunately, to such wretched creatures God offers (or lures us with the prospect of) release in the Gift of the Christ—a Gift, of course, we may, and generally do, reject (Rom. 7.13ff), maybe not in its totality but just the inconvenient parts, or more to the point, just the parts we find inconvenient *today*. Tomorrow—or next year or in a couple of decades—we may respond differently to the Gift, for ever the Hound of Heaven, the heavenly Lover continues to pursue us down the corridors of our lives.

From the Christian perspective, the all-loving God, through the agency of the Word, becomes flesh and "tents" among us (the marvelous Prologue to the Fourth Gospel, John 1.1–18, esp. v. 14). Additionally, the ideal aims of an all-loving God would introduce saving and healing characteristics or elements in the relationships involved. In that respect, whether speaking of Christ as the embodiment of Love made visible in the world or the ideal aims offered by an all-loving God to actual entities (that is, persons) in the world, we are essentially affirming one and the same reality, a Love so profound as to transform human being itself. This is barely the tip of the iceberg of a properly developed Christology, but perhaps it can suffice for present purposes: that the divine lure breaking into our consciousness presents new possibilities, the name of which is Love.

Of course, the divine lure only becomes effective or actual if we respond to it and in responding to the divine lure, we introduce creativity into our human experience. Moment by moment, the past and the future come together and to the extent that we respond at all do we exercise our creativity. The process philosopher Alfred North Whitehead would have us think of this in terms of two poles present in any single occasion of experience. The "Physical" pole represents the given from the past, the determining influence from the intricate complexity of interrelationships between the myriad of entities that make up the world; the "Mental" pole represents the multiple possibilities among which the individual may choose. What separates higher entities (like persons, say) from lower entities (electrons, for example) is that the latter have only a Physical pole and so "prehend" (or "feel") only the past (subsequently conforming to it) whereas in addition to "prehending" (or "feeling" the past, the Physical pole) higher entities, humans, have the Mental pole and so "prehend" (or "feel") perhaps a multitude of possibilities for self-actualization in the future.

Responding to other possibilities and so having exercised their creativity introduces novelty into the universe, supplementing and so changing the complex interrelationships that comprise the past. In the next moment of experience, individuals now must reinterpret the past in light of the ways God lures each of us to actualize new possibilities in the present. In other words, the present is not exhausted by a synthesis of the past; rather, the past serves merely (but importantly) as the prelude to the future; it shapes the future but does not determine the future because self-actualizing persons, sharing power with God, are free to choose from a multitude of possibilities, including the one that represents God's ideal aim for that individual in that moment.

What we call the past is, of course, the result of a vast, incomprehensibly complex network of interconnected relationships, the interactions of which are recorded as historical narrative. As the "poet of the world" (Whitehead), God's artistic impulse invites these innumerable participants, themselves an incomprehensible array of entities ranging from electrons to persons, to engage in the unfolding drama we call life, but God does not act upon the creation as a potter might act upon the clay. We recall that God's power is persuasive, not coercive, that God may have a vision for the "clay" but honors the freedom of the "clay" to choose whether and to what extent it might respond to the invitation.

The choices themselves range all the way from acceptance of God's ideal aim through lesser gradations (the multitude of possibilities, say, approximations) to the trivial (none of the above). The greater choices give greater, more intense value; essentially, the movement from chaos to life (and in particular, human life). Greater value means greater varieties of life (like the diverse ecosystems so seriously threatened today), an increasing range of possibilities within life (think of the rich tapestry of interconnected cultures available in the interconnected network of the digital age), and a heightened intensity of "feeling" for life (not just awareness of and sensitivity toward but actually embracing this tapestry).

The other choice—the trivial—gives little or none of the above. Trivial choices might be morally suspect and possibly even ethically wrong, but more generally, such options are more in line with a missed opportunity (indifference replacing love, for example) or settling for the mediocre as opposed to the exceptional.

Depending on how one chooses, the ideal or the trivial, the future will evolve accordingly. The ideal will focus on ever-greater and more intense value, the trivial something less: choosing love, say, as opposed to indifference and certainly hate will tell a different story and create a different future from what would otherwise have been the case had a lesser choice been made.

But, as astonishing as it sounds, not only will our choices—good, bad, or indifferent—impact the future as reflected in the historical narrative, so too will those very same choices impact God, for as a God of love (1 John 4.7–21), so intimate is God's relationship with the Universe that as we exercise our freedom, God receives our decisions and the actions that follow, retains them, and then feeds them back to us in the form of new ideal aims, appropriate for the present in light of the past—the Hound of Heaven engaged in a creative process that persists over time, for all time, for that which God creates, God cannot lose and those whom God loves, God does not forget. We would expect no less from an intimate God. The mother who died along with the three students she killed while driving intoxicated is no less a part of God than the three victims.

This is not to excuse her for what happened or any of us for our lapses in judgment and flawed decision-making that result in bad things happening to good people, unintended or not. What justice demands and love delivers in the wake of the horrors humankind visits upon one another and the creation is hardly incidental to a process theodicy: *doing* justice (Micah 6.8), restoring right relationships, is the work of a lifetime, the gift of love as a way of life, and I repeatedly return to this tragic episode because it so graphically illustrates how the abuse of freedom can so quickly result in such tragic consequences for both agent and victim of the abuse and how the process of recovery necessarily spreads to all those affected by (in this case) the irreparable damage to their relationships brought about by the death of these four persons. In how many ways in the course of everyday life are all of us both agent and victim when it comes to the consequences of the misuse of our freedom?

Maybe eventually, over time, eons of time, humankind will grow or evolve and develop an increasingly cooperative attitude with regard to God's own ongoing creative purposes. As with the theory of evolution generally, a specifically evolving and presumably increasing intellectual and spiritual capacity resulting in ever-higher orders of human being is attractive; descriptive language for such a creature itself needs to evolve, but for starters we might think in terms of humans with a more "cosmic consciousness" or better (and borrowing directly from the German theologian Friedrich Schleiermacher, often called the father of modern liberal Protestant theology) a "God-consciousness" on the order of Jesus himself for whom his self-consciousness and his God-consciousness were effectively one. In that respect, Jesus at once serves as the Sign of humanity's destination and, at least for the foreseeable (if not distant) future, its Guide.

And in the meantime…? In the meantime, my increasingly familiar companion, something about a mission. I frequently speak of that moment in the classroom as a conversion experience and not only for its answer to the problem of why bad things happen to good people but also because it clarified so clearly, ever so clearly, the purpose of the church and not incidentally, it provided the framework and impetus to continue in pastoral ministry for another quarter-century. As I said above, what to say about God was becoming problematic for me with the theodicy question hanging overhead, an ominous shadow. I never saw myself as leaving the Christian faith, or even the church as a participating member, but I had begun seriously to question whether I had anything meaningful to contribute to the discussion about how God relates to the world, why it matters, and what—if anything—we are to do as a consequence.

By this time, I had been in the parish ministry about fifteen years, much of it dealing with conflict. I was certainly not tired of the whole thing, but clearly I needed something (or felt the *church* needed something) more compelling to keep our interest—not to mention passion—than a numbing preoccupation with its own institutional maintenance, its creeds and articles and forms.

In that moment, all those troubled misgivings evaporated and I understood with absolute clarity how God first invests us with freedom and then invites us to become co-creators with God in this unfolding, unknown drama of tomorrow—a purpose for the people of God, indeed! It turns out that it matters not only that we live but why, to what ends, because so seriously does God take human freedom that God does not—God *cannot*—deflect those missiles into the heavens and thereby save us from ourselves any more than God can cool down a warming planet or temper our enthusiasm for the dictates of Genesis 1.28. If the missiles go up, the planet heats up, or the population bomb blows up…well, we have none but ourselves to blame.

Having charged us with the responsibility to share in the ongoing drama of life as co-creators with God, suddenly it mattered a great deal that we begin to pay more attention to God, if only for our sake. In that realization, I answered a second of what I called the "Big Three," the key, critical questions the mainline churches must have the courage, wisdom, and language to tackle if they have any hope of addressing the occupants of the 21st century. Failing there, the mainline church will probably fail utterly, undoubtedly no one the wiser. At issue:

- The nature of God, by which I mean not whether God exists but why God matters even if God does exist;

- The problem of suffering and evil, or why are there earthquakes and what does it mean when bad things happen to good people;

- The challenge of pluralism, or whether it matters what we believe so long as we believe something (unless, as some say, humankind would be better off believing nothing and thereby solving the challenge of pluralism).[11]

A century and more ago, humans fretted over the question of God's existence—did God really exist and how could mere humans possibly know? The question today, though, is that the world functions and humans get along in the world as if God does not matter even if God might exist. The variable here is not theology but pragmatism and pragmatically speaking, everyday people manage to get along quite nicely day to day without much reference to how God might improve the course of day-to-day life and especially what God might prefer we do with our lives.

Our currency proclaims that "In God We Trust," but we count on an employer, Wall Street, the pension board, the Social Security Administration, or some combination of them to make such dollars as we can claim available for our use. In reality, we trust absolutely in the clunky bureaucracy of a complex social system to meet our needs, in God not so much, unless to receive

---

11. While not speaking further of the problem of pluralism in this chapter, the inherent issues are anchored in post-modern culture and the inherent challenge of relativism where subjective experience becomes the arbiter of the so-called real world and truth, including religious truth, becomes a matter of one's own choosing, my truth as opposed to your truth, both having status quite apart from any external or authoritative standard for testing their authenticity, validity, and legitimacy. Most (but can we say all?) would agree that the world has no tolerance for a religion that would placate an angry deity by tossing virgins into volcanoes but beyond that, does not tolerance rather demand accommodating all manner of creedal affirmations, their numerous contradictions within themselves and between one another simply part of a post-modern landscape?

us at journey's end or some such. Having no importance in everyday life, the question of God seems almost quaint, like church attendance, a relic belonging in a museum. Inevitably, God fades from view altogether. This condition effectively makes most of us, including most religious people, *functional* atheists. It is not that we do not believe in God but that believing in God hardly matters. The Roman Catholic Louis Dupré, who for many years taught the philosophy of religion at Yale, said it well: "We have all become atheists, in the sense that God no longer matters *absolutely* in our closed world—if God matters at all."[12] Similarly does Rabbi Abraham Heschel note that "God is of no importance unless God is of supreme importance."

On that otherwise quiet afternoon, all that suddenly changed. Not only did God matter absolutely but so too did the people of God absolutely matter. Working together, we would keep the missiles in the ground…or not. In God we trust, but in a moment of madness, there they go, those missiles, and there goes the creation, back to the evolutionary stage where crabgrass and cockroaches ruled the world.

It turns out that God trusts us to keep that from happening.

A little naïve, maybe, but no pressure. In a way, it seems so simple. In the beginning, creative energy draws (lures) the churning chaos of the Big Bang to take shape according to the divine vision. Eventually, humans (our understandable preoccupation) come along. It turns out that we are not a random accumulation of atoms and molecules whose complex electro-chemical reactions have given rise to a peculiar but otherwise meaningless experience called self-consciousness. Quite the contrary, God envisioned that from the stewpot humans might emerge, purposefully and intentionally, loved and valued for who and what they are, endowed with freedom and power of their own, and so invited to share in the continuing drama as it evolves into the perfected vision God shares with all the co-creators, including electrons.

---

12. "Seeking Christian Interiority: An Interview with Louis Dupré," *The Christian Century*, July 16-23, 1997, pp. 654-660. The full quote: "We have all become atheists, in the sense that God no longer matters absolutely in our closed world—if God matters at all. To survive as a genuine believer, the Christian must now personally integrate what tradition did in the past. Christians are responsible for the culture in which they live, however unlike-minded it may be." He goes on to connect a "benign atheism" with a growing cultural secularism beginning in the 18th century.

Well and good, humans appear—call them the First Couple—and to the humans, God gives an assignment, to till and keep the Garden (Gen. 1.15), but along the way a rift developed in the human soul and things began to spin out of control. On the one side, humankind's intellectual advancement and technological prowess soared, but the capacity and even the desire to control the mounting horsepower lagged tragically behind. Humans grew smarter, but not necessarily wiser; they filled vast libraries with their knowledge, but were not always clear about its proper use; they acknowledged the moral dimension built into the fabric of creation, but found it easy to ignore its contours. As a measure of their own success, they may well have unleashed the very forces that will lead to their own extinction, what with missiles set to go up, their planet heating up, and a population bomb on the brink of blowing up. Already, too many people chase dwindling resources across the face of a planet tipping toward its own exhaustion, a dystopian future taking shape in *our* present.

Whether they—that is to say, whether we—can extricate ourselves from our own recklessness remains to be seen. *Remains to be seen*…because it all depends. It depends on innumerable decisions by countless persons acting individually and collectively, and so the outcome is yet to be determined. Certainly, things look a little grim, certainly for millions of the world's poorest and most vulnerable peoples who will feel the impact of climate change first (and probably worst) as unpredictable weather patterns affect food production and distribution and sea levels rise. Eventually, within a century or two, perhaps all peoples will succumb; but at this point, we cannot say definitively how the climate crisis will unfold, not so long as God continues to lure us toward creative and loving possibilities to which we give our attention and respond accordingly.

We call this creative transformation, by which we mean that religion does not reduce us to mere passive bystanders in a cosmic drama but empowers us to participate with God at a cosmic level in the drama's outcome. Creative transformation places the accent on what we do and how we act. To a confession of faith, creative transformation responds with the essential challenge, "Now What?" or "So What?"—that is to say, what difference does it make that we claim a faith, espouse a doctrine, or identify with a creed? More to the

point, in the aftershock of learning that if missiles go up, they do also most definitely come down, creative transformation invites God's co-creators so to discern the divine lure as to remove the mere possibility of their release from ever
happening…perhaps because the weapons themselves have ceased to exist.

Creative transformation recognizes that God needs us as much as we need
God; it places front and center the question of our goals and priorities and
values; it asks us to consider the ends to which we work and the causes to
which we give ourselves, and why; it emphasizes the importance of the present
because of its impact on the future.

Creative transformation inspires hope by enflaming the very passions
that give meaning to our days, to the end of our days; it sends us on the fool's
errands (cf. 1 Cor. 1.18ff), for which we are grateful; it makes everything seem
so important, even as it scares and intimidates us.

Creative transformation liberates individuals and the church alike, infusing
both with renewed purpose and the energy to respond courageously and purposefully to the divine lure.

And one more thing: creative transformation reminds the church on just
another Wednesday to take itself with utmost seriousness. Usually, we hear it
the other way around: *Don't* take yourself too seriously. I could never quite get
the hang of that, *not* taking ourselves too seriously. After all, if one did not take
one's own self seriously, who would? Same for the church: a church not out
to save the world will probably not be struggling with Standing Room Only
crowds on Sunday.

Paul identifies the pathway: having the mind of Christ (Phil 2.5–11), a spiritual renaissance to complement the renaissance in the arts and sciences and
technology. Taken together, creatively applied, who can say what tomorrow
may bring? So it looks like the church needs to get to work. We have a story to
tell, placing humankind in a cosmic context where the ultimate resolution of
life's many conundrums points to the saving grace of a divine love expressed
through the conscious decisions of a people to live that love. Mystic and sci-
entist Teilhard de Chardin called such a love a force stronger than gravity, a
discovery-in-waiting more transformative than the discovery of fire. Not long

enough out of the cave ourselves, we are mere neophytes in the ways of love. We dabble in the laboratory called church but go home to a world whose creative imagination has equipped the planet with the capacity to destroy itself.

Quite a challenge, addressing the disconnect between promise and reality.

In addressing that disconnect, I find myself drawn to the mystical side of the faith venture and its intimations of the Cosmic Christ. Sometimes theological liberals distinguish the Jesus of the Gospels from the Christ of the Epistles, the preference for the former clearly taking precedence over the latter, but it is a false distinction. The Bible presents both and so if we are to take the Bible seriously, we must honor its integrity and deal with the totality of its message. Thomas Jefferson may have created his own Bible with a pair of scissors, excising the sticky parts in favor of the accessible words of the Rabbi, and we all certainly have our favorite passages to which we turn when encountering the more troubling sections of our Book, but cut-and-paste is not a generally recognized Bible study technique.

Besides, sometimes we find that not just the world is too much with us (as the English Romantic poet William Wordsworth put it), but so too is the earth-bound Jesus of the Gospels. As our Rabbi, he instructs us to address its interminable ills with his profound ethic and compelling social conscience and to advance the Reign of God by loving our neighbor—the neighbor, of all things, who turns out to include just about everyone, friend and foe and stranger alike. Yes, we heard him say that he shows up in the hungry and the naked and the infirm (Matt. 25.40), and of course, we paid attention when the lesson was that upside-down-first-shall-be-last-and-last-first business and the curious economics of discipleship (Mark 10.17–31, par.)—not that we understood it, but we did pay attention—but sometimes we need a respite from the demands, a little relief from the press of the world's ills, nourishment along the way. For the Way is hard, as he himself points out (Matt. 7.13f), but to whom shall we turn when we feel the need to replenish the well? Can he who defines discipleship also have the food that nourishes the disciple? Or conversely, how could he who sets disciples on their path not provide the nourishment that feeds their souls and keeps them going?

Of course, hints of the "something more" were already evident in Jesus' power to heal the sick and cast out demons, and the capstone to the public ministry, the Resurrection followed quickly by Pentecost, confirmed that Jesus was not just one more itinerant prophet and rabbi in a succession of prophets and rabbis passing through the religious landscape. Perhaps more interesting than most, and certainly more troublesome to existing power structures, had he been only a prophet and rabbi, he would have disappeared as little more than a footnote in Jewish history, if even that. As we say, no Resurrection—no Church.

To appreciate fully the "something more" to the Person of Jesus, though, the biblical narrative invites us to go beyond the public ministry, or perhaps *behind* the public ministry, where we catch a glimpse of the Cosmic Christ. The Revelation to John, for example, describes Jesus in his cosmic setting as Alpha and Omega, beginning and end, the Christ of God who is present at the dawn of creation and who will preside over its fulfillment (Rev. 1.8, 22.13). Similarly, the Prologue to the Fourth Gospel, so different in tone and style from the so-called Synoptic Gospels of Matthew, Mark, and Luke, identifies the Jesus of history with the preexistent Word, present at and agent of creation itself (1.1–4, 14a, NRSV):

> In the beginning was the Word, and the Word was with God, and the Word was God. He was in the beginning with God. All things came into being through him, and without him not one thing came into being. What has come into being in him was life, and the life was the light of all people…. And the Word became flesh and lived among us.

More colorfully, the *Cotton Patch* version translates that last line, "The Idea became a man and moved in with us." Others take a more literal translation of the Greek, that "Jesus pitched his tent among us."

Paul is even more effusive (Col. 1.15–23, NRSV):

> He is the image of the invisible God, the firstborn of all creation; for in him all things in heaven and on earth were created, things visible and invisible, whether thrones or dominions or rulers or powers—all things have been created through him and for him. He himself is before all things, and in him all things hold together. He is the head of the body, the church; he

is the beginning, the firstborn from the dead, so that he might come to have first place in everything. For in him all the fullness of God was pleased to dwell, and through him God was pleased to reconcile to himself all things, whether on earth or in heaven, by making peace through the blood of his cross.

For years I followed a lectionary that placed this text in the middle of summer when no one was paying attention instead of the first Sunday in Advent when the grand mysticism, zealous metaphors, and spiritual exuberance might have helped save Christmas from its cultural captivity, an oversight I frequently corrected in my own preaching schedule.

Teilhard de Chardin offers his own parallel leap into what the secular world can only dismiss as fantastic (from, with some minor variations in language but not meaning, *The Mass on the World*, 1923, XIII, 131–132):

Glorious Lord Christ: the divine influence secretly diffused and active in the depths of matter, and the dazzling centre where all the innumerable fibres of the manifold meet; power as implacable as the world and as warm as life; you whose forehead is of the whiteness of snow, whose eyes are of fire, and whose feet are brighter than molten gold; you whose hands imprison the stars; you who are the first and the last, the living and the dead and the risen again; you who gather into your exuberant unity every mode of existence; it is you to whom my being cries out with a desire as vast as the universe, "In truth you are my Lord and my God."

All this almost feels like a foreign language in our overly intellectual and underpowered liberal churches, which only underscores the need to get back to or recover it. We hunger for some experience of the Holy, a sign, not to reveal heaven's every contour but simply to confirm its existence.

My interest in wilderness spirituality is motivated by just such a desire, and perhaps this same yearning explains why Ann can be found so often just staring up at the night sky. Her most expressive (I am inclined to say *mystical*) language generally takes shape as notes on a musical score—listening to her musical compositions all these years, I hear clearly the story they tell—but occasionally she resorts to mere words, poetry apparently music's nearest kin. Sometimes words and music come together as in "A Cosmic Conversation," where the two languages set the stage for the leap beyond the captivity of time and space. Alas, in this space, words alone must suffice:

Oh Lord in the morning you hear my voice.
Bright planet Venus,
Bright Venus gleams a good morning.
Jupiter, Saturn, a Crescent Moon, Mars,
Polaris in place. We're set for the dawn.

Chorus:
It's a cosmic conversation,
It's a daily jubilation.
All my cares subside as I gaze up high.
And as light is revealed, my soul is healed,
For I know God is by my side.

Oh Lord in the daytime I'm warmed by your sun.
Bright dazzling planet,
Bright brilliant sunbeams alight on my face.
Energized, vitalized, greeted by rays,
Our work to be done. We're set for the day.

Chorus

Oh Lord in the evening I rest in your peace.
Jupiter glitters good evening, my friends.
Orion, Pegasus, Cygnus, the swan,
Polaris in place. We're set 'til the dawn.

Chorus

© 1999 Ann Marie Kurrasch

It feels as if the mystic yearnings that may at least lie latent in every person's essential self (the soul or the spirit) and do take flight in some are an invitation, a kind of provocation of the cosmos, by which we dare God to speak in our time as God sometimes spoke in biblical times. Picture Elijah on Mt. Horeb, having been chased into the wilderness by Jezebel, there to wait for God (1 Kings 19.1–18): the story tells of wind and earthquake and fire, and then a still small voice.

We call the manifestation of a deity to humankind, here in the frightening phenomena of nature, a theophany. Terrorizing, perhaps, but having stood on the edge of the mountain, the divine presence swirling all around, would not one be rather inclined to get back to work, addressing the world's innumerable ills as a result? Not many of us get to stand with Elijah on Mt. Horeb, but we can immerse ourselves in the Word that became flesh and "tented" among us, and in a moment's quietness catch a vision of the eternal Christ, Alpha and Omega, present at the moment of creation's explosive Big Bang and its eventual collapse. The Word is inseparable from both the Jesus of the Sermon on the Mount and the Man on the cross who (in the words of the 19th century Jesuit George Tyrrell) sends us back again and again. "Lent to be spent" is how the Quaker philosopher Douglas Steere concludes his wonderful little book, *Dimensions of Prayer*. About the time we are ready to give up on the whole human enterprise we are reminded of that unfinished task, perhaps something about missiles and the need to keep them in the ground lest they go up.

In a word, the Cosmic Christ and the Jesus of the Gospels are but two sides of the one coin, each is incomplete without the other. Together they pronounce the creation sacred, and ultimately the sacred creation, of which humans are an integral part (and not separate, independent, and generally irresponsible caretakers) compels us to continue along the Way so long as breath remains in our bodies.

CHAPTER 5

WHEN IS THE GOOD, GOOD ENOUGH?

"The worship of God is not a rule of safety,
it is an adventure of the Spirit....
Without the high hope of adventure,
religion degenerates into a mere appendage of a comfortable life."

~ALFRED NORTH WHITEHEAD

"The best is the enemy of the good."

~ATTRIBUTED TO VOLTAIRE
quoting an Italian proverb

EVERY PARISH MINISTER DESERVES THE opportunity at some point in his or her career to serve a congregation like the First Congregational Church of Royal Oak, Michigan. I would turn 40 shortly after our family moved from Southern California to suburban Detroit in January 1986, and I count my nearly 15-year ministry at "First Church" (as I affectionately continue to call it even today) as my most productive, by far the most fulfilling and rewarding, and generally the happiest pastorate in my career.

This is not to suggest that the value or meaning of the work in other places I served (internally conflicted or their survival in question—maybe both) is thereby less significant, their people subsequently and easily overlooked. Done right, ministry in these congregations demands one's best effort and entails good work, but it does not and cannot offer the full range of duties and responsibilities that make parish ministry attractive in the first place and so it is not as personally rewarding or fulfilling as serving a stronger and healthier congregation. Mayflower is a case in point. It offered neither the outcome nor the personal satisfaction for which I had hoped, but I nonetheless recorded some very good work during those years (an affirmation likely to go unchallenged, there being so few left to mount one).

To listen to the old-timers tell the story, in the early decades of the 20th century, Detroit was one of the great urban, cultural, and manufacturing centers of the country. Henry Ford had founded the Ford Motor Company in 1903, followed by others that established Detroit as the world's automotive capital. The factories brought rural Blacks from the South and even larger numbers of southern Whites in the so-called Great Migration; their numbers increased further by Catholic and Jewish immigrants from Europe. Predictably, like other places in the United States, Detroit experienced racial conflict and discrimination.

The second wave of the Great Migration (1941–1943) brought some 400,000 people to the city, mostly from the South, to work in the factories that produced the planes and tanks for the war. The population peaked in the 1950s at nearly 2,000,000 and then began a long, slow, debilitating decline to less than half that by the turn of the century. As the people fled, the city's fortunes began to change and worsen accordingly. The loss of public transportation, for example, in favor of an extensive roadway system encouraged the movement of persons and jobs to the sprawling suburbs, decimating the city and its tax base and leaving behind the urban poor who lacked both jobs locally and affordable transportation to jobs regionally. The 1967 riot and the condition of the schools exacerbated White flight and aggravated the decay of a once-great urban center. The next decade saw the gas crises of 1973 and 1979 and the decline in American automotive manufacturing as people wanted smaller, more fuel-efficient cars, which at the time were pretty much limited to imports manufactured elsewhere. Plants closed, further eroding the Detroit tax base and the prospects of good paying jobs.

Notwithstanding that its roots stretched back to the competition for jobs and housing in the First Migration, I was shocked to discover the *overt* racism that defined a considerable piece of the culture of Metro Detroit. It was hardly the case that other places where I had lived were free of racial tensions—I've always held that to grow up American was to grow up racist—and we certainly had our racial and ethnic problems in the greater Los Angeles area from which I had just moved, but I comforted myself with the thought that at least in California we had the good grace to recognize our racism and acknowledge that something must be done about it. Not that we ever did anything about it, but at least we gave it the name it deserved.

Detroit conveyed no such embarrassment (making Detroiters a tad more honest, perhaps?), and I have since recanted my kudos-to-California naiveté. Racism is racism, and racial, ethnic, and (where part of the package) religious intolerance is the cancer that continues to eat away at the fabric of American society. Our participation in the institution of slavery predates the founding of the country and the grievous failure of the Founders to excise slavery from the Constitution (1619 a commonly accepted date, although captive Africans were likely present in the Americas in the 1400s and as early as 1526 in what would become the United States). That piece of unfinished business resulted, three-quarters of a century later, in a bitter Civil War. The battle for civil rights would take another hundred years and still the task remains unfinished. In fact, at this writing, racial justice seems to be in retreat as a repugnant White nationalism, like a cancer no longer in remission, has suddenly inflicted itself upon the body politic.

We do well to remember the voyage of the St. Louis. On May 13, 1939, the German transatlantic liner sailed from Hamburg, Germany, for Havana, Cuba, carrying 937 passengers, almost all of whom were Jews fleeing the Third Reich. Neither Cuba nor the United States wanted them, and they were returned to Europe and almost certain death in the concentration camps—something about "quotas" and "waiting their turn," not to mention economic conditions (coming out of the Depression) and the competition for jobs. Three-quarters of a century later, the "others" are still not wanted.

In any event, over the years Detroit had become a leading stronghold of the Ku Klux Klan, and folklore even had it that at one point the Royal Oak chief of police headed the Klan. I never bothered to research whether the story was apocryphal or not, but it was certainly in keeping with the racism that defined the Metro Detroit region. Even in the late 1980s, people felt that DWB (Driving While Black) in Detroit's suburbs after dark was not a particularly good idea for African Americans. The better choice was getting below the infamous Eight Mile Road which served as the northern boundary separating the City of Detroit from its older suburbs like Royal Oak. More than a line in the sand, easily ignored, "Eight Mile" meant something: one side designated where White people live, the other side where Black people belong. It represented an established order, a social and economic caste system, a long-standing rule, the violation of which was not expected—and even less tolerated. At least on the north side of Eight Mile Road, that established order was not questioned—that was the part I found so shocking, its acceptance.

Not surprisingly, Royal Oak was solidly White and middle class. Founded as a village in 1891 and incorporated as a city in 1921, it formed part of the older, protective ring of northern suburbs that separated Detroit from middle America north of Eight Mile Road. Its population peaked in 1970 at about 86,000, had declined to something less than 70,000 by the time we arrived in 1986, and seems to have stabilized since in the upper-50,000 range, a reflection of the transition from two-generation homes and neighborhoods teeming with children to single-generation households of older empty-nesters. Perhaps the premier sign of the end of an era was the consolidation of the two high schools into a single campus about the turn of the century.

The northern suburbs are highly stratified economically, the price of real estate increasing with each Mile Road going north toward the newer, more exclusive zip codes, but we wanted to live close to (not next to but near enough to walk to) the church. Coming from Los Angeles, we discovered that we could get twice the house for about half the money in our part of town, which translated to a lovely four-bedroom tri-level that served our family well. Years later, we would move back to California where we got far less than half the house for considerably more than twice the money, with a mortgage that will undoubtedly outlast us.

Though I did not recognize it at the time, Royal Oak offered a snapshot that explained why the post-war Boomer generation (born 1946-1964) was so highly privileged. Among my Royal Oak parishioners was a group of retired men, mostly from the automotive plants. Members of the GI and the Silent Generations (the young men and women who came of age during the Depression, went on to win the war, and came home to build a life for themselves and their families), they called themselves the "Odd Job Squad," and they would gather at least weekly at the church depending on the "odd jobs" needing their attention. They would tell stories about themselves and their friends who would graduate from high school, have a big party on Saturday, and on Monday walk into one of the Big Three and get a job, a good job—a union job, a job that supported a family living in a modest home in the suburbs. Two parents with one income between them raised their children in safe neighborhoods, sent them to good public schools, and saw them go on to college. They bought a new car every three or four years and not infrequently spent summer vacations and long weekends at their cottage "up north." Forty years later, they retired with a good pension and excellent continuing medical care. The engineers and managers did better financially, but blue-collar and white-collar families alike formed the backbone of the broad middle class and for four decades following World War II enjoyed a level of prosperity that was unprecedented historically, a blip on the screen probably never to be repeated.

We, my generation, often caricatured the world of our youth as the socially superficial realm of "Ozzie and Harriet." We noticed and would soon correct its shortcomings (among them, unaddressed racism, unacknowledged gender imbalances, and soon, an unjust war that would dare to draft us). Had we looked deeper, though, we would have noticed as well the work already underway, particularly in civil rights. This work included the momentous Supreme Court decision, *Brown v. Board of Education* (1954), and the equally significant day a certain Black woman refused to give up her seat on a Montgomery bus to a White man (Rosa Parks, 1955, the "first lady of civil rights," according to Congress). By the time he left office in 1961, President Eisenhower was warning us about the "Military-Industrial Complex," an ethical issue we Boomers and everyone else since have failed to tackle.

Shortcomings, yes, socially superficial, without a doubt, but from the platform of history does a measure of humility take form, for the fact remains that through no merit of our own but rather from the happenstance of the time and place of our birth, we Boomers were only too happy to take advantage of the unparalleled social, economic, and educational privileges it offered.

Very slowly, that would change as economic development spread to more places. Manufacturing, for example, and commercial vitality eventually returned to a rebuilt Europe following the devastation of war. Globalization moved good manufacturing (read "well paid union") jobs to places where labor cost pennies on the dollar compared to the United States. This benefited greatly a developing middle class in other countries (India, Brazil, and China, for example), but lifting huge populations of the economically marginal elsewhere on the planet left behind an increasing population of the economically vulnerable at home; the retail and service economy that emerged just did not pay as well as the assembly line in Detroit. Further, whereas a high school diploma once practically guaranteed the willing a job, within two generations a relentless automation of the means of production and other technologies, coupled with a disastrous decline in the quality of public-school education, rendered that same high school diploma practically useless. Sadly, tragically, absent a national commitment to excellence in public education for the individual and lacking a similar commitment to lifelong learning from the individual, large swaths of the American people will be underemployed, marginally employable, or unnecessary altogether throughout their working years.

Throughout this transition, the American economy would reign supreme, the dollar the currency of choice well into the 21st century, but its wealth increasingly, alarmingly, would find itself concentrated in an ever-decreasing slice of the American workforce and households; those highly skilled in computer science and technology (Silicon Valley the poster child) and especially those who can master (if not manipulate) the financial services marketplace will do well—everyone else, less so. It did not have to turn out that way. The nation's wealth could have been directed to the priorities typically voiced in the public square (access to adequate health care and decent public education, for example) but overshadowing the public square is the financial tyranny of corporate greed and unregulated capitalism, coupled with the vast military-industrial apparatus and its own "national security" propaganda machinery. Add the threat of the Other to the mix (political and environmental refugees, say) and any meaningful conversation about redistribution of wealth (aka, tax reform) never gets off the ground.

My Odd Job Squad taught the lesson well. For a brief moment, the GI and Silent generations had opened the door for the Boomers to feast on a can-do, men-on-the-moon arena of possibilities, supported in the public square which paid the freight to make it happen. It made possible the four-year Liberal Arts degree I earned from a public, four-year university and from which I graduated without any debt whatsoever. From there I went to seminary and from seminary into the pastorate—privilege indeed.

At its peak in the late 1960s, First Church had about 1,000 members. Over the next twenty years, a slow erosion of membership gradually reduced the numerical strength of the church (still measured by names on the role and not bodies in the pews in those days) but when I arrived, the church still claimed to have about 800 members (a figure undoubtedly inflated but substantial nonetheless).

By its own account, the church's theology was self-consciously liberal, and the church itself was recognized as the most liberal in town. Of my three immediate predecessors, two (with a combined tenure of about three decades) were Unitarian, and one of the strongest members of the Search Committee was actually a Deist. A substantial number of the church's members had come from Unitarian backgrounds, and I always felt that a fair number would have easily identified as Unitarian had its tenets been defined (Closet Unitarians, I called them). They placed themselves within the Christian umbrella (many in Unitarian-Universalist fellowships today do not), and so they found a comfortable enough home in the noncreedal Congregational church (or better, the Congregational church with the liberal creed). We only celebrated Communion quarterly, but I always noticed a dip in attendance on those occasions as some chose to sit out the opportunity to "eat Jesus," the barbarism of which belonged to a religious past best forgotten.

A word about Christian Unitarianism. The movement traces its roots to the doctrine of the Trinity, rejecting the classical formulation that God is one being in three persons (Father, Son, and Holy Spirit) in favor of an understanding of God as one singular entity. This position has particular implications for the person and purpose of Jesus whom Unitarians see as a man, even a great man and a prophet, the bearer of profound moral teachings and certainly a model for living one's own life, but not otherwise possessed of a unique measure of divinity unavailable to any other human being. As I use the term in the context of the Royal Oak church, "Unitarian" and "liberal" are almost interchangeable in that each sees no necessary conflict between faith in God and the findings of reason, rationality, science, and philosophy. Further, each holds that humans have and are responsible for the ethical expression of their free will. They deny the infallibility of the Bible and are open to the teachings of other religions. Neither is tied to creedal formulas.

Note that I specified the *Christian* context for this characterization of the historic roots of Unitarianism. Over time, other religious and non-theistic views became part of Unitarian and Unitarian-Universalist congregations, many intentionally standing outside a specifically Christian context, but this was not the case of the Royal Oak Unitarians. From the 19th century, James Freeman Clarke's Affirmation of Faith states the Unitarian position well: "The Fatherhood of God, the brotherhood of man, the leadership of Jesus, salvation by character, and the progress of mankind onward and upward forever." Later I will question such an optimistic spirit in light of the bloody 20th century and the dismal start to the 21st century, and clearly my Christology, or understanding of the Person of Jesus, goes far beyond the "leadership of Jesus" model as Clarke affirmed, but as a theological liberal, I nod my head mostly in approval, as did my liberal and Unitarian members alike.

As if to balance the theological continuum somewhat, the congregation also included a small number of members with more conservative-evangelical tendencies, and not comfortable with either label (Liberal or Evangelical), most of the members really considered themselves "Moderate." A rather nondescript term, theological Moderates know where they do *not* belong on the theological spectrum, namely, on the Right where we find the enthusiastic, praise-the-Lord, are-you-saved Evangelicals and such. Moderates will stop short of *that* but will quickly step back from the *other* if they get too far Left, especially when it strays into social-cultural matters (as we will see presently).

Moderate-to-Liberal with a goodly number of Unitarians, but not to the exclusion of those who placed themselves further out on both ends of the continuum, together they formed the backbone of the church. Perfectly willing to accommodate Darwin and Jesus (science and religion), generally preferring the language of Jesus the Rabbi to that of Christ the Savior, and somewhat puzzled in any event by the implications of carrying this Person too far, together they were also a constant reminder not to grow complacent with my own comfort zone but to push, ponder, explore, and otherwise think about my own theological boundaries and what, quite possibly, I was still missing, to my and my parishioners' detriment.

A wonderful place, First Church. A privileged people, they were, given where they lived and worked and raised their families, with friendships in many cases that extended over decades. They raised their children together, grew old together, weathered their illnesses together, and when the time came, attended each other's funerals. They were white collar and blue collar, business and professional, homemaker and breadwinner, and while some lived a little higher on the socioeconomic scale than others and enjoyed somewhat more exclusive zip codes and took definitely more exotic vacations, none was pretentious. Pompous I would see later, but never at Royal Oak.

Preaching to such a congregation was both a challenge and a joy of which I hardly ever tired. I was taught never to preach down to the people but rather to honor their intelligence, education, and experience—which I did. I took them seriously which meant taking sermon preparation with utmost seriousness. I finished my Doctor of Ministry program that first year in Royal Oak, and I was grateful for the process-informed theological orientation: acknowledging God's intimate and loving relationship to the creation with whom the Creator shares power was ever a fruitful way to frame that challenge.

We—pastor and parishioner—understood that church people did not have to leave their brains outside when they walked in the church on a Sunday morning; neither science nor the increasingly secular landscape was the enemy; one could read the Bible without concluding that the world was created in 4004 BC. Overall, we were quite comfortable in and with a 20th century Western *Weltanschauung*. It meant that we, the liberal church and the modern world, might actually talk to each other.

Admittedly, that conversation became a little more difficult as a new phenomenon, the postmodern age, began to break into our consciousness and conversation. Vaclav Havel for one gave the idea currency in his 1994 Liberty Medal acceptance speech at Independence Hall in Philadelphia. He noted that the modern age had died and that something new was in the process of being born. We live between those two worlds, the world we have known and the world yet to be. He calls this middle ground "postmodern," a time where everything is possible and almost nothing is certain. Specifically, he said that "there appear to be no integrating forces, no unified meaning, no true inner understanding of phenomena in our experience of the world. Experts can explain anything in the objective world to us, yet we understand our own lives less and less. In short, we live in the postmodern world, where everything is possible and almost nothing is certain."[13]

In other words, all the rules, anchors, expectations, mores, certainties, not to mention the attendant stability, of the old, modern age have given way to a time of an essential subjectivity born of uncertainty where the rules, even truth itself, are those of one's own choosing. Cast free from the old anchors, we each have our own truth; maybe they overlap—maybe not; either way, we cling to the vestiges of the world we have known, all the while aware of a lurking chaos dogging our every step.

Havel says the modern age ended in 1969 when we landed men on the moon. I would date it to the 1945 unleashing of atomic power which, as Albert Einstein has famously said, "has changed everything except our way of thinking." It hardly matters when, for at issue in the last half century or so is a

---

13. The speech can be found at the National Constitution Center and online generally.

massive, global upheaval at every level of society, social, economic, and political. Religion's role: to make sense of a time of cataclysmic change.

This is a tall order because the religious quest in its various institutional expressions suffers from the same postmodern subjectivity it is supposed to explain. A cacophony of truths results. Sometimes a benign tolerance allows them to share a common space; at other times, bitter conflict pits one version against another. Surely, the spectacular growth of conservative churches in this time period (and religious fundamentalism generally) lies in its promise that the sacred and veritable truths of the faith are just that, sacred and veritable.

In any event, churches exist as front-line, down-in-the-trenches schools where the local theologian in residence, the rabbi-teacher, connects the "ways of God" with the real lives of everyday men and women. Following its in-house conversation with each other, liberal Protestants could then walk outside and have an intelligible, meaningful, relevant (I still like that word) conversation with the wider community. We expected such of our people, that they would see and make a connection between what happened in the church and its implications for how they lived in the world.

For a church that has no creed, no binding statement of faith, and no authoritative voice or agency external to the local church, the key to that conversation both in and out of the pulpit was finding a way to address a theologically diverse congregation with a solid biblical foundation. To think theologically and develop spiritually, we desperately needed the Bible's language, a challenge for many moderate-to-liberal Protestants who had grown skittish toward biblical language. Congregationalists may be a people of the Book, but the Book was facing some pretty stiff hurdles in a world increasingly defined as culturally secular, socially diverse, and now vaguely postmodern as well.

Of course, the in-house conversation is only half the life of the church. The rest of our Story asks the "Now What?" or the "So What?" question, or to use the familiar acronym, WWJD?...What Would Jesus Do? In other words, having come to church to *rehearse* the drama, now the church must go forth to *live* the drama! The Danish theologian Søren Kierkegaard, ever the burr-in-the-saddle to establishment ecclesiastical types, applied the image of the drama to the life of the church.[14]

Any dramatic production, he said, includes three categories of participants: performers, cue-givers, and the audience. Front and center, we find the performers, the actors on the stage who tell the story; off to the side, out of sight, cue-givers direct the actors, offering the prompts that keep the story flowing; the audience takes in the story, responding with applause or laughter or tears as appropriate but otherwise remaining passive.

Television expands the nature of drama to include entertainment generally and reinforces the same division of labor: performers are still front and center, "performing;" behind the scenes, out of view of the camera, cue-givers serve as the "production crew;" some still watch "live," but the real audience, the audience that counts (the audience that buys the sponsor's products), sits at home passively, grateful (or not) for the entertainment but having no role in the performance other than changing the channel or boycotting the sponsor's products.

Inevitably, when it comes to the drama performed in the sanctuary, the same three roles—performer, cue-giver, and audience—apply and inevitably are assigned according to their counterparts in the secular world whether in the theater or on the stage: acting out the story are the people in the chancel, preachers, musicians, choirs, and liturgists; behind the scenes, out of sight, God gives the cues; sitting in the pews, the parishioners take it all in, passive consumers of the drama.

Kierkegaard offers a correction: those people in the chancel, self-importantly accepting the starring roles...call them cue-givers; the people in the pew, passively absorbing the Story presented...instead, make them the actors; watching the drama unfold...that would be God.

Talk about role reversal! Actors performing for God in their everyday lives sounds suspiciously like...mission. Mission, the Gospel drama at work in the world. Kierkegaard was right—the focus of the church properly falls not

---

14. From his book, *Purity of Heart Is to Will One Thing*, Chapter 12: What Then Must I Do? The Listener's Role in a Devotional Address.

on the clergy but the laity. How to get that point across? Once again, process thought came to the rescue: with its emphasis on freedom, and so the necessity to choose among competing options, we need to pay attention to that particular option that constitutes the Creator's lure or aim for each of us individually as persons and corporately as a church. Such is our mission as people of faith, a mission as central to our existence as fire is to burning (paraphrasing Emil Brunner).

As I frequently said, it matters not only that we live but why, to what ends. The church is not a club from which one derives certain benefits by virtue of having a name on the membership roles and paying the necessary "dues" (pledge). Quite the contrary, the church equips the saints for the work of ministry in the world (Eph. 4.12). Ultimately, the church's goal and so the individual member's purpose turns on Jesus' peculiar economy, whereby in losing ourselves do we find ourselves (Matt. 16.24 ff., par.). Like Amos, we would heed the summons to replace the form of worship with its substance (Amos 5.21–24), and like Micah, we would remember that at its best religion is a verb, *doing* justice, *loving* kindness, *walking* humbly with God (Mic. 6.6–8).

Not my needs but the world's hurts, to that cause (mission) does the church literally give itself away.

Or such we said, anyway—its execution told a different story. It's as if having gotten it right in the worship hour, we then retired to the coffee hour, the mission if not accomplished then at least deferred…or if not deferred, then ever marked "Incomplete," like a class at school, its grade and so the credits withheld, until the student satisfied some as-yet unmet class requirements.

The problem, of course, is Jesus. WWJD?—What Would Jesus Do? In his book, *A Short History of the World*, H. G. Wells provides an answer. A little more in keeping with what Jesus *wants* than what Jesus *does*, the chapter on the "Teaching of Jesus" describes his "resolve to revolutionize the world,…to change and fuse and enlarge all human life." A revolutionary, changing and fusing and enlarging all human life? Who can stand such a thing? Certainly not the "rich and prosperous [who] felt a horror of strange things, a swimming of their world at his teaching." Little wonder, for taken to their conclusion,

Jesus' teachings turn the world upside down. Wells goes a little further in his Christology than most:

> He was like some terrible moral huntsman digging mankind out of the snug burrows in which they had lived hitherto. In the white blaze of this kingdom of his there was to be no property, no privilege, no pride and precedence; no motive indeed and no reward but love. Is it any wonder that men were dazzled and blinded and cried out against him? Even his disciples cried out when he would not spare them the light.

What to do about such as he, the revolutionary? Wells is masterful in describing what can only be called the horror elicited in that first moment of recognition. The clergy, for example, knew that "between this man and themselves there was no choice but that he or [they] should perish," the disciple not just supplanting the master (Matt. 10.24) but replacing the master altogether. The soldiers, "confronted and amazed by something soaring over their comprehension and threatening all their disciplines," could not say why, but the presence of this Man drove them mad such that they "should take refuge in wild laughter, and crown him with thorns and robe him in purple and make a mock Cæsar of him." From this telling, Jesus comes with a warning: "to take him seriously [is] to enter upon a strange and alarming life, to abandon habits, to control instincts and impulses, to essay an incredible happiness."

The terrible moral huntsman digging the self-satisfied and privileged out of their snug burrows resonates with many of us who came of age in the '60s and it speaks to me still. It underscores the whole of the prophetic voice of both the Hebrew and Christian Scriptures, racial, economic, and environmental justice still hanging in the balance. The resolve to revolutionize the world nurtures the idea, the vision, of the wider community as well, a new community where everyone had enough and where the new covenant of which Jeremiah spoke would take root (Jer. 31.31–34). An educated, prosperous, privileged people of God, the very people who comprised so many of our urban and suburban mainline congregations in the second half of the last century, were the messengers; surely they would see the possibilities; together we would bring in Jesus' radical vision of a New Age.

Or maybe not, for somewhere along the way, the message got muddled and we agreed that talking the talk and sort of walking the walk was good enough—definitely more reasonable and much more comfortable. Quoted with some minor variation in language, Dom Hélder Câmara, Brazilian Catholic Archbishop of Olinda and Recife, makes the point succinctly:[15]

> When I give food to the poor, they call me a saint. When I ask
> why the poor have no food, they call me a Communist.

Feeding the hungry is good and eliminating the reason people are hungry is better, but addressing the cause to which the symptom points takes us in directions we would rather not go, and so we agree that the good is perhaps good enough.

Jesus tells us to clothe the naked, which is a prime purpose of every church rummage sale, and we rightly celebrate our good work in doing so, but we cannot help but note that were the labor of the families who buy our castoff clothing sufficiently, fairly, and justly compensated, these same families could shop where we shop. Is it not better to anticipate charity by eliminating poverty (as Maimonides taught us[16])? And if that is better, why is the merely good, good enough?

We light candles at the outbreak of each new war and pray for peace, which is surely good, but why do we not tax the profits from waging war and direct that bounty to the causes that make for peace, which is better? But who would dare voice such an outrageous notion, and so at least the good is a start…and maybe enough?

With more guns than citizens in the country, gun violence represents a kind of war on ourselves, although now that the incidents of such violence are too numerous to light candles each time it erupts, we no longer know what the good is, not to mention when it becomes good enough.

---

15. Following here Zildo Rocha, *Helder, the Gift: A Life that Marked the Course of the Church in Brazil*, p. 53, Editora Vozes, 2000.

16. Maimonides Golden Ladder comes from the 12th century Rabbi Moshe Ben Maimon, one of Judaism's great philosophical, theological, and scientific thinkers. In writing on the Jewish obligation to give, he develops stages by which the giver is lifted to increasingly higher steps on the spiritual ladder, the highest of which is eliminating the conditions that make the gift necessary in the first place.

During the Cold War, it was missiles (lest we forget, it still could be)—by the middle decades of the 21st century, it could well be irreversible ecological degradation. Even at this point, two decades in, it nonetheless looks like greenhouse gases will increase the planet's temperature dangerously past 2°C, perhaps moving into the catastrophic 2.5–5°C range where really bad things begin to happen to all the world's good people. Minimally, changing weather patterns and excessive heating in certain regions around the globe will produce food and water scarcity for millions and induce mass migrations of the desperate. Without adequate advance planning and preparation, we can only…well, the scenarios are not encouraging. One more layer of gloom is the prospect of the Sixth Extinction, presumably now underway, the only question being whether humankind itself will become one of the victims, and civilization before that.

It is, of course, quite possible that humankind is not the first of the evolutionary experiments involving so-called higher intelligence beings to have reached the critical crossroads that ended badly, so to speak. That others of similar or even greater intelligence have pushed some button or transgressed some catastrophic tipping point, causing the grand experiment to reset and begin again, all sounds like nonsense, the stuff of science fiction and the contemporary spate of dystopian novels, but at some point some beings will emerge with the spiritual intelligence of Jesus himself and the accompanying capacity to do as he did, if not even more (like commanding stinky Lazarus to come forth from the tomb). The contemporary version of human being is indeed quite smart enough—we have the science and the technology—to meet the challenge. Our only variable is whether we are good enough to put it to use quickly enough to carry the creation over the threshold to a healthier place for all living things. As people of faith, we look to the transformative power of love as the missing but necessary ingredient, working in and through us and our calling as co-creators with God, and if not us, maybe the next incarnation of a still-higher order of creature will overcome that deficiency.

Whether acknowledging it or not, both church and society face the same conundrum—are we good enough and if so, why aren't we doing better?—when it comes to racially bifurcated metropolitan Detroit. Our faith traditions uphold the inherent dignity of all persons and extol the virtues of simple respect as the essential glue holding a civil society together, but the 400-year legacy of slavery and what became America's Original Sin continue to poison the social fabric in the form of prejudice, fear, and intractable socioeconomic divisions.

An opportunity to address our Original Sin in Royal Oak came in the form of a bold initiative from the Metropolitan Detroit Council of Churches to establish partnerships between White suburban churches and Black Detroit churches, and with courage and good intentions, we responded. I would later pursue a similar agenda with the Tongan and English sides of my church in Maui (a true melting pot—if it can work in Hawaii, it can work anywhere) and the Korean and English congregations of a downtown Los Angeles church. The Maui experiment would show promise. In retrospect, the Los Angeles version was doomed before it began and so failed miserably.

I continue to believe such programs belong in the church, but racism is systemic in our country, and building substantial and meaningful relationships across racial and ethnic lines is terrifically hard work. It may begin as an affair of the mind, but very quickly it needs to become an affair of the heart, passionate and deeply anchored at the core of a congregation's life, as routine and natural as the Sunday offering. Most congregations lack the will and the energy (the former more than the latter) to sustain that level of heavy lifting. We were paired with a Baptist church, and I give us high marks for trying, but after sharing a few meals, enjoying friendly conversation, and exchanging pulpits (once), the effort gradually faded and nothing really came of it.

Something was missing. We had good intentions but in this case, good intentions were not nearly good enough. As with any mission, so with the intractable problem of racism, extending ourselves into the world below Eight Mile Road may have necessarily started as an affair of the mind, but it clearly could not end there. As we were about to learn, the mission requires a missionary.

She arrived quite unexpectedly in the person of Ann. At the time, she had completed what would be the first of three degrees, an achievement all by itself but not quite sufficient by itself to equip her to teach music, band in particular. So having just settled our family in Royal Oak, she enrolled in

Oakland University and earned a second bachelor's degree, this time in Music Education. Later still, she would earn a Master's Degree in Music Composition from Oakland.

We treat the arts as discretionary in our educational systems, just one of our shortsighted deficiencies in how the Village prepares children for adulthood, but in time Ann landed a band position in the Detroit Public Schools system. Since she would teach strings as well as band instruments and serve as *the* music resource for such events as assemblies where music was part of the program, it would be more accurate to say she was the music department. Initially, she traveled between several schools before finally settling at one with some 1,100 students.

Talk about pushing the boundaries of your comfort level! This was Detroit; Detroit was predominately Black, the public schools even more so. The color barrier, though, was only the beginning, for zip code segregation imposed socioeconomic overtones on top of race—she being White and suburban and her students mostly Black and inner city, the network of relationships were predictably layered with the attitudes and prejudices that a racist culture had nurtured over decades of discrimination and experience had confirmed within the ranks of its victims. Pointedly, the music teacher from Royal Oak felt the sting of reverse discrimination from her own colleagues, mostly Black, some of whom made it very clear that her White, privileged presence was not appreciated in the troubled environment from which she escaped at day's end. (We would again experience reverse discrimination from native Hawaiians while living on Maui.)

Money was equally problematic—money to buy and repair instruments. Imagine a band and orchestra program lacking both enough working instruments to outfit the students who wanted to play in the band or orchestra and the funds to purchase even used instruments and fix broken ones. Uniforms were out of the question.

Or maybe not. Ann has a knack for sales, and it occurred to her that the members of the church might want to participate in her program. In a flash, the Detroit Instrument Project at the First Congregational Church was born.

It turned out that the church very much wanted to participate in what one of their own was doing below Eight Mile Road, and the members responded very generously. Collecting dust in closets were all kinds of musical instruments children left behind when they moved from their family home, and eventually some 80 instruments in playable condition found their way to Detroit schools.

They wrote checks, too, mostly through another of her innovations at Royal Oak: the Alternative Christmas Fair. A rather new concept at the time, these fairs raised significant amounts of money for any number of nonprofit organizations, faith-based and secular alike. The idea was simple: many people try to avoid the commercial side of Christmas; a growing number of others want to refrain from purchasing things for the sake of purchasing things that will only end up in the landfill and degrade the environment in the process of getting there; and virtually everybody has friends and family members in that have-everything-need-nothing category—what to do? The Alternative Christmas Fair provides the solution to this problem whereby the giver can make a donation to a humanitarian organization or religious mission in the name of a friend or family member who then receives a certificate or card acknowledging the gift. Heifer International continues to be one of our favorites, the generations of chickens, bees, and goats we procured still serving communities all over the world.

Ann created a fundraising arm for her program that she called "The Ten Dollar Club." The idea was to help a student learn to play an instrument by purchasing a mouthpiece, which cost $10.00. Donors became members of the club and had their names listed in the newsletter. Over the nine years she taught in Detroit, she received about $11,000 from church members, which covered about half of the actual operational expenses year-to-year. The balance came from the district and (as with her colleagues everywhere) the music teacher herself, but the generosity of the church meant Ann could then purchase used instruments and supplies like reeds and mouthpieces that would otherwise be out of reach. She had taught herself to repair most anything that might go wrong with the moving parts, like malfunctioning keys of a delicate flute. "Give it to Ms. K, she'll know what to do," was the mantra, and usually she did, but on other occasions when she could not repair it herself, the Ten Dollar Club footed the bill.

The most remarkable thing to me, though, was the fruit of their efforts, teacher and students alike, during the seasonal concerts. I attended most of them, sitting in the back of the auditorium while ensembles and soloists would offer their contribution to the program, Ms. K conducting, accompanying, and encouraging as necessary to support the performance. As families do at the end of the day, sharing highlights and maybe a little gossip from classroom and workplace, Ann would tell me how her students were doing and what was going on in their homes, and I remember at one point reaching my saturation point in dealing with the endless struggles and challenges inner city kids and their families faced day after day just to survive, much less thrive. I had to ask her to be a little circumspect in what she related, maybe just the big picture without all the dreadful details. I still feel badly about that. After all, she was the one who lived it, and I could not let her unload the burden?

Of course, it was not all hardship and burden. Kids are kids everywhere and the kids loved their music program—and responded to the expectations their teacher placed on them. Having their hand on a musical instrument that they could actually take home was a high point for the members of the band and orchestra. ("No, Ms. K, you cannot possibly trust them to take the instrument home," everyone said, as the kids took their instruments home…and brought them back.) In fact, one of the most memorable comments Ann ever made about her work was discovering that for some of her students, making music was the first time they experienced success.

The discovery for the church was the personal nature of mission, or what increasingly we would call the church's outreach—the ways it extends itself into the wider community. While it's good to talk about such things, like peace or racism, and even better to talk and write checks, nothing can take the place of simply being there—the ministry of presence. For the next ten years, until we left Royal Oak, one of our own lived that lesson. She did not go to her Detroit school "in the name of the First Congregational Church of Royal Oak" and did not offer the church's gifts "in the name of Jesus," but she extended a love—or better, she lived a love—that was in keeping with the church's teaching, and in that respect, she was the church's missionary, as were several hundred other brothers and sisters in that mission station, the First Congregational Church. Every one of them sent "in the name of Jesus" to extend—or better, to live—a love that lies at the heart and is the soul of any church bearing his name.

I doubt many of our people actually saw themselves as missionaries, either thinking themselves unworthy of the calling or finding the prospect too horrifying even to contemplate (religion a private matter after all, best kept to oneself), but in the daily round of activities, our local *missionaries* assumed responsibility for scores of decisions that necessarily touched the heart and soul of family, community, and nation alike, and each act flowing from even insignificant decisions in its own way bore the mark of the Christ whose words and ways they committed to follow by virtue of their membership in his church. We might call this the Project of Love, by which we mean that members of the faith community embrace one another and the whole creation with the same Love that first embraced them. Call it our mission individually and corporately, to live the Project of Love in the Drama of Life.

Living out our individual callings as disciples of Christ is a matter of orienting ourselves to the words and ways of Jesus in our daily routine. So easy to say…at least until we hear echoes of H. G. Wells spelling out the words and ways of Jesus, something about a "resolve to revolutionize the world…to change and fuse and enlarge all human life," but for those so oriented, all that stands in the way is personal resolve. Fusing and enlarging life does not need first to go before the Council for inclusion in the Mission Statement or the Trustees for funding or an ad hoc Commission to study the matter and return with a recommendation. Forget the minutes and listen instead for the still small voice speaking directly to anyone brave enough—foolish enough—to pose the question, WWJD?

Posing the same question for the local mission station, the church, however, is an entirely different matter, a complicated matter, and as the decade of the '80s unwound, the churches and their leaders began to see just how different the times had become as a post-Christian America began to take shape.

Loren Mead and the Alban Institute described it for us as the end of Christendom itself. Having previously acknowledged the role the Alban Institute played in my work at Mayflower Church, San Gabriel, it will be readily apparent that I offer no token appreciation to Loren Mead and his colleagues for his *Once and Future Church* series. It was an incredibly important gift to the church at the very time the church needed his analysis and insights. That series and other Alban studies linked theology with history and culture, the combination of which brought to light the early signs of a complex socioeconomic, demographic, and generational tidal wave working its way through post-modern and now post-Christian America. With a new Reformation in its infancy, but apparently underway, the missional question was not so much theoretical as strategic: of course we will address needs and hurts with a healing love…but which ones and how?

A heavy lift, the end of Christendom. You could see eyes glaze over when the subject appeared on board agendas. Perhaps our members (and clergy?) found the language too alarming, the concepts too foreign, and the implied prospect of change too uncomfortable. Sitting in our little boats, the surrounding turbulent seas just overwhelmed us, all of us. Alvin Toffler's *Future Shock* (first published in 1970) said it well: "too much change in too short a period of time." Nobody came to church to hear about Future Shock and sinking boats.

Maybe not, but the Drama of Life has a way of bumping into the Project of Love anyway. For the First Congregational Church of Royal Oak, the one collided with the other the day Doug and Brian knocked on the door of my study and requested a few minutes of my time (at their request, I do not use their real names). Their purpose in meeting with me was to ask if they could be married in the church, specifically, in the sanctuary. They were very clear: this was to be a marriage ceremony (not a benign blessing or recognition service) in the sanctuary (not someone's backyard).

As I write this, same-sex marriage is the law of the land. Some churches refuse to participate (the law does not require differently), and here and there a few businesses will quote the usual biblical verses to justify why they cannot possibly do business with such people; apparently the usual biblical passages connecting divorce and remarriage with adultery posed no impediment when it came to ethical business practices, probably for the simple reason that excluding such people would put them out of business (Matt. 5.31–32; Mark 10.2–12; Rom. 7.3; et al.). Wedding cakes for adulterers, scorn for LGBTQ+ lovers.

A quarter-century ago, though, things were different. Not many—certainly not many churches—were even talking about same-sex relationships (unless it was to condemn its practice), much less performing same-sex marriage ceremonies in the sanctuary. The wider community largely looked upon homosexuality as a matter of choice, a freely adopted lifestyle, not a matter of genetics, and ruled that such relationships were contrary to human nature. End of subject.

I had been in the ministry about twenty-five years by then, and never once had the question found its way to a board meeting agenda or study group. (Quite frankly, I do not remember ever having discussed it in seminary.) Over the years, I had gay and lesbian members and members with gay and lesbian children—I knew it and so did everybody else—but no one knocked on my door to talk about it. Looking back, this was not too surprising since institutional religion had rendered its judgment on the matter and prescribed repentance or therapy for its practitioners, so why risk the pastor's ire bringing to the foreground that which had already been consigned to the underground? Content to say on the subject what Jesus said on the subject, I felt no compunction to dive into sticky passages in Leviticus or Paul and so there the matter rested, consigned to the closet (so to speak).[17] Of course, no request for a church wedding had found its way to my desk, the very concept unthinkable...until it did.

Interestingly enough, a colleague in town had challenged me just a few months earlier to prepare for this moment. A similar request had come to him and he had a book to recommend, which I quickly bought and read, an excellent choice called *The New Testament and Homosexuality* by Robin Scroggs, Professor of New Testament at Union Theological Seminary. In that book,

---

17. The Gospels are silent on the subject of homosexuality.

Scroggs analyzed the relevant Leviticus and Roman texts in the cultural context within which they were written, including other laws and social strictures governing same-sex relationships generally. Among his findings was this: that at issue was not sexual contact between two persons of the same gender *per se* but the abuse of that relationship, typically where an older man takes advantage of a younger boy. In other words, the issue is power, concentrated in one, virtually absent in the other. The abuse of power—the powerful taking advantage of and otherwise exploiting the vulnerability of the powerless—is the condition of rape generally, sex seldom if ever the objective. (One avoids reluctantly the parallel exploitation of labor in the marketplace.) At issue is the absence of love, mutually given and received.

In something of an understatement, since I knew absolutely nothing about the subject, I was grateful for my colleague's advice, and more grateful for such a resource.

With the matter now on the table, the question was what to do? As a Congregational minister, called to my position as Pastor and Teacher and serving as Resident Theologian, most definitely not a presiding bishop, it never occurred to me to give Doug and Brian either an impetuous Yes, as if the congregation did not and need not figure in my deliberations, or a perfunctory No, the children in the pew unequal to the challenge of deliberating on the subject and reaching their own conclusion. I was taught to respect the integrity of my people and for half a century I never wavered in that commitment.

Predictably, then, I proposed to both Doug and Brian and subsequently to my leadership that we undertake a study. This being a reasonable approach, I outlined a process that began with an examination of the biblical texts themselves, the Scroggs book serving as the primary resource. We had several persons who felt safe enough in the church to "come out" and for one session, a gay man and his parents talked about their experience as a family and answered our questions. Near the end of the study, my colleague and I engaged in a dialogue, two pastors talking between themselves about our experience as pastors helping our local churches deal with a volatile subject without blowing the place up. We ended with Doug and Brian themselves talking about their own experience growing up gay, closeted, and rejected by their families. More than two decades later, their pain still brings tears to my eyes.

I must say it was a very good study—clear, concise, and well received by the church. I do not remember that the attendance was very impressive, but it offered a frank appraisal of what was then just beginning to surface as an issue for churches.

It was understood from the beginning that I would make a recommendation to the Board of Deacons (the combined Diaconate) and that the Deacons would make the decision about granting or denying the request. As with any decision of any board or committee, this one could be (but was not) referred to the entire membership called to a special meeting to review the action so taken, but the spiritual life of the church generally, especially as it took shape in its worship, was the responsibility of the Deacons and so the initial decision fell to them.

On the surface, the decision was a matter of clarifying its wedding policy: essentially, we opened the doors to any couple intent on establishing a marriage covenant. That we might discriminate based on race, socioeconomic status, a history of divorce, or even creed and religious affiliation (if any) was unthinkable. In latter years, the presence of children was not even an impediment, as couples who had been living together long enough to start families involved their own children in their wedding. It was not terribly common, but I have baptized children for parents in advance of performing their wedding service. Y'all come, God's joyous grace is extended to each and every person.

Or was it? That, of course, was the test. On the surface, the decision was a simple matter of policy: by opening the doors "to any couple intent on establishing a marriage covenant," do we really mean *any* couple, gender not an issue, or do we draw the line, requiring a man and a woman to show up at the altar?

Suddenly, a matter of policy became a test of a much different sort, one that for starters raised questions about the definition of marriage and challenged the comfort level of individuals and congregation alike. With regard to the Gay and Lesbian community (the LGBT and LGBTQ+ affiliations had not emerged in the public's consciousness at the time), the congregation had long employed a don't-ask-don't-tell approach and was proud of its cutting-edge tolerance for diverse peoples (this all-White, middle-class, suburban congregation), but tolerance *for* is not the same as acceptance *of* diversity. Our tribal instincts will only bend so far—and not very far at that. Generally speaking, as long as the numbers of the differently oriented (in race, creed, and who they love) remain small, quite small, and so marginalized, a façade of acceptance covering a veneer of tolerance is easy to maintain.

That façade began to dissolve as the discussion developed. How could it be otherwise? Generations of cultural conditioning, with its layers of ignorance—especially the view that homosexuality is a choice—and prejudice collided with the request before the membership. Gay men stayed in the closet for a reason and used clandestine measures to meet in social settings, like bars: it was just too dangerous to do otherwise. Predictably, as our discussion continued, an undercurrent of conflict began to surface, and eventually it reached the point where some, the anonymous "they," threatened to leave the church were the request to be granted. I never knew exactly who "they" were or their numbers, but presumably "they" were among the major contributors and were the church to split over this issue, which I considered a real possibility, the financial fallout would most likely have been more consequential than the numerical decrease in the membership.

Having come into churches that had fought bitterly and split, I did not want to see FCC, a large, strong church, go through that devastating experience. I was prepared personally to support Doug and Brian in their request and believe it to have been the proper message from the Pastor and Teacher to his people and so the appropriate recommendation to the Board of Deacons, but my actual recommendation to the Board was to deny the request on the grounds that to do otherwise would split the church. The Board accepted my recommendation with just one dissenting vote. I suspect the Deacons would have said no even if I had recommended otherwise. In any event, while some questioned their decision and one family did subsequently leave the church because of it, no one challenged their prerogatives to make it, which I took to mean that everyone was glad someone else had to do it and now that it was done we could get on with our business.

Remarkably, Doug and Brian stuck with the church that had rejected them—I give them lots of credit for that and their underlying willingness to work for change from within. They continued in that effort for several years after I had left, focusing some effort on the question of leadership for the church's Boy Scout troop. For many years, the church had chartered a highly regarded Boy Scout troop, but the troop's local committee took seriously the ruling from the national body that refused to allow gay men to serve in any leadership role. One year, as charter renewal approached, Doug and Brian asked the Council to send a letter to the local Boy Scout Committee asking its members to consider the possibility—just the possibility, nothing more—that good adult leadership could come from the gay community. Apparently, they had hoped that at least the church's own leadership would have evolved sufficiently in the ensuing decade to move beyond the narrow prejudices of the Scouts' policy at the national level (not the least of which was the continuing view that gay men posed a greater risk for child abuse than their heterosexual counterparts), but they did not ask the troop's local governing committee to *change* its policy, only that the troop's governing committee *review* the policy that had governed their leadership choices for decades. The Council refused to write that letter, and with that final rebuke, they left.

I have struggled with my recommendation for more than twenty years now, and fifteen months after having first offered it, I revisited the issue in a sermon. I quote myself from that sermon:

> Every church is actually two churches, an inner, spiritual body and an outer, temporal structure. The former we wish we could see and often cannot; the latter we can easily see and sometimes wish we did not. The inner, spiritual church is a living organism, the very body of Christ; the outer, temporal structure is an organization, defined by its history and traditions and bylaws and worship books. The organism is the ideals of Jesus transforming human personality and human relationships; the organization is the social institution of brick and mortar on thousands of street corners across the country. Hopefully the ideal and the real overlap and someday they will become one, but at times it seems as if they are impossibly distant from each other.

Or as I have put it more simply elsewhere, the distinction is between the Jesus Movement (the spiritual, ideal church) and the Jesus Club (its momentary manifestation, at best an approximation of its Founder).

My recommendation was that we side with the welfare of the institution on this matter, and acting on behalf of the membership, the Deacons agreed. I went on to say (now fifteen months later) that having faced an incredibly difficult issue with potentially serious consequences, I do not second-guess my recommendation as such, but I took ownership of an error on my part which I lamented then and have continued to lament ever since. Again, my own words:

> The problem is not that we took seriously where we are as a people, not that we assessed what is possible and realistic for a people to embrace at a given time, not that we looked at the politics operating in a given situation (politics being the art of the possible), not that we chose the organization over the organism, the real in favor of the ideal. In and of itself, that was not the problem. The problem was that sacrificing the ideal—or what I will call here sacrificing the realm of pure possibility—will almost certainly create an injustice. Creating an injustice and (worse) ignoring an injustice so created places us under judgment. *That* is the problem.

The ideal, of course, is embodying the words and ways of Jesus; essentially, the way of love, and extending that love individually and corporately. Certainly the church can aspire to no less, celebrating that love among themselves as a faith community and then going forth to live and tell that story in the wider world. Simple.

Simple, that is, until the church says that gay and lesbian persons and their relationships lie beyond the reach of God's love. Do LGBTQ+ persons and their relationships qualify as objects of God's loving grace and the church's loving affirmation? Do they have a place in the church of Jesus Christ? Apparently not. For our decision in effect said that there are limits to God's love, that God does not love limitlessly and unconditionally, that there is at least one group of people or one category of behavior that disqualifies some people from receiving the benefits of God's good grace. I would say that the church's self-righteous embrace of such people under the don't-ask-don't-tell mantra does not get the membership off the hook and is in fact a form of hypocrisy, for if in fact God does embrace LGBTQ+ persons, then the church can do no less than to recognize their full humanity and their relationships. Even more, must we not tell the world that at least to this church belongs a people who are inclusive of all persons by nailing an "Open and Affirming" sign (or its equivalent in other denominations) on the front door.

That part is simple…and surely what the people believe. Surely.

But the decision was otherwise, to preserve the church which was already in conflict and would almost certainly have split, and in that moment when we sided with the institution, certainly for good and substantial reasons, at the expense of the persons most directly involved, an injustice was committed.

How often does this happen, this compromise, to know and understand what God hopes and dreams and prepares a people of God to do on the one hand and on the other for those same people to choose a lesser path on the grounds that the organization is not ready to take the leap and then to compound the sin by ignoring the injustice so created? *That* was the problem which I left in the wake of my recommendation, the error of which I repented fifteen months after placing it before my people, and the conundrum with which I have struggled in this and so many other ways throughout my entire ministry. As I concluded then:

> I have a suggestion, a mission statement…simultaneously an act of repentance and a name for the road to redemption: it has been said before…to do justice (Micah 6.8). Our mission, the measure of our activities: to be engaged in the ministries of justice.

> We have some unfinished agenda on our plates. When we pick it up, individually and corporately, the renewing, transforming wind of the Holy Spirit will blow through our lives.

Finally, an answer: when is the good, good enough? When the good work in the moment connects with the ultimate goal of justice, in which case the good work in the moment becomes a stepping stone along the way. The problem with our intermediate steps is not that they are the wrong steps—what can possibly be wrong with, say, feeding the hungry and clothing the naked, as Jesus taught us?—but that having taken them, we consider the job done until the next time.

Feeding the hungry is good, but the pursuit of justice as a goal leads us eventually to ask, as did Dom Hélder Câmara, why there are hungry people in the first place? A tough question, to be sure, for at that point the church addresses not just symptoms (food scarcity for certain people, say) but the relationship of food scarcity to such social issues as poverty, racism, and militarism and the economic forces and spending priorities that overlook the needs of vulnerable populations.

I cannot say that the sermon had any impact—none I could detect anyway, but it did clarify one point; that doing justice is the ultimate good work and that justice workers are a good definition for the church's missionaries. Its completion always just over the horizon, justice work can never rest, and from that perspective, our work can never be enough, but at the same time, what we do to that end is itself good, dare we say, even good enough.

One of the ever-nagging challenges I faced at Royal Oak was how to keep a strong church strong. Not that it was all up to me, but it was my watch and I felt the responsibility deeply. Fortunately, both the church and I could count on a competent and committed cadre of lay leaders to take their governing and program responsibilities with the utmost seriousness, and fortunately for me, I had an exceptionally competent and committed staff in whom I could place my utmost trust and confidence. Looking back, to have worked with such gifted leaders was one of the high points of my entire ministry.

Well before my arrival, the church adopted the model of filling staff positions with so-called paraprofessionals. The term is pejorative, the qualifier *para* suggesting something close to or resembling a "real" professional but not quite cut from the same cloth. In the church, *real* professionals have seminary and denominational credentials, everyone else is a paraprofessional. We later borrowed from a different model which identified the training and skills and other qualifications staff members would need to lead specific programs or departments and called them Directors. Although we did not require that they have formal religious training (setting the theological context for their work was my job), their interest in religion (and more, that they liked churches and church people!) was self-evident, and as we would quickly learn, our program Directors brought with them not just the skills and expertise appropriate for the position but an equally self-evident passion for the work and the desire to explore its creative potential.

Gifts and passion, coupled with a generous measure of creativity, bear remarkable fruit. It seems so obvious: ask people what they want to do and then set them free to do it. Such is the legacy of our program Directors at Royal Oak and the people with whom they worked.

Upon my arrival, the staff included an uncommonly talented young man in charge of the Music Department and a triumvirate of strong, competent, self-assured, and (choosing my words deliberately and carefully) grand ladies. I hold them and others of their generation in special esteem and honor their memory, commitment, and (yes) style because we shall not see them again and the loss is ours to mourn.

Their successors began to feel the effects of what (for shorthand purposes) we can now simply call the end of Christendom, and with its complex web of challenges the need for an evolving program became increasingly evident. The result touched every corner of the life of the church: in effect, we reinvented the church school, redefined our understanding of pastoral care, and reimagined worship. In the first instance, the church school adopted the Workshop Rotation Model, a hands-on, learning center approach to Christian education where a single lesson rotates through a half-dozen or so different stations incorporating a variety of learning styles that reflect the different ways in which students learn. With a little luck, one station will include the theater and its popcorn machine. The program never lacked for volunteer teachers.

All churches will affirm their love in general for one another. The Pastoral Care Ministry program prepared lay members to serve as Pastoral Care Ministers (PCMs we called them) who would carry that love on behalf of the church to individuals experiencing a difficult moment in their lives: the loss of a family member, perhaps, or a serious illness. If my role in the church was that of a generalist, the PCMs were specialists and between them, they committed multiple hours of care to individual members that I could not possibly carve out of a typical week. Lay ministry at its finest.

To say we reimagined worship may touch on the hyperbolic, but at this time the Church Renewal Movement did not ignore the worship hour and the result came to be known as blended worship. I should perhaps say that those *daring* to bring Church Renewal into the sanctuary often created blended worship, for nothing will cause the foundations of a church to tremble like adjustments to its worship, particularly with regard to music. I have often compared the challenge to that of walking a tightrope downhill while blindfolded. That we had a very strong music department with equally strong leadership willing to push its envelope was key to our success in this venture, as was our ability to accommodate a less-formal style without compromising our integrity. Whole books were written on the subject of how to avoid the trap of dumbing down the church's worship as the price of keeping members in the pews. Walking a tightrope, indeed! Understandably, from my perspective our ventures in blended worship exemplify one of the great successes of my tenure at Royal Oak.

Each of these innovations is a story in its own right and each encompasses a Who's Who of First Church lay and staff leadership. I still see in the church's newsletter the names of some who were present from the beginning and nearly three decades later are still active in these ministries. My anxiety of keeping a strong church strong found much of its resolution in this network of church leaders. I would naturally be involved in what are actually five major emphases in this time period (these three projects and two others focused on Administration and Outreach), but I would also be the first to give credit where credit is due—to the gifted, competent, and committed leaders and volunteers in the respective departments who took charge of an idea and made it real.

In 1996, I marked my tenth anniversary with the Royal Oak congregation, at which point the church surprised me with a three-month sabbatical to use as I wished. That year, I turned 50, had 25 years of solid pastoral ministry behind me, was Chair of the Executive Committee of the National Association, and could (and did) entertain the notion of retiring from Royal Oak some 15 years hence.

My emphasis on Church Renewal as summarized above had kept us on our toes; we had fine-tuned some structural issues that improved our Congregational governance; and their respective conclusions notwithstanding, it was gratifying to address emotionally challenging subjects (chief among them was my proposal to adopt a new hymnal which went down in inglorious defeat and the question of gay marriage), air differences of opinion, and survive a decision in good Congregational fashion. Objectively—measuring membership, attendance, and dollars—we were holding our own. Subjectively—a theologically moderate-to-liberal-to-Unitarian congregation of White, prosperous, middle-class, Midwestern Protestants—we were doing splendidly.

Personally, during this period I received periodic affirmations in the form of invitations to apply for Senior Minister positions in what at that time were flagship churches and for Executive and Associate Executive Secretary positions in the National Association itself. While an initial invitation to apply is not the same as an actual offer in hand, the mere suggestion that I might join what would certainly be a fairly select group of serious candidates for such positions was very gratifying.

Upon subsequently declining one such invitation, one colleague responded that I was "the most spiritually-sensitive, intellectually sound minister we have." (High praise given his intellect, education, and stature). He went on to observe that "you exemplify my thesis that not ecclesiastical organization but personal closeness with the Holy Spirit is our guide. When you have prayed over the matter and not felt the Spirit directing you, I have to accept that as real. I am sure you have enough presence and ability to handle that congregation, but if you do not feel spiritually guided you are right to decline." At the risk of boasting less of the Lord than of myself (1 Cor. 1.31), a member of the Royal Oak Search Committee of equal stature echoed something of the same sentiments, noting that I was the only intelligent candidate for the Royal Oak pulpit. Held in such esteem by my highly esteemed colleagues and declining their encouragements to move, if not advance, in favor of remaining where I was, retiring from Royal Oak seemed almost inevitable.

Not that all was rosy, of course. *Covert* ingredients—contrary voices, counterproductive sniping, and everyday irritants—always lurk in the recesses of the stewpot that is the life of any church, invisible even to those who are looking for them until they break through to the surface. Only the unimaginably naïve could even pretend to ignore their certain presence, but then, having come to appreciate Oscar Wilde's observation that no good deed goes unpunished, not many of us suffer from naïveté.

Obviously, I did not retire from Royal Oak. Over the closing years of that decade, things began to change—the mood or feel of the place as well as my mood and how I was feeling about ministry and the church generally. I could point to no single deed of individual consequence, no clear and concise "Aha!" moment, that in and of itself might *overtly* account for a shift in my attitude. I only knew that like encountering turbulence at 35,000 feet, the ride had become less comfortable.

I will turn to the sources of the turbulence next and want to close the Royal Oak chapter with the assessment with which it began, that this was my most productive, by far the most fulfilling and rewarding, and generally the happiest pastorate in my career.

One might say that it was good, very good, indeed.

CHAPTER 6

CHURCH PEOPLE
ARE DIFFERENT

"History belongs to the intercessors
who believe the future into being."

~WALTER WINK
American theologian

"If one is lucky,
a solitary fantasy can totally transform one million realities."

~MAYA ANGELOU
American poet and civil rights activist

I AGREE WITH THOSE WHO say that parish ministry is a wonderful calling and a terrible job. As I have tried to capture in these pages, serving a people in the capacity of pastor is an extraordinary privilege and a humbling and daunting challenge. It encourages creativity in mind and generosity of heart, both of which are frequently in short supply, and dependence on an underlying and nurturing hope. As resident theologians, ministers bring the ways of God to bear upon the human odyssey. As spiritual guides, they voice the possibility of faith when so much in the human odyssey resists the summons to faithfulness. As rabbis, they bring to light the words and ways of the Rabbi who was crucified for his words and ways, suggesting theirs is often a thankless and sometimes even a dangerous calling, but so did they do to the prophets. Privilege indeed.

As a resurrection people, together we proclaim that Good Friday did not get the last word on Jesus and neither does it get to offer the benediction on humankind itself, for as I like to put it, the last chapter has yet to be written. Giving voice to all this is the privilege and opportunity of ministry. A wonderful calling, indeed.

Professional ministry, however, typically involves a salary and performance expectations and all the accouterments that come with the employer-employee relationship. In other words, for ministers who depend on their ministry for some or all of their income, their calling is also a job. Employees are expensive in any business and the business of religion is no exception, so understandably, the congregation-as-employer wants its money's worth and a good return on its investment for which institutional stability (measured superficially by attendance and finances) is a pretty good indicator for the employee and the employer alike.

All quite reasonable, I suppose, but it does create a potential conflict where considerations of, say, job security might overshadow and compromise the minister's calling as servant. Perhaps that explains the seldom-noted counsel to Timothy and the church that its workers deserve their wages (1 Tim. 5.18); at one time that was understood to mean that clergy "wages" are offered not for *what* they do (performance) but so that they *can* do (service). In other words, the work is one thing, the means to sustain one's life for the sake of the work is quite another, and applying the latter as leverage shaping the former serves neither the church nor its workers because it sets the stage for a subsequent and inescapable political calculus that ministers simply cannot ignore, not if a mortgage and children are part of their home life.

Pragmatically speaking, how can it be otherwise, but then juxtapose that with a Jesus resolved "to revolutionize the world...to change and fuse and enlarge all human life" (H. G. Wells again). A "terrible moral huntsman digging mankind out of the snug burrows in which they had lived hitherto," campaigning for a kingdom with no property, no privilege, no pride, no reward: who can stand such a thing? On his economics alone, we know the world cannot possibly tolerate such a Jesus...but can the church? WWJD?—Yes,

What *Would* Jesus Do? Or Micah and his mantra capturing religion at its best, *doing* justice, *loving* kindness, and *walking* humbly with God. Mindful of the advantages of job security, the minister might want to find ways to temper that…without sliding too much down the slippery slope of compromise.

Ministry: a great calling, a terrible job that learns along the way to live with ambiguity and not give up on living into God's future at the same time, reminding the people week by week that this is their calling, too.

The summons to live into God's future is by another name a not-so-veiled invitation to grow and to change—that word again, change—and with it the struggle of herculean proportions, like Jacob and the Angel, a struggle with ourselves and one another, with dreams and visions, with God (Gen. 32.22–32; Hosea 12.3–5), our interest in so bold a project as living into God's future ever colliding with our capacity for and the limitations of our ability to reach the distant horizon in the first place.

The political calculus having entered the ecclesiastical arena, ministers of necessity need a modicum of political instinct. Our power is persuasive, not coercive, and surveying the congregation's political landscape is an essential component of knowing when and how to introduce innovations or propose even modest adjustments to priorities and missional emphases. Personal survival and institutional integrity alike can hang in the balance.

I found it helpful to think in terms of a political capital account from which I would make periodic withdrawals. Some argue that the minister's political account allows only withdrawals and that once depleted, the account is closed. These "funds" may be spent wisely or foolishly; they might bear good, bad, or indifferent fruit; but since the account permits no deposits to counter a declining balance, when the fund is gone, it is gone. It would be nice to think that a congregation might forgive a bad investment and deposit at least some replacement funds, but politics is a messy business, and church politics especially so.

The closing of the Royal Oak chapter illustrates the point. For all the commendation I rightfully directed to that congregation, in the end, my depleted political capital fund played a part in coloring both the time and manner of my departure. I had gladly spent a fair amount of my capital on the innovations described in that chapter, particularly with regard to blended worship. For example, our sanctuary already had a grand piano and a modest but superbly designed pipe organ, and to enhance the worship experience, we added an electronic keyboard as well (both music and liturgical reform were key components of blended worship at that time). What we might have anticipated as a high-risk venture proved to be a low-cost innovation. As one parishioner put it, she did not like the new instrument but recognized the reason for it and so tolerated it for the sake of the many others (including me) who found their worship experience enriched with its addition.

On the other hand, I also attempted to introduce a contemporary hymnal alongside the venerable *Pilgrim Hymnal* that proved to be a costly failure. (If ever the doldrums seep in under the church door, the minister only needs to suggest a new hymnal or prayer book to awaken the troops.)

Because it introduced a subject with which the church was ill-equipped to deal both intellectually and emotionally, the request to recognize a gay relationship as a marriage covenant, celebrated in the church's sanctuary, came with a sizeable price tag, although it might have been considerably more had I initiated the conversation and undoubtedly more had I recommended we provide the service requested. I would note that it is not to our credit that we ignored an important issue until we could ignore it no longer, but when it found us we turned and faced it, and that is to our credit. Not every church could—or would—do the same, even today. Still, addressing a subject of that magnitude was like moving a mountain with a shovel, and the political and emotional cost was real.

I hesitate to include what ostensibly is a strange expenditure of capital because I cannot see it but others wiser than I on the matter insist it shows up on the balance sheet. I (they) call it the Daddy-Left-Us Syndrome. In celebration of *our* ten years together, the church gave me a sabbatical. It came with no expectations of burying myself in a seminary library, and we did not have the financial resources for an extended tour of exotic places of culture and urbane sophistication, so we piled into our truck camper, we three (the two of us and Hobbes, our Golden Retriever), and for seven glorious weeks toured the middle and western regions of the country from Detroit to Seattle. Our Associate Minister was on board by then, so the pastoral bases were covered, and while I seem to recall taking some books with me having to do with church and ministry, and even reading some of them, the summer hiatus really turned out to be an extended time for rest and renewal.

The people certainly seemed happy enough upon our return, but something had changed. Things felt different. When I voiced vague feelings of contrary vibrations disturbing the cosmos that I could not name, I received this retort, "What did you expect? Daddy left them!"

I feigned ignorance, incredulity. "But," I protested, reasonably enough, "they gave me the gift." (Surely, logic would carry the day. Surely.) I suspected my good people would find the mere notion of having, wanting, or needing a "Daddy" mildly offensive to their understanding of our Congregational Way and with the merest hint of self-righteousness so did I say on their behalf, only to hear echoing in my ears the same refrain, "Daddy left them!" Drip, drip, drip.

A steady drip eventually shows up on the water bill, but our experience with adding an Associate Minister to the staff was the episode that drained the well. I gloss over the analysis—theological, sociological, and organizational—that brought us to the decision to call a second ordained minister. Suffice to say, the church's leadership and I had done our homework, and we carefully crafted a job description and then waited upon the search committee to do its work; I had been an Associate Minister myself and had had firsthand exposure to the rules and expectations on both the Senior and Associate sides of the equation; on balance, the prospect looked very promising.

It turned out, though, that a considerable gap separated promise from reality. Our Associate had the gifts and the training to succeed personally and could clearly have facilitated the church's development, but almost from the start, it became apparent that the "rules and expectations" component did not apply to her. One day, for example, I asked her to attend to a particular matter within her purview and perhaps without even thinking, she immediately quipped, "You do it." I imagine that had I said something like that to Old Ben, I would have spent the afternoon updating my ministerial profile and looking into available pulpits. Not that he would have fired me…not that he could have fired me, for technically I did not work for Old Ben! I worked for the church—a big difference. In proper Congregational fashion, the *church* had *called* me (in our system, ministers are never hired by, say, a Board of Trustees or a committee with personnel responsibilities but rather are called by the members to serve as "pastor and teacher"), and so it was the members to whom I was beholden, but make no mistake: I gave primary attention and reported to certain boards and worked with specified departments within the church as outlined in my job description, but as the senior administrator responsible for the day-to-day life of the church, I worked for Old Ben. He was the Senior Minister, I was the Associate, a subordinate role…as everyone knows.

Or almost everyone, it appears. As an isolated event, we might have taken a breath and reviewed how things work in a Congregational church but unfortunately, this was not an isolated event but one episode in a pattern where the nuances of Congregational polity along with the "rules and expectations" of day-to-day staff relationships did not apply. I generally included a few minutes with the children in the worship service and one such moment featured a tube of toothpaste which at my invitation one lucky volunteer squeezed onto a plate. It was great fun! I then asked another volunteer to put it back. In the silence that followed, I simply suggested that so are our words, that once spoken we cannot pull them back, and such were her words, "You do it," for they named and clarified the pattern that up until that moment had remained in the tube of toothpaste, as it were, its existence obvious, its nature and purpose apparent, but its impact within the community not yet clear. In three little words, all that changed and there was no way to put it back.

When Congregational polity works, it works very well…until it doesn't, and over the years, it worked very well indeed for me and the church alike. Give credit where credit is due: to the members and the staff who made it work. Our Way is highly nuanced and enough members have generally understood and applied its nuances to keep us pretty much on track. For the staff, competence in what each does coupled with commitment to the church and respect for one another kept the lines of communication and account- ability open, essential in a system where no one is really in charge and the lines of authority can quickly become muddled, the environment muddied. On paper, the Congregational system is awkward and inefficient when the seas are calm, but for real sport, try to set the sails and hold the helm when the wind roils the waves. They were few and far between, but this was one moment when I would gladly have handed the problem over to a bishop had we had one.

We did our best (I did my best) in clarifying how the system worked, how job descriptions and bylaws shape the structure, how accountability and supervision identify lines of authority, how governance includes built-in protections to shield employees from the capricious, if not malicious, whims of the minister or errant subgroups in the church. I appealed to the obliga- tions of staff members in particular to honor the intent of the members who, having set the sails, then placed their trust in us to stay the course. Perhaps as a measure of their own desperation, if not exhaustion and possibly disgust, some of my lay leaders thought maybe the two of us could work things out in counseling, a suggestion I pronounced both absurd and insulting.

In the end, a way forward was not found and the staff situation continued to deteriorate, and as I had feared, this chapter in the life of the church that had begun with so much hope was not going to end well.

But life moves on and so did the church...or at least I *thought* the church had moved on. Apparently, the church's leaders had not moved on, not without first having opened the tap and draining the balance of my political capital, in effect cutting me off at the knees, and so skillful were my Trustees with the surgery, the Council standing by in the gallery, that I did not even learn of its having happened for more than a year!

The surgery took place in the budget. Preparations for the next year's budget had begun closely on the heels of the Associate Minister's departure, and enough revenue had been anticipated to give the staff salary increases.

During this period, the church was clearly in a disagreeable mood, and the Board of Trustees decided that I was personally culpable for all the discontent connected with the Associate Minister's tenure, its disruptive resolution, and its lingering aftermath, and so had to be punished. My punishment was to have reduced by 50% what to that point had been an agreed upon salary increase. I only learned of this a full year later and as reported to me, the proposal from the Board of Trustees met no challenge from the Council.

I was speechless and not because of the dollars involved. I had always prided myself on strong working relationships with my Moderators and key lay leaders (board Chairs especially) which always meant a good working relationship with the Council. The Council always reviewed the Trustees' proposed budget before it went to the members for approval, and for the Council to acquiesce passively to a vindictive mentality, obviously in support of it, and then have neither the courage nor the simple courtesy to discuss their censure with me, indicates that I had not connected some pretty important dots. For more than a year, this antagonism festered unaddressed, a disruption in the ethers that should have taken shape but did not and should have been quickly resolved but was not. Speechless and disappointed…not to mention bankrupt.

Ministry: a great calling but a terrible job.

I do not argue that the buck stops on the minister's desk. It happened on my watch and under my (allegedly careful) direction and so my responsibility is apparent. I accept that and maybe I got off easy. The leaders could have washed their hands of both of us and started over, and had they named the real burr under their saddle, they might have done just that. On the surface, the Trustees' (and the Council's) anger zeroed in on me for not producing a better outcome to this chapter, but what if the real anger was directed at me for introducing the chapter in the first place and leading the church in a direction it never wanted to go? What if I had asked the members to reach beyond their grasp and the cost—months and months of planning and waiting and a goodly expenditure of time, energy, and treasure—was more than they could bear, more than they ever wanted to bear? At the time, it seemed like the right—and necessary—call, religion at its best; all these years later, I'm not so sure. Maybe they were not so sure, either.

A peculiar business, the church.

In any event, having belatedly learned of my leadership's action regarding my salary, the question was what to do about it...if anything. Was it even imperative that I should end a 15-year pastorate? Probably not. At least they did not exactly tell me to fall on my sword for what I had put them through, and so I might have licked my wounds and carried on, but I thought then and conclude now that it would not have been good for either of us were I to remain in place and not just because of this incident. Remember, I counseled myself, political capital spent is political capital gone, but it was still a very hard decision. On the one hand, I was approaching my mid-50s and felt ready for another challenge; at the same time, the mid-50s put me at the end of what the life-cycle people call middle-age, not exactly prime time for the job market. On the one hand, I could stay another ten years, theoretically, and retire, sliding across home under the tag, safe; on the other hand, I have seen plenty of ministers hang on past their "sell by" date, and I vowed never to fall into that trap.

As in telling a joke, so in life, timing is everything, and I kept hearing the words of a parishioner who used to talk about her internal bell that signaled an approaching shift in her life journey. "You can't ignore the bell," she would say, and she was right. Was I, too, hearing a bell, I asked myself, perhaps several bells, and if so, what songs were they playing? The church song was the loudest, clanging away, some notes off key, but the home front had a tune going as well. By this time, our children were on their own, which found the two of us (and a big dog) rattling around in a four-bedroom tri-level, more house than we needed and far more than we wanted to maintain. Our sabbatical trip had taken us through the Pacific Northwest and subsequent vacations added the Dakotas and Coastal California and Los Angeles, and along the way we found ourselves asking the "What if...?" question, that is to say, when the time comes to retire, what if we decided to move to this locale or that part of the country...? Oh, and the dawn of a new millennium and century seemed to dangle its blank slate. Putting it all together, we found ourselves looking West.

It is one thing to take the high ground on reading the tea leaves and seeing a change on the horizon, but at a certain age, the high ground begins to look less inviting, and as I indicated above, I was at that age where we all become less marketable. Complicating the picture immensely for my generation of parish clergy, age coupled with decades of mainline decline restricted the simple availability of other opportunities. As one colleague put it, "the National Association does not have a sufficient number of good pulpits to which you might go." By "good," he did not mean socially prominent or financially attractive but rather churches offering a good theological fit (precisely what I had come so to cherish about Royal Oak with its theologically moderate-to-liberal-to-Unitarian membership). Where would I find such a congregation in our small fellowship? At that moment, none was open and ministers in relatively stable positions were themselves opting for stability.

I am not given to melodrama and so will not blame a handful of members for serving as the catalyst, but neither do I put much stock in coincidences, and the fact is that six months later, I found myself "on loan" to the California Pacific Annual Conference of the United Methodist Church and on my way to the Lahaina UMC, Maui, Hawaii, and the decade unexpectedly ended much differently from how it had looked at its mid-point.

A peculiar business, the church, and I separate the close of the Royal Oak story in this chapter from the detailed, appreciative consideration of that church in the previous chapter because I did not want the twists and turns at the end to overshadow what had essentially been for nearly 15 years a very good journey together. The passage of time offers the gift of perspective, and from its vantage point I continue to honor the Royal Oak church and hold its people in very high regard.

There were times when they drove me to distraction, and I suspect that they could cite occasions when I returned the favor. Early in this pastoral chronicle, I mentioned a midweek Lenten study where some of us pondered the conundrum of violence against the backdrop of a Clint Eastwood western while down the hall some of the ladies enjoyed a lingerie party. I discretely omitted any reference to which ladies and what church but I suspect if by chance any of these words would find their way to Royal Oak, a number of my former parishioners would agree with my assessment that they did more good for their home life that evening than I did.

As for the ending recorded here, well, maybe the lesson is that we delude ourselves into thinking we control the general trajectory of our lives, that the speed bumps notwithstanding, with our hands on the wheel, we go where we choose to go. The reality, of course, is much different. Zip code and skin color have huge ramifications for how the drama even begins and certainly unfolds for each of us. A lucky break or somebody pulling the right string at the right time can open a door that otherwise would have remained forever closed. Avoiding the fatal bullet in a military campaign means coming home to the rest of your life, but those bullets do not bend to the will of the targets against whom they are flying. Those four fearsome words at the end of the annual physical—let's run some tests—remind us that maybe we control far less than we think, until at the end we control nothing at all.

My even receiving the call to serve the Royal Oak church bears that out. I never knew how many profiles the search committee received, but given the church's history and stature in the National Association, the number would have been large and mine was about to be removed from further consideration except that a member of the search committee suggested that doing so might be a bit premature and upon his recommendation the committee kept it active. It just so happened that I had met this member of the search committee and his wife more than a decade earlier while serving the Mukwonago, Wisconsin, church where he had deep roots and a number of relatives who were my parishioners. That bit of history played a crucial role in my call to the church and had that not been the case, had I not received the call to Royal Oak, I would have continued to explore pastoral opportunities in the United Church of Christ where I had Privilege of Call, very likely our family remaining in Southern California. Talk about divergent trajectories and the complex interactions of events that would have produced very different outcomes! I had very limited control over those two pathways and to this day I remain grateful for the events that came together in favor of Royal Oak.

Life is complicated. People are complicated. The web of factors that influence our countless decisions and their uncontrollable outcomes is unfathomably complicated. Exhibit A: the last eighteen months or so at Royal Oak. For so many years, so much went so well for that church and then the ambiance turned rather sour fairly quickly and brought about an unexpected ending. Nobody planned it. Nobody connected a complex array of dots leading to a preconceived end. Nobody wanted *that* ending, but that ending is the one that developed which, as I suggested, in a way painted all of us as victims to some extent, our Associate most of all but not exclusively, for the web snagged me and the church as well. Well, so be it, but our chapters written, we—all of us—pick up the pieces, scars and all, and the journey continues, sometimes in unexpected ways, and so did I—pick up the pieces, that is—and the journey did continue, though in a most unexpected way.

This rather abrupt ending to a generally happy chapter serves as the backdrop against which I would finally find some resolution to the ever-nagging issue of a mission worthy of the message, or more to the point, why we, the members of the church, struggle so when the conversation turns from faith to faithfulness, what I characterize in general terms as living into God's purposes, the words and ways of Jesus giving shape and direction to that life. Not that we don't struggle with the matter of faith itself and just what we do believe, but once what we believe becomes reasonably settled, what to do with it and how to live it comes up next on the agenda. Faith and faithfulness are but two sides of the same coin, and while we can and do struggle with both sides, I give the nod to the latter as the more vexing.

These days I call this struggle the Câmara Conundrum in honor of Dom Hélder Câmara, the former Brazilian Catholic Archbishop of Olinda and Recife. From an earlier chapter, I reprise his observation:

> When I give food to the poor, they call me a saint.

Saint-like, churches and other religious communities (and, not incidentally, a host of secular organizations) do a commendable job giving food to the poor. Food banks and local food pantries and soup kitchens depend on such for support. Achieving sainthood is as close as writing a check.

The intriguing—and troubling—part of the Archbishop's quip follows: "When I ask why the poor have no food, they call me a Communist," he notes. Bullies that they are, of course *they* will call him a name, in this case a *Communist*, for now the saint has overstepped his bounds, challenging the social structures and economic policies that find poor people without food languishing in the community. How can this be, he asks? Who is responsible for the social systems that distribute society's goods and services so unjustly? Who has such power? Well, now we know; a mere cleric with a simple question has them quaking in their boots. Well, maybe not exactly quaking, but sufficiently rattled to respond, for the question puts the spotlight first and foremost on the System and those who put it in place and benefit from its continuance and so maintain it against all intruders. Challenge the System, the System stirs in response—no surprise there.

But in addition to questioning the System, we note that the Brazilian pastor speaks on behalf of his church (or more to the point, speaks on behalf of *the* church), reminding the rest of the flock that it is not enough just to feed the poor. Equally incumbent upon the church is to ask why this is so, why we find poor people without food languishing in our own community?

The church at work.

And the church…hearing the question, what does the church do? Typically, seemingly, nothing, and understandably so. After all, no one likes being called names, and challenging the prevailing systems and structures that control the community at a given time can generate any number of names and other, even more unpleasant consequences. The struggle for civil rights is a case in point. I had a colleague who served a church in a Midwestern university town. He marched with Dr. King in Selma and upon returning home found himself fired.

The church at work?

How we struggle with the meaning of faithfulness and the limits we place on its expression in our personal lives and the life of our churches. The Master calls us to the life of discipleship, but how far will we and our churches take it—how far *can* we and our churches take it? Having learned the lesson from Jesus, we easily go far enough to warrant sainthood but will stop short of martyrdom. He took the extra step and challenged the religious and secular structures of his day, and look what it got him!

Sainthood, yes; martyrdom, no—the church at work.

When it comes to following in his ways, the church at work seemingly settles for mere approximations (and sometimes pretty faint ones at that) of the Original. When we ask why we settle for so much less, feeding the hungry today without solving the systemic roots of poverty that will leave them hungry tomorrow, the default answer points to the choices we make. In other words, we choose not to explore the matter further. The bishop may challenge us to confront the System—we ourselves might even agree that Jesus expects no less of us!—and who knows, we just might, but then again, we might not. After all, the choice is ours, and when it comes to challenging the Systems operating in the community and the power of those who maintain them, the we *might* not very easily becomes we *will* not.

But as I tentatively asked in an earlier chapter, reflecting there on the problem of choosing to implement midcourse corrections in light of new possibilities that benefit the community (for example, addressing climate change...or not), what if the issue has less to do with a matter of choice and more a matter of fundamental limitations germane to human being itself compounded by personal circumstances and abilities? In other words, what if a defiant *I won't* has a humble counterpart—*I can't*?

Admittedly, saying "I can't" does have a way of softening the harsher, more shrill, "I won't," but I do feel the weight of perhaps having placed unfair and unrealistic expectations on my people from time to time, pushing all of us into that realm of self-awareness where our limitations do come to the fore and "I won't" just gives way to "I can't." Challenging injustice or changing its embedded Systems? Maybe someday, possibly on that distant day when humankind will have evolved more fully in the way of the Christ, but right now, some things are just a step too far, a change too great.

Take, for instance, that strange economy where Jesus talks about how we find our lives, our true or higher selves, only by a process of self-denial and (for lack of a better term) radical discipleship (Matt. 16.24ff; par.). Jesus illustrates his point by telling the story of the young man who asks him to name the key to eternal life. Jesus tells him to keep the commandments, which the man has done from his youth, whereupon Jesus then invites him to take the next step and divest himself of his possessions, giving all to the poor, and then to come and follow him. The text indicates that the man went away sorrowful, for he had great possessions (Matt. 19.16ff; par.).

Talk about a step too far! Maybe a tithe but self-denial? Perchance generosity but sacrificing real pleasures on earth for an anticipated "treasure in heaven," as Jesus offers the young man? Is he serious? Rare are those who will even ponder such a thing, rarer still those who might take it literally.

The more measured approach, of course, recognizes that between *I won't* and *I can't*, there is a qualified *Yes...but*, an *I will...* up to a point. From this perspective, as disciples we can accommodate the Câmara Conundrum (committing to the pursuit of justice by reforming oppressive systems, for example) but recognize that at best such reforms occur very slowly, incrementally, one baby step at a time. With time and the contributions of others, we might make progress on the justice front. Maybe not, but we take a cue from Martin Luther King and make peace with the privilege of having seen the Promised Land even if we ourselves will never get there.

By another name we might call this pragmatic discipleship. Admittedly, it carries clear overtones of compromise until we realize that the pragmatic, judicious allocation of our powers in the pursuit of justice today equips us to continue the pursuit in coming days, perhaps even as a way of life, agents of transformation sustained by our own transformation. As we see in Jeremiah's wonderful Allegory of the Potter and the Clay (Jer. 18.1–12), God works the clay, patiently shaping and transforming the raw material of humanity out of which there begins to emerge a people (co-creators with God). Repressive Systems do well to take note.

Of course, our transformation occurs so slowly it scarcely seems to be occurring at all. Under the most encouraging of circumstances, our completion as persons is always in process. No wonder our missional calling to carry the Jesus Movement into the wider world only approximates the full idea of what Jesus brought us in the public ministry. Slowly, over time, maybe we will come more and more to have the mind of Christ (Phil. 2.1–18) and then perhaps we will master how to do the things he did, and then some, as he promised the first disciples (John 14.12). Until then, we do what we can, *as we can.*

An interesting prospect, having the mind of Christ. Paul describes it in Philippians (2.5ff), what we call Kenotic Christology or the self-emptying Christ who gave up the form of and equality with God in order to take on the form of a human being and the role of a servant (the better translation is slave) in order to plant the healing, saving, gracious love of God in the midst of the world where it can address the human condition.

Whole theologies follow from this action, but for our purposes, think of having such a mind as can do such a thing as give up essentially everything in favor of becoming nothing, all to the end of serving a greater purpose.

A formidable project, working toward and developing the mind of Christ! Who could manage such a thing—and how? Typically, we would name here desire and discipline as the key variables, that we must want the mind of Christ badly enough to work for it, to live into God's purposes for our lives actively, purposefully, intentionally. Like success on the athletic field, so here: commitment and exercise become the order of the day, every day. Cutting corners in the training room will bear its predictable fruit for athletes and disciples alike.

But what if having the mind of Christ does not reduce to mere desire and sufficient motivation to persist along that path? What if the underlying issue is less an *I won't,* a lack of motivation and sustained commitment over time, say, but an *I can't,* because I am just a different order of being and lack the simple capacity to climb that mountain?

One of the endless Christological debates about the Person of Jesus asks if he is but a better version of ourselves—a Rabbi with a profound teaching and a revolutionary vision within reach of any one who but chooses to walk his path—or whether he is so qualitatively different from mere human beings as to represent a different order (and way) of being altogether, unreachable at least until such a time as the upward thrust of creation's inherent evolutionary impulse delivers a higher order of a thoroughly transformed humanity.

I tend toward the latter perspective, that while we can emulate the model of the (kenotic) self-emptying Christ, we will at best only approximate (and most likely, faintly at that) his mind and even less so his work, what he did and what he invites us to do as well. How can we expect otherwise? Our place on the evolutionary scale just lags too far behind.

This is not to let the church off the hook, though. We need a church that is not satisfied with feeding hungry people unless at the same time it is addressing—and correcting—the very systems that leave them hungry the next day. Church people must insist that their faith communities hold before them the grand vision where we actually beat those missiles into plowshares and pruning hooks (Isa. 2.4), where the harmony of the peaceable kingdom (Isa. 11.1–9) actually heals a planet in peril, and where humankind finally discovers fire for the second time in the power of love, a force greater than gravity (as mystic Teilhard de Chardin reminds us).

In the meantime, if we have such time until a new humanity develops a higher order of consciousness closer to that of Christ, we need a people who point the rest of us in that direction. Such a people will not have arrived themselves at the goal (how can they, lacking themselves the capacity) but having begun the journey *as able*, they will to some extent stand apart, different, Sign Bearers of the New Way. How did they get that way—what made them…different? We might be inclined to say that, nurtured and sustained over time, their faith made them different, but nurturing and sustaining faith over time very frequently involves a close church relationship, so we might just as well say that hanging around the church made them different, as it should. The Southern novelist Flannery O'Connor may have said it better: "You shall know the truth and the truth shall make you odd," but different or odd, either way, one of the continuing and significant accomplishments of the church is to fashion such a people.

Church people are different. Imagine all the ways that simple statement can be misunderstood! High on the list, that in saying church people are *different from* the Others, we also seem to imply that they are thereby *better than* those Others. A close second, that the difference is unique to those with a church relationship.

History, if not personal experience, suggests otherwise, of course. Church people may well be different, but not necessarily in ways that make them good dinner guests (what was it Mark Twain said, heaven for the weather, hell for the company), and those qualities that set people apart for all the right reasons (honor and decency and personal ethics and integrity among them) are certainly distributed among those who have nothing whatsoever to do with the church, if not religion as a whole.

So, to clarify, declaring church people to be different in no way asserts or pretends that church people are thereby better than unchurched people or that apart from the church one cannot be different in quite the same way. Still, all the disclaimers notwithstanding, I have lived with church people all my life, and I can testify, that while church people are only too human, church people are also different.

At first blush, what makes church people different may surprise the churched and unchurched alike, for it has little to do with their religiosity as such, like which church and how often they attend, the doctrines they do—and do not—espouse, the disciplines and pieties that define their daily practices, or where they stand on the great theological and ethical controversies of the day. These distinctions are all certainly important because they leave their imprint on the spiritual pilgrimage in very different ways. They give shape to a wide variety of churches and church people, but their variety as such is not what makes church people different.

So, what *does* constitute the difference? The answer is deceptively simple: language. What makes church people different is the church's language, the language of the Christian faith as captured and employed by the particular church (or the type of church, liberal-conservative-evangelical-fundamentalist) to which they gravitate over the course of their lives. Over time, church people absorb this language and its application to such an extent that it plays a key role in defining the nature and purpose of their lives.

To put it in the vernacular, their church's language becomes part of their DNA.

Probably the single most important word in the church's language is love, especially the third and highest form of the three Greek words typically translated as love in English. The lowest, *eros* or erotic or self-love, focuses exclusively on the self and views the other as an object whose purpose is to satisfy the self. Pornography is the obvious example but the gratuitous sexuality that pervades so much of popular culture at the expense of women is ultimately more destructive.

The middle form, *philos* or *philia,* has an obvious connection with family and connotes a love shared equally and mutually between members, whether they belong to one's organic family of birth or any community where its members think of themselves as family (the church family, say).

The highest form, *agape*, describes self-giving love and puts the needs and interests of the other as subject above any concern whatsoever for the interests or satisfaction of the self. *Agape* love asks not what pleases me but how I can serve you and (with some references to filial love) is the form love takes almost exclusively in the Bible: we find it in the love we owe the neighbor (Matt. 22.39, et al.), the life we sacrifice for the friend (John 15.13), and the example of Jesus (John 15.12). Although the word itself does not appear in the passage, the mind of Christ (Phil 2.5–11) and the scope of New Testament generally reflect a foundation of *agape* love, Christ's love a mirror of God's love.

The language of love is not limited to the church and so strictly speaking it is not the church that makes church people different, for wherever self-giving love is heard, received, and practiced, such persons will be different.[18] What does make church people different by virtue of their connection with a church over time, though, is the language of love as it takes shape specifically in Jesus and how it subsequently shapes their relationships at home and their neighborhood and the wider world generally. As Oliver Wendell Holmes said, a mind shaped by a new idea can never go back to its original shape and the Idea of Jesus is no exception. Extending the invitation to begin and continue the pilgrimage along that path that makes a difference for a lifetime is the work of the church and the privilege of ministry.

Odd...different: such indeed were my people at Royal Oak...and I thank them for it.

---

18. Some may object that my emphasis on Jesus sets in place a hierarchy of language systems, or religions, with those at or near the top better able to capture the nature and power of love as a moving force in human personality and world affairs than others. Such is not my intention and only illustrates what I have called elsewhere the challenge of pluralism. I deflected addressing the challenge there and will do so again here other than to acknowledge the following: first, that I am speaking only of the church and its people, which is not to say other religions or philosophical and ethical systems have no claim on the subject; second, that church people have hardly captured the market on the meaning, much less the expression, of the love made visible in Jesus and so do well themselves to listen to those other voices; and third, that as confirmed in the simple affirmation, God is love (1 John 4.7-21), a divine, universal love has permeated the creation from the moment of the Big Bang, such that where love is, so too is God, the Source of love. Similarly, a God intimately related to the world would make love an inescapable component of every relationship, action, and occasion: where God is, so too is love.

CHAPTER 7

MY DARK NIGHT
OF THE SOUL

"The more one is given, the more is expected of him;
the more somebody is entrusted with, the more he must account for."

~JESUS
(Luke 12.48, *Cotton Patch Version*)

AS CHILDREN, WE BRING HOME colds, lice, and assorted viruses from school; later, as adults, we bring home work from the office; while the Interim Senior Minister of the First Congregational Church of Los Angeles, I brought home a ghost. As it turned out, though, the ghost was the least of my concerns, for I went to this deeply troubled congregation in July 2002 and was dismissed twenty-eight months later.

I had, of course, served in conflicted situations over the years, and I certainly cannot claim ignorance of what awaited me. After all, with its reputation so well entrenched in National Association circles, one just had to utter the words, First Church, and eyes would roll. Beyond that was the obvious factor that I had lived with the San Gabriel offspring, Mayflower Congregational Church, two decades earlier and as I suspected—and later confirmed—the child does indeed inherit the DNA of the parent. There is no escaping: I was warned (among those pleading for sanity was Ann) and I knew better than to so much as pass within view of the Mother Ship...and went anyway. My mistake...and a big one, a blunder on my part that I continue to rue to this day.

Generally speaking, I have no regrets when it comes to the course my life has taken and its countless decisions big and small. For good reason does Emerson counsel us to forget the "blunders and absurdities" and all those regrets that creep into everyday life so we can greet the new day with the enthusiasm it properly deserves. We all have things we would do differently given the chance, words we would recast or avoid saying altogether if only we could, but this decision is the exception: it is not for nothing that I look upon it as the dark night of my soul, the scars of which I still bear.

In the end, though, it was the challenge itself, how to be church and do ministry in such a time and place, that outweighed the other considerations and drove my decision to give it a try. For years, the Los Angeles church struggled with the related challenges of a declining membership and a neighborhood in cultural transition. Nothing unusual about that in metropolitan Los Angeles, but what was unusual in their case was the magnificent Cathedral, complete with the largest, church-based pipe organ in the world, the forebears had bequeathed to subsequent generations. I shall not attempt to describe either the building or the musical instrument—think splendid, grand, imposing. In addition, the members had at their disposal enormous financial resources to engage the challenges creatively—talk about a mission to match the message!—if they would but choose to do so. First step: a willingness to rethink everything.

A willingness to rethink everything? Really? I will later describe my work in Congregational Revitalization which involved on-site visitations with congregations facing exactly the same dynamics of cultural marginalization vis-à-vis its surrounding neighborhood, coupled with herculean efforts to preserve the treasured past against a difficult present and a threatening future. Small rural congregations in simple wood-framed Meeting Houses and this small urban congregation in a splendid cathedral, and all congregations in between, confronted the same challenge to rethink everything, reimagining mission and purpose in light of changing circumstances. Outward circumstances notwithstanding, these congregations are so alike in so many ways as to be rather unremarkable in almost every way.

Except, of course, that the Los Angeles variation included a splendid cathedral and campus on the famed Wilshire Corridor of Los Angeles, a private school, a mountain campground near Big Bear, and considerable financial assets. Understandably, those charged with the stewardship of those substantial resources exercised considerable power in determining the ends to which they would—and perhaps more to the point, would not—be directed. This in turn introduced a defining and largely debilitating dynamic into the internal life of the church, for predictably, maintaining that power took center stage and the ensuing struggle to occupy key offices and control votes on select boards created a culture of unceasing and unremitting conflict between two primary factions. The balance of power might shift from time to time, but the partisan divide remained so firmly entrenched and the battle lines so deeply imbedded that the church's elected leaders were identified not by their office or board but by their connection with one of the two parties, their office an incidental avenue keeping them in the game. Except that they provided the necessary façade, stated meetings were largely irrelevant because desired decisions on selected agenda had been reached and sufficient votes had already been secured behind the scenes.

As for the two parties, each had a handful of core members and an easily identified circle of allies. While I was there, one was slightly larger numerically and could garner more votes on most any issue than the other which was crucial to its agenda because this party functioned as the guardian of the church's traditions. So fiercely did its members defend the past and maintain its dictates in the present that the merest hint of modifying a practice—or worse, introducing a new one—would invariably run into a brick wall of resistance and disappear from the conversation.

Rethink everything? Or for that matter, rethink anything? Not so fast.

The other party was somewhat smaller numerically and controlled fewer votes and, like their counterparts, its members fully supported the church's traditions as well—for all the fighting, no rogue iconoclasts in sheep's clothing were anywhere to be found. It is one thing, though, to appreciate tradition and quite another to be bound by it, and this group was equally open to the church's creative potential. On multiple occasions, for example, I heard a wistful acknowledgment of the many activities my predecessor had brought to the attention of the members, a clear signal of interest in a wider agenda. This attitude introduced something of an entrepreneurial spirit to the church's conversation. We can only imagine how the church's trajectory might have changed had they been able to release some of its latent creativity.

Rethink everything? Maybe not everything but certainly some things.

In any event, another church in conflict. Having waded into that swamp before, why not take the cue from Jesus and consider this as the one from which to walk away? In his case, teaching in the synagogue at Nazareth Jesus had so enraged the folks that they wanted only to toss him over the cliff. Instead he chose to pass through their midst and go away (Luke 4.28-30). Jesus—who stared down the devil, delivered the possessed of demons, healed the broken, and feared neither the secular nor the religious power brokers—seemingly had had enough. Like Jesus, his followers presumably have the wherewithal to stand up to the devil and all other manner of economic and political structures, but like Jesus, sometimes this frightful world is just too brutal, human brutality just too frightful.

Obviously, I failed to take the hint, in part as I said because the challenge of coming to grips with urban ministry in metropolitan Los Angeles appealed to me, but in consulting with others before making the decision, another factor played a role as well—that this time things were different. Settled opinion had concluded that unlike all the other times when things looked a little grim for First Church, *this* time the church was on the ropes financially and, having finally come to terms with its situation, was focused on doing something about it. Naturally, there were no guarantees that in the end it would actually change direction, even to save itself, but economic reality had removed the last vestiges of the shackles of denial and a glimmer of light now beckoned on the near-term horizon, or so I was told.

I had no way of judging the credibility of this view, other than the source from which it came, and my instincts told me to listen with a healthy measure of skepticism. As it turned out, the church was anything but "on the ropes," at least financially. The depth of that financial well was never clear to me, but it must have been deep enough, because I never heard so much as a whisper about closing the doors for any reason, certainly not for a financial one.

Also missing from the agenda was much concern about membership development. The membership had dwindled mightily over the years. The rolls still claimed some 900 members, about half living within a reasonable commuting distance of the church, but based on worship attendance, pledge support, and available hands to do the work, we considered ourselves subjectively, if not realistically, to be a 100-member church. Some might still remember when theirs was the largest Congregational church in the country, now reduced to just a handful rattling around in its cavernous chambers, but the remnant never seemed particularly perturbed.

This seemed strange to me, an anomaly among an otherwise seemingly universal concern in church circles for declining memberships, but in looking back on my experience with this church, I recalled the decorative fence the members had installed around the campus and the security fence surrounding the parking lot. Both symbolically and functionally, the fences created a barrier between the church and the world and sent a clear message to its neighbors, and I began to wonder if this was by design, its message intentional? Had the remnant given their church a new mission after all, now seeing itself—and more importantly, now *functioning*—quite literally as something of an oasis? What comes to mind are those early desert fathers and mothers who retreated to the wilderness so as to live their faith untainted by the world. So dangerous were the world's snares and compromises that for the sake of one's soul, the faithful had no other option but to flee its clutches. In a similar vein, might some want to escape the cacophony and dissonance of the surrounding urban confusion and take refuge in the towering cathedral if not to save the soul, then perhaps to savor a moment of quiet and calm?

A retreat center, or better still, something like a monastery, a Congregational monastery—is that what the people wanted? I cannot say that the members themselves ever alluded to such a portrayal of their identity, so I would not want to press this characterization too far, but in terms of the church's internal culture and the generally accepted (or at least largely unchallenged) priorities of the members, outsized attention centered on the traditions of the past and very little on the outline of the future. Understandably, membership development would necessarily play a minor role in the life of the church at best, for new members represented the very change from which the church otherwise needed—and sought—protection.

I confess that a part of me finds the idea of the monastery—an oasis in the midst of this messy, noisy, and confusing world—rather appealing, but I also recognize that the idea may provide a convenient escape from having to rethink everything. What if the cacophony and noise of the contemporary urban environment was the reason for the church's being, its purpose and mission, in the first place? Not fleeing the world but engaging the world, not building fences but tearing them down…I detected that voice, too, a minority voice, to be sure, more diffuse, less organized, virtually powerless, but nonetheless present. Taken together, the pendulum strongly weighted toward the status quo, other ideas and interests still managed to circulate, and with so much at stake—nothing less than control of the church and its assets—a power struggle ensued. Over the years, the fighting among the various voices and the several interlinking undercurrents becoming at times so intense, not just a few of the members suggested that what the place really needed was an exorcism. In that one respect alone, First Church stood alone in my experience.

Maybe time has muted some of the intensity of the conflict, but what stands out nearly two decades later is the toxicity of that environment. Certainly, from my earlier experiences in conflicted churches I had learned the lesson that church politics is no less brutal than secular politics. Even in more harmonious situations, the bumps and bruises that come with life in the parish were second nature to me, but I was out of my league here. I knew it and my Kitchen Cabinet knew it.

It was never an official body, the Kitchen Cabinet. There are no minutes of meetings. They had no recognition in the church and so no authority and no power except the power of persuasion. They were few in number, just some key local and national leaders with whom I felt comfortable consulting from time to time and whose counsel I took seriously. I will respect what I assume is their wish for anonymity by not naming them here.

I might note in all honesty that if naiveté did not cloud my judgment in accepting this position, neither did hubris. The fact is that the church had never really lacked for talent over the years, both lay and clergy, and preceding my turn at bat were a dozen or so ministers and interim ministers with whom I was personally acquainted or of whom I was aware by virtue of their reputation, and I can say that pastoral competence over these years had not been an issue. (Some have said all of these have been interim ministers, some intentional and the rest unintentional, but interim nonetheless. Without putting too fine a point on it, the average tenure between them lends substance to the observation.) Others must have noticed the common thread of competence as well because during a Kitchen Cabinet conference early in my tenure, the discussion turned to the illustrious ministers who graced this church before me. With reference to one in particular, someone said, "Well, if he couldn't do it, what makes you think you could do it?" A worthy question at which I might have taken some umbrage had I not already (and often since) pondered it myself. Given how things ended, the moment would prove uncomfortably prescient.

Admittedly, I did seriously consider leaving this chapter out altogether—shaking, as it were, this church's dust off my being (Matt 10.5–15, especially v. 14). That which is not named thereby ceases to exist, and the ease by which I might dismiss the time and the place by ignoring both serves as my judgment on the episode, that the scars notwithstanding, some things are best forgotten.

At the same time, the fact remains that I did go there; these things did happen; ignoring them does not change history, and as I reviewed my voluminous files of notes, correspondence, and reports, my compromise was to give my brief moment in its shadow a decent and fair hearing (from my perspective, naturally), and let the story speak for itself…good, bad, or indifferent.

I must say too at the outset that having lived with the drama and its aftershocks, it is inevitable that I would comment first on its intensity, but in another sense the problem at First Church was neither novel nor remarkable. Actually, it was quite mundane. Lots of oars were going in the water, but not at the same time and not with any sense of a shared enterprise or a common purpose. Between its people and the property and wealth at their disposal, the church certainly did not lack potential. There was sufficient power to drive any number of possibilities, but without a common goal or mission to link different groups and members, the energy expended produced no discernible benefit to anyone. Occasionally, fighting would break out, eventually settling down into an ecclesiastical version of a Cold War before the next skirmish erupted. Such it was at the Cathedral—such it had been for years.

Given the situation, what would a successful outcome to my efforts look like? Clearly, I thought in terms of finding a shared thread that would redirect the narrative from the past with a view to the future, but was that definition of success shared and for that matter, was it even reasonable? As I came to understand as I left Royal Oak, was I once again asking the members not only to reach beyond their grasp but also to reach where they did not want to go? Potential, yes, but was it available to rethink everything?

And what could I do about it in any event? What was I *supposed* to do about it? What about my power and my choices about its use? Clergy and laity alike often fail to appreciate the power attached to the office and thereby to the person of the minister-priest—even the keys to the kingdom itself according to one Authority (Matt. 16.19). Power indeed, and respecting our office and its power and the people we serve keeps most clergy on an even keel.

Whatever its potential, I never thought of myself as using my power in ways that would threaten my parishioners or give them reason to question my motives. I was ever-vigilant about boundaries and the ethics of pastor-parish relationships. I believed in and respected the integrity and dignity of my people. I honored the Congregational principle that placed responsibility for the church in the hands of the members and *their* elected representatives who in turn were accountable not to me but to the membership—talk about power to the people! Whatever influence I was able to add to the discussion came through my role as the resident theologian, its *persuasive* power filtered through my work as pastor and teacher—not much of a threat there.

Or so it seemed from my perspective, but even with the best of intentions, clergy make decisions that will be praised by some and criticized by others. I lost count of the times my Los Angeles detractors accused me of "wrecking the church" with my decisions, the cloud of their suspicions and distrust lurking like a plague in the crevices and dark corners of the entire enterprise. Survive all that and one still must be on the lookout for the outbreak of "unintended consequences."

Jesus may have had the Keys to the Kingdom theoretically in place but the real-life lesson came from a parishioner who offered a rather frank appraisal of my pastoral power and of my potential for its abuse. This parishioner was one of two sons whose mother, also a member of the church I served at the time, suffered from Alzheimer's disease. He himself lived about a five hour's drive from the church but his brother and his family lived in town and provided the level of attention and care necessary to allow their mother to remain in her home as her disease progressed. The geographically distant son was no less caring, but he was less visible week-to-week. I made frequent calls on her in her home and in due time, we had her memorial service.

Shortly thereafter, I spoke with the son who lived some distance away. He was a lawyer, and he informed me that he was of the opinion that my intention in calling so frequently on his mother (if anything, he might have complained that I paid too little attention to her) was to get my hands on her house for the church and were that to happen, he would fight me over it in court.

It was a new experience, the accusation that I was taking advantage of a vulnerable woman for the church's financial gain and I was, of course, suitably incensed. Who was he, this lawyer, to insult me, a man of the cloth, particularly with regard to my pastoral response to his mother. Indeed!

In time, however, I began to look at it from his perspective, and from his perspective not only did I have my clutches on his mother's house (and the family's inheritance) but also (and this was the new revelation) that I might just get away with it. He let me know that he was up to the fight and intended to win, but it was equally clear that the outcome was in doubt. What power—who knew?

Admittedly, my profession does count its share of dubious characters among its ranks and tragically, some do cross the threshold of the morally reprehensible and the criminally liable, their victims often the young, the innocent, and the vulnerable, but I never determined why my parishioner harbored such dark suspicions of my designs on his mother's house, what I might have inadvertently said or done. Fortunately, such episodes were rare (or rarely came to my attention, which is not quite the same thing), but in a back-handed sort of way, it did drive home the inherent power that comes with the position and it pointed to a unique and potentially far-reaching application of clergy authority, the power of a new idea to reshape one's mind and possibly even to redirect the trajectory of one's life.

Ideas are the minister's stock-in-trade and as the resident theologian, one might rather expect the pastor to have ideas about the words and ways of Jesus and their application to the life of the church, shaping a mission and an agenda. It's then that tensions and conflicts between pastor and parish often emerge. Not that the pastor's agenda is necessarily adopted, but the mere appearance of a new idea taking root in a different agenda may not exactly find favor within the congregation. After all, new ideas challenge us to reach beyond our grasp and go where we would rather not. They stretch the boundaries of our individual comfort levels and can even threaten well-anchored social, political, and religious commitments.

Power, indeed, the power of a new idea, and when new ideas become the source of tension and even conflict between pastor and parishioner, communication and transparency are critical in preventing a creative and healthy disagreement with the minister's agendas from tipping over and spilling into a suspicious and destructive distrust of the minister's motives. A good illustration here was the suggestion to my former congregation that we add another hymnal to our worship. A very sound idea from my perspective, and I made a strong case for its adoption, but the people had a different idea and rejected it. They disagreed. The question was not divisive because we talked it out, took the vote, and moved on. Had the new hymnal just shown up one Sunday, simple disagreement with a new idea would have quickly transmogrified into a very divisive distrust.

At the same time, entrusting the people with a new idea, pushing their boundaries into the emphatically uncomfortable and definitely unwanted zone, can produce a reaction of a different sort...not just to dismiss the idea but the person introducing it. Such was the case early in my second year when the core leaders of one of the First Church factions met secretly off campus to plan for my departure and arrange for my successor. Here, too, I was never sure exactly what I had said that provoked the conspirators' subterfuge (it was probably an accumulated cluster of things gathered under their occasional charge that I was on the verge of "wrecking the church" and perhaps my interest in developing a stronger relationship with the Korean congregation which I will describe shortly), but they went so far as to phone their candidate to replace me, a lay person who had the good sense to decline the opportunity. There was, of course, no vacancy in the office of Interim Senior Minister at that moment and even if there were, the bylaws outlined the process for first dismissing the minister and then selecting a committee charged with the task of identifying a successor, but to this party, the bylaws did not matter. What mattered, the only objective on the table at the time, was my removal by any means necessary.

Words fail to describe my sense of shock and disappointment at discovering their duplicity and its implied betrayal of the congregation, for this cabal included longstanding defenders of the principles of historic Congregationalism and by their secret manipulations, they traded the voice, vote, and authority of the congregation for a few pieces of political silver, a Faustian deal with the devil that cost them their soul and my respect.

The disillusionment brought to light a strategic error I had made in assuming all this time that the name on the door, Congregational, still meant something to the members on both sides of the partisan divide, that they took their Congregational heritage seriously and would abide by its governing principles as the alternative to brute force and anarchy. As a Congregational minister, I would naturally work with the leaders elected by the congregation to represent and serve their interests, but this was not really a Congregational church, not when secret meetings and behind-the-curtain manipulations led to policy decisions.

Having learned of one side's machinations to remove me from my office put me in a state of high alert. As the months bore on and their vitriol became steadily worse and the attacks on my person and integrity more painful to endure, I came to fear some of them. I lost plenty of sleep over my financial vulnerability (for good reason, it turned out), and the nearly constant emotional assault and spiritual turmoil left me wondering at times about my own mental health.

It is not my place—and they did not ask me—to argue the case for the other staff members, but from my perspective, all the employees, the "servants of the servants of God" (as we used to say of paid church personnel), experienced a toxic work environment. Criticism from officers and board members to whom staff members were variously accountable typically flowed quite freely and staff morale generally ran pretty low. Neither side trusted the other which only fueled the toxic atmosphere day to day. A cloud of suspicion fragmented the church's employees along departmental lines and lay oversight kept us in our respective silos and precluded any possibility of the staff functioning as a team. The best I could do was listen to staff grievances, apply Band-Aids to gaping wounds, and send them back to the front.

As the downward spiral worsened, stress levels increased (two staff members actually qualified for Workers Compensation because of the toll it took on their health), and there was even talk about some employees filing lawsuits against the church and the Trustees for harassment and constructive discharge (the latter refers to a situation in which a harassed employee is justified in quitting his or her job due to intolerable workplace conditions that force the employee to leave). These were all competent and committed people with much to offer a troubled church but in the end, their potential was tragically squandered.

I suggested earlier that ideas are the basic commodity in the minister's work, but so too are ideas the basic commodity in the *people's* work as well, and for a fractured church, such ideas have the potential to steer the church's conversation about its future. That was the sole purpose of the interim period, to interrupt the dysfunctional patterns of the past long enough for the members to contemplate the desirability of putting their oars in the water at the same time and pulling together toward a common goal.

To encourage just such a conversation, I proposed the so-called 7-7-7 program, seven groups of seven people meeting for seven weeks to talk about the Bible and matters of faith and the nature and purpose of the church. We came close enough to involving 49 people for most of those seven weeks that I deemed it a success, but the significant thing about the number of participants is that they accounted for about half of the active (or what we called our *functional*) membership of 100 or so. This was quite remarkable.

Even more remarkable were the results, essentially two. First, their work, the *people's* work, bore fruit. Admittedly, it was not much, but people were talking and hope was in the air. While initially much of the discussion focused on complaints and criticism, the focus quickly shifted to the church's biblical basis: who are we as a people of God; what does God need of us in this time and place; what gifts do we bring to the table; what is the nature of our individual and corporate ministries—with such great and important questions to consider and ideas to evaluate, who has time to complain? Though hardly definitive and a long way from compelling a consensus, a faint outline of the shape of the future had begun to take shape on the distant horizon.

Second, it became apparent that these study and fellowship groups were places of leadership development, their number—49—representing more candidates for elected office than there were offices to fill.

Physicist Isaac Newton had predicted three centuries earlier in his Third Law of Motion what would happen once I declared the 7-7-7 program a rousing success: "When one body exerts a force on a second body, the second body simultaneously exerts a force equal in magnitude and opposite in direction on the first body," or as formally stated, "For every action, there is an equal and opposite reaction."

In this case, the reaction took place under the aegis of the Council, which decided that the time was right to seat a search committee and get on with the business of selecting a permanent or settled minister. I had urged the church to commit to a minimal three-year interim period (five years even better), and after only eighteen months, the same forces that had met secretly off campus just a few months earlier now put their cards fully on the table. The intervening variable this time was the 7-7-7 program which they argued was merely the vehicle by which I was imprinting my agenda on the church. Not to quibble but credit for the threads of an emerging agenda went to members participating in the 7-7-7 discussion groups. Besides, the real problem was the emergence of *an* agenda at all since it would expand participation and spread leadership responsibility among more people, a challenge to existing power structures.

Of course, no one put it in those terms. Instead, my critics expressed great alarm that a mere *interim* minister was usurping the work of the *real* minister who now would have to undo and repair so many of my errors, they said. Best to get me out of the way before (here it comes again) I further "wreck the church."

Fueling their fire was the conviction that I was about to hand the keys to the kingdom to the Koreans. Demographic change in the Wilshire corridor of Los Angeles had by this time positioned the church between two very large populations, one Korean and the other Hispanic. I still believed that since gender, color, and ethnic distinctions no longer apply within the body of Christ (Gal. 3.27–28), the church should (I seldom use the "S-word," *should*, so when it appears, it really applies) embrace and was especially equipped for cross-cultural, multi-ethnic ministries, and the opportunity so to work was actually a key reason I agreed to accept the position. (I still believe it *should* but I no longer believe it will.)

A few years earlier, a Korean congregation had begun meeting in the church, but it was never clear whether the relationship was merely landlord and tenant or whether it was designed to bring two communities together in a shared partnership and common ministry. My sense was the latter, that a partnership was intended (this was subsequently confirmed by some of the leadership instrumental in establishing the relationship), and so I invited the Korean pastor to join staff meetings and participate in the early Sunday service. I also urged the Deacons to install equipment that would allow for the simultaneous translation of the second, formal service into Korean so that the Korean community could begin to feel a part of and participate in the life of the church at large.

Not everyone viewed these steps favorably, but the coup de grâce that ended the whole exercise in building a bridge to the Korean community was the decision by the Board of Deacons (which had jurisdiction over the worship services) to prohibit the Membership Committee (which had jurisdiction over the preparation of new members for covenant fellowship within the body of Christ) from scheduling a service of Reception of New Members, the candidates for which were…yes, Koreans.

I was dumbfounded. Flabbergasted. Speechless. Never in my experience had the spiritual direction of a church (the overall responsibility of a Board of Deacons) been so severely compromised, a congregation so poorly served (talk about "wrecking the church!") as was represented by that single decision. Though not reflected in anyone's minutes, the sentiment behind the decision (actually voiced in a meeting) was that if the church opened the door to just one Korean member, the masses would follow.

Such overt racism was reminiscent of the open housing and civil rights struggles of the 1960s. Thirty-five years later, the same fortress mentality had apparently survived intact. In a report on the matter of Korean membership, two of the church's clergy-members wrote:

> [We might question the motives driving] a group of people from another culture [who] wish to become full members of our church—not understanding our language, not compatible with our theological position, and not conversant with the meaning of the word "Congregational."

That report went on to conclude:

> Might not the Korean Christians be better served if they were to affiliate with already existing and established Korean church groups?

This from a Christian church in racially, ethnically, and culturally diverse Los Angeles, California. It makes one weep for his church as Jesus wept for holy Jerusalem (Luke 19.41–44). One might have expected that sophisticated Congregationalists would have an inkling of understanding of the process of assimilation as immigrant populations develop to the second- and third-American-born generations.

Instead, they insulted the Koreans (that they were not wanted after all and would be happier with their own kind) and not incidentally, they insulted those of us charged with the task of membership development (that we had neither taken the acculturation process into consideration nor had given any thought to the time it would take and the steps we would follow in building bridges to the Korean community). Of course, the church did not really need members (at least to pay the bills) and it turned out that, walking away in disgust, some of the members no longer needed their church.

Following upon the heels of the Korean debacle I allowed my name to be placed in nomination for the position of settled minister. This came about not as a request by interested supporters that the search committee consider my candidacy (the committee would have had a good laugh over that one). Quite the contrary, by petition, those backing this effort bypassed the search committee altogether, calling instead for a special meeting of the membership to take action on my candidacy.

A suitable metaphor to capture the reaction eludes me. As if the heat under the church's cauldron were not high enough already, imagine the emotion of this period once my candidacy was proposed.

This was the second of the two colossal blunders I made with regard to this position. The first of the blunders was the decision to accept the position in the first place. The second blunder was agreeing to put forward my candidacy as the permanent (or in our Congregational tradition, the "called") minister. If my mental stability was in question in committing the first, my going over to the Dark Side would be suspected in the second, for in Protestant circles interim ministers are never—as in under no circumstances—to be considered or to allow themselves to be considered for the permanent or settled position. This almost has the status of the Eleventh Commandment.

I do not discount in the least the seriousness of this step, but—and this is extremely important—the decision itself to take the step anyway was not the second of the two fundamental errors in judgment. This was actually a carefully calculated decision, not made lightly or in isolation but only after careful consideration and with the support and encouragement of my Kitchen Cabinet with whom I had consulted on other issues in this turbulent period.

I had raised the question of my eligibility for the permanent position before accepting the interim position. Nothing was put in writing, but an understanding of sorts left that door open if circumstances warranted. And in my (or more to the point, in our, the Kitchen Cabinet's) judgment, circumstances warranted it: a search committee prematurely seated and biased in favor of the faction in control all but guaranteed a continuation of the dysfunctional past into an inglorious future. The church had started on but not yet completed the process of identifying its mission and purpose, what today we call a congregation's missional commitments, and we concluded that for this interim period to make a difference in the life and trajectory of the church, an intervention was necessary. I would serve as the sacrificial lamb (if not now, when; if not me, who?), take the senior minister's position if the church voted to extend a formal call, and remain in position long enough to complete the "interim" agenda, at the end of which I would call for the formation of a representative search committee and step aside.

Right or wrong, agree or disagree, that was the theory.

The vote of the congregation did not sustain the theory…or did it? We will never know. Officially, I fell a few votes short of the two-thirds necessary to extend a call to a candidate. (Under normal circumstances, a candidate would most likely reject a call with a favorable vote less than 90%, virtually unanimous, but then these were not normal circumstances.) Complicating the outcome, however, were charges from each side alleging that the other side had stuffed the ballot boxes. Reportedly, witnesses had seen specific persons aligned with the two warring factions compromise the process. That the charges were not investigated or that a second balloting under more controlled conditions was not suggested, much less scheduled, lends credence to the accusations, although an equally viable and more likely explanation is that the losing side was too exhausted to carry the fight to another level. More than one voiced the thought that I was surely better off having lost the vote, and with that assessment I had to agree.

I said that putting forth my candidacy for the settled position was an error in judgment on my part, though not for the usual reason cited (that it violated the Eleventh Commandment). Actually, it was something far more fundamental, that in violating the Eleventh Commandment I had first compromised a core principle, a theological pillar defining my approach to and practice of pastoral ministry. That principle simply affirmed that when acting theologically (that is, when making decisions at least partially informed by one's faith, however inadequately), the efficacy or impact of that action or decision on another person or the wider community is at best persuasive, never coercive. I can bear witness to the words and ways of Jesus, but I can never compel another to do the same. I can aspire to love my neighbors but can never require my neighbors to join and even expand the community of love.

Well, maybe in the church such talk makes sense, and at a minimum, living faithfully within that unique community called church, would certainly distinguish coercive from persuasive power, the accent falling exclusively, or nearly so, on the latter, but far more common to any number of interpersonal relationships in everyday life is coercive power, the kind we typically see, for example, between parent and child, employer and employee, men relative to women, and majorities with racial, religious, and cultural hegemony and their minority and marginal counterparts. Vast inequalities exist in the coercive power by which one individual or group forces compliance with or otherwise limits the freedom of another person or group without due consideration to what each needs and might choose given the opportunity.

History records the results, including the accumulated injustices, but history does not necessarily get the last word on how we might alternatively structure more equitable, more just, and more holistic networks of interpersonal relationships. Key to that project is learning to distinguish coercive power from persuasive power and open some space whereby persons and communities, societies and nations, might have a conversation on the nature of equitable relationships—what Jesus called the Kingdom (or Reign) of God—and how to build equitable communities.

It sounds hopelessly utopian, building equitable communities, but that conversation is the work of the church. It is certainly not limited to the church, but churches acknowledging Jesus Christ as the cornerstone of their faith (Eph. 2.19–22) will follow and model his Way—the path of justice, peace, healing, and love—in their interpersonal relationships, and these relationships in turn become the building blocks of the equitable community.

Such a project can hardly be coerced. At best and over time, usually a great deal of time and maybe not even then, the germ of an idea having to do with just relationships and new models for human community will emerge from the words and ways of the Christ, but neither their implementation nor for that matter the prior conversation that gives birth to the idea itself can ever be legislated by fiat. Yet my decision to set aside the Eleventh Commandment was legislation by fiat. If I could not persuade the members to continue the conversation, which the Council effectively vetoed in seating a search committee, then I would achieve the same end by other means. The power of persuasion, a pillar of my theoretical and practical theology, took a back seat to the power of coercion. It was a grievous error on my part because at that point a most grievous transformation occurred. Instead of the free exchange of ideas as the medium for an extended conversation about new possibilities (which to some germinal extent had taken root in the 7-7-7 program), politics-as-usual took over, setting the stage for a zero-sum game. Gladiators in the arena, once again the church would choose sides and count votes along party lines the process necessarily competitive and decisively combative and the outcome most definitely divisive.

In its wake, pragmatism took center stage for Ann and me. In the midst of all the skirmishes, battles, and the concluding apocalypse, I had labored under the impression that my contract protected me from the politics of the place and the arbitrary actions of those who determined that I had overstayed my welcome. Theoretically, such protections would have given me the freedom to maneuver among the political landmines without undo fear of blowing myself up, a necessary prerequisite for any serious interim process to succeed.

Unfortunately, thinking I was protected financially, I got a little sloppy. I delayed the start of my own search process for what I would do when the interim agenda was complete. Typically, that takes a year and not infrequently more and should have begun my first day on the job. The consequences of having delayed became painfully evident one morning when the cabal of lay leaders and clergy who had been plotting against me for months met me in the parking lot and announced that my services were no longer needed. I was marched to an office for the formalities of paperwork and then escorted to my office, the lock having been changed and my computer disconnected. I gathered my personal effects and was escorted to my car. A couple of weeks later, I returned for my library, never again to set foot in or eye upon the place.

An interesting experience, getting fired. Not only had I never been fired in my life but also had I never been treated as a pariah, all but handcuffed and dragged to the gate lest I walk off with the silver after desecrating the holy shrine. I remember how following my term as the Chair of the Executive Committee of the National Association, the phone stopped ringing and the email slowed to a trickle. One second I was somebody; the next second, I was nobody. A colleague coined a term for the experience: Instant Splaticide. We laughed about it.

This was Instant Splaticide on steroids, and no one laughed. For one thing, no sooner had the vote been announced, my usefulness buried under the suspicious clouds of voter impropriety, than my own supporters disappeared. It took almost a nanosecond for my Kitchen Cabinet to evaporate, never to be seen again, almost as if a black hole gobbled them up lest their ties to my tattered coattails come to light, as it were. The hopes of supporters snuffed out, hopes that I would not rekindle, noticeable holes started appearing in the pews on Sunday. Some told me of visiting other churches, others of having joined a new church. After all, in the church or out, life does go on, and even at First Church, life seemed to go on...a fitting and even a hopeful note on which to end a sad tale.

Or almost a fitting end. At the beginning of this chapter I casually noted that in addition to a laptop and briefcase, I brought a ghost home from my office. A bit later, I added the conviction held by various members and not infrequently voiced to me that what First Church really needed was an exorcism. These were outwardly sane and balanced individuals, seemingly in control of their faculties, arguing that the years and years of fighting signaled not so much a church in conflict as a church possessed. Apparently, the place was both haunted and possessed...another combination missing from the seminary curriculum.

I had actually heard the judgment repeated from time to time over the years (or was it a not-so-veiled plea for help...I was never quite sure) that an exorcism was in order, and I was always grateful that I could count on more immediate concerns to distract me from such a disagreeable subject. After all, in the postmodern era, safely ensconced within Western mainstream Protestant circles and its historically liberal theology and its reasonable and rational members, what does one say about demons, the devil, and demonic possession?

Modern-day people tend to treat any reference to the devil and the demonic as a remnant of a pre-scientific worldview where ignorance and superstition held sway over an unenlightened populace, but my experience from the inside of this congregation taught me to appreciate C. S. Lewis' classic observation (perhaps quoting the 19th century French poet Charles Baudelaire in *The Generous Gambler*), that "the greatest trick the devil ever pulled was convincing the world he didn't exist" (*The Screwtape Letters*). No exorcism was ever conducted to my knowledge, the diagnosis of its necessity notwithstanding. I certainly never entertained the slightest inclination to do the deed myself. There are some things mere mortals touch to their peril.

As with the devil and the demonic, normal people similarly look the other way out of a sense of embarrassment for those who bring ghosts into the conversation, and yet having agreed to stand for election as the permanent minister of the church, what should appear *in our home* but something from the *other* side. Not necessarily demonic, but clearly paranormal, and in any event clearly not of what we think of as *this* world, Ann and I called the visitors our ghosts.

Noting the correlation between the fateful decision to apply for the office of permanent minister and the arrival of the ghosts was inescapable but hardly an explanation, for it seems to suggest that decisions of a certain kind (violations of community standards, say, or other taboos) open the door to the appearance of ghosts. This is nonsense, of course—nonsense, that is, until the reaction of those opposed is factored into the equation, because the reaction was immediate and intense, and in looking back on this period with the help of my notes taken at the time, I have come to hypothesize that the intense energy of the reaction provided a platform or context out of which this paranormal phenomenon emerged. In no way do I make light of this; the conflict was incessant and the emotional toll like nothing I had ever experienced. It taught me that ghosts and such are nothing to fool with.

Not incidentally, perhaps our experience offers something of a clue for those who wonder if what this church needs is an exorcism: that the best exorcism is removing the platform by which one might become necessary.

In any event, not exactly a precise science, the paranormal, and at the mere mention of "ghosts," some will think more of disruptions in my mental stability than visitations from beyond the grave. But for an intense eight-month period beginning about six months before my dismissal and then ebbing in the weeks immediately following, Ann and I recorded manifestations that correlate with a paranormal "presence" in our home. In discussions of this sort, a "presence" can refer to a demonic entity, evil in origin and intent, but we feel fairly confident that the "presence" detected in our home was a nonthreatening fragment of a human personality that remained on this side of the dividing line that separates what we understand as life from what we call death.

This understanding recognizes that the building blocks out of which the universe is created ultimately reduce to energy. As the fundamental reality, then, the energy organized in a human being by the principle of self-consciousness (more traditional language speaks here of a spirit or soul) is released at the moment of the person's death. From the Christian perspective, that energy would be received (absorbed) by God (the Creator who loses nothing and forgets no one). Quite apart from the philosophical and theological issues that accompany the question of biological death, however, humans generally understand the experience itself to be complete and final. That is, whatever awaits (if anything), nothing remains "behind" (as it were)...except that on occasions, and normally undetected (at least by normal human beings), a fragment or perhaps collections of psychic energy, a piece of self-conscious personality, does not fully release at the moment of death and (indulge me the language) "go where it is supposed to go." Instead, not knowing or unwilling to accept its new status (no longer living but not completely dead), this "presence" takes up residence where access affords itself, an uninvited intruder walking through an open door. These "energy fields" are usually benign or mildly problematic but can be evil, even dangerous, and in any event, again, are nothing with which to meddle.

Interestingly enough, Ann and I had had a somewhat parallel experience with a "presence" years earlier. We had moved into a house that we later learned had been the scene of serious and injurious family conflict resulting in a divorce. As reported, the trauma was sufficient to inflict one of the children with anorexia. So far as we knew, the conflict had left emotional scars but did not include physical abuse. In any event, this child's bedroom became our daughter's bedroom when we moved into the house and our daughter began noticing phenomena that had all the characteristics of a "presence," and we invited an individual experienced in these matters to spend some time just sitting in the room. He later reported having felt an "entity" in the bedroom which he attributed to the severe conflict surrounding the disruption of family relationships—such disruptions are often the "open door," he said, by which these things take up residence—and he subsequently dismissed it with a common command, essentially, to go to the place where "you" need to go (I will come back to this momentarily). There being no further manifestations of this or a related paranormal nuisance that had initiated the request for further explorations in the first place, the episode was quietly shelved and not recounted outside our own family.

Now years later, when a more troublesome and possibly malignant "presence" took up residence in our upstairs guest room, I naturally connected the phenomenon with the church's mounting conflict, its intensity providing the "open door" or platform by which this unwanted and uninvited intruder found access into our home and lives.

An interesting question is whether, unbeknown to us, this entity, our ghost, was already in the house, a lingering presence from some earlier trauma involving a former resident, or whether my own inner turmoil provided the platform to which the entity attached itself and followed me home. My own view is the latter because we had been living in our home for nearly eighteen months before any manifestations of the "presence" became evident. Naturally, since the church was alleged to need an exorcism anyway, we looked upon the church's turmoil as the platform from which this "hitchhiker" in effect followed me home, taking up residence in our upstairs guest room. Either way, though, the point is that intense and prolonged turmoil, conflict, and anger correlated with the various manifestations of our "presence," regardless of its point of origin.

As for the manifestations themselves, our log of this eight-month time period records a series of two different categories of experiences. We call the first of these the Attention Grabbers, many of which involve electricity. For example, one time the vent fan over the stove came on without the switch turning it on (the stove not in use at the time). Another time, the computer keyboard stopped working and the computer had to be rebooted (and then functioned normally with the same keyboard). The doorbell might ring with no one at the door or nearby (this happened frequently). A phone call disconnects; while on a phone call, the phone rings continuously; the phone rings and we can hear the caller who cannot hear us. In and of themselves, each has a reasonable explanation (whose computer has never frozen, say, or what phone company has never caused a "problem"), but when these events suddenly occur in a relatively concentrated time period, mere coincidence is itself a suspect explanation.

Other Attention Grabbers were physical, dynamic, or even kinetic in nature and include such phenomena as:

- the sound of running water when faucets are off and toilets are not flushing

- the creaking sound of a rocking chair on hardwood floor (our floors are carpeted)

- doors slamming shut that are normally held open by heavy door stops

- objects disappearing from the counter only to be found in drawers, under the sink, and even behind the washer

- strange smells, like urine, appearing in stairways and closets

- CDs that were stacked on the desk falling on the floor

- the hammock hook snapping in two
- a picture dropping off the wall, breaking the frame
- something falling on the floor while our grandson sleeps in our room
- something going missing from the clothes closet
- most disturbing of all, the opening of the valve from the gas grill under our sliding bedroom door, the smell of propane filling the upstairs area

Again, in isolation, each might have a reasonable explanation, but when otherwise unusual, seemingly random events occur in a relatively confined time frame (so far, all within this period of intense turmoil), one begins to connect other dots.

Added to electrical and physical phenomena were personal encounters. On two occasions, I see a wisp of something, a gray shadow fleeing up the stairway. The outside lights playing tricks? Another time I watch a dark shadow move from the study to the guest room—not the dog who was asleep in the corner. Ann reports a sore spot on her back—just a muscle? She sees something move, an unfocused double-vision in the corner of the closet—a dust ball? Ditto on the "reasonable" explanation.

Speaking of the dog, some of the people with whom we consulted about these events advised us not to rule out our dog's bizarre behavior, like the various times he seemed to be watching the ceiling as if there was something moving across it. On several occasions, he would scratch at the door, as if something was behind it, or bark as if possessed, or cower and shake as if... well, as if he had seen a ghost. Of course, it could have been anything—after all, a dog is only a dog...unless a dog is more than a dog, something akin to a barometer, say? You never know.

The second category of encounter with our "presence" comes from unsolicited reports, principally, from a friend (I'll call her "Mary") and her daughter ("Sally") who was about ten. They stopped by one day and while Mary did not report it at the time, Sally told her mother after they left that she was afraid to go into the upstairs area and in fact would not go into our house ever again because she sensed something that frightened her. This was before we started logging the events catalogued above.

Might we just dismiss this as the runaway imagination of a child? Maybe… except two weeks before we started logging the events catalogued above, Mary had had the same experience. Another two months would pass before she shared with us her own conclusion about the nature of our "presence," which she described as a man and, based on the events listed above, not a good man at that. Mary had felt him in the upstairs study, in its closet, and in the guest room—a very strong feeling, she said.

Mary has an aunt who had died some years earlier but who still made periodic contact with her niece. The aunt took this a step further and said the "presence" was actually a "low-level demon" and that Mary was to have nothing to do with it or to be in our house ever again.

How do you get rid of such as this? We explored our experience and Mary's conclusions with several people who were conversant with the subject but who also had their feet firmly planted in the real world. Among them were a couple of Catholic priests who were willing to perform exorcisms but felt it had not yet come to that and instead counseled us to follow a more routine, if not mildly mundane course (given the subject). This consisted of "being nice" to the "presence," informing him that he was dead and needed to go to the place where he now belonged, and then sealing the episode by burning sage. Long term, we were counseled to protect our home by nurturing a healing ambiance, the conflict at work not finding its way into our home.

We did all this, and with regard to burning sage, a plant used in purification rituals, one final observation: we carried the burning plant from room to room throughout the entire house and its flame remained constant until we got to the guest room, at which point the flame burned higher and higher and seemed to take on a life of its own, finally setting off the smoke detector…the guest room where a young child had felt something so frightening that she would not return to our house ever again. We did ask her mother, Mary, to return one more time, which she did, wandering throughout the house, feeling nothing anywhere, including the guest room.

This was not necessarily the end of our entanglement with ghosts. That this particular "presence" had "gone to a better place" seemed self-evident, but other suspicious manifestations did appear from time to time, though with much less frequency and of the there-it-goes again sort. More to the point, these manifestations themselves correlated with the more intense eruptions at the church, the stress and emotion of which I failed to keep out of our home.

Renewed attention to the light, which casts away all manner of darkness (John 1.5), and greater intentionality regarding a healthful environment, kept these moments, if not at bay, then at least under control through the remaining months of my tenure and in the long slog that was our recovery following its rather abrupt—and insulting—end. We do exist in a relational universe where all entities (not just persons and other living creatures) are intimately interconnected, and the health of the network it creates (a network of interconnected souls is how Evelyn Underhill describes it) has a direct impact on both the well-being of each participant individually and the whole of creation collectively. Healing from and keeping out the dark takes an uncommon concentration on the light, a lesson we humans are slow to comprehend.

Uncommon concentration and eternal vigilance. As I would quickly learn, the flip side of writing is editing, and while I have had some good coaching along the way, the hard work (the rewrites and dealing with the editor's observations) falls to the writer. Some sections have required more effort than others, perhaps none more than this sad tale. I had hoped I could just tell the story and then set it aside, presumably locking these things away where they might stew in their own juices but not continue to touch mine. That, too, was a false hope, and instead what I found was that each of the several times I returned to this narrative, its juices very much touched and stirred mine—not a pleasant experience and not uncommon, having had my daytime disturbed by yet another rehearsal of these things, so would I find my sleep disrupted. Two AM and wide awake. Sigh. I pick up my book and go to the living room to read.

And then this: one night during one such period of revisiting this chapter (this was long after we had retired and moved to the Central Coast), both Ann and I are awakened at the same time from very sound sleeps by four loud bangs, knocks, thumps, the kind that you associate with someone at the door, like the police with orders to evacuate…except that they sounded more like very loud bangs, knocks, thumps on the wall. I investigate and find nothing untoward, as it were. The next day some people report having heard gun shots that night. We live in gun-crazy times and guns in the hands of the crazed do go off at odd hours, but mostly around holidays, not on just another ordinary Wednesday. Besides, what woke us up did not sound like gun fire any more than it sounded like four loud bangs, knocks, or thumps on the *door*. It sounded like four very loud bangs, knocks, or thumps on the *wall*.

The kind of sound that along with the other attention-grabbing phenomena we had logged during an eight-month period of intolerable stress and conflict preceding and immediately following my dismissal from *that* church. The log that has had (had had?) no additions for some fifteen years.

Just saying….

Earlier in this chapter I referred to two very serious mistakes I made with regard to First Church. The first was the decision to accept the invitation to serve as the Interim Senior Minister. The second was agreeing to run for the permanent position which required a prior theological compromise on my part.

Invariably, that history now duly recorded, some might wonder if I would do it again? In a way, it's a pointless question—the decisions having been made, we do not get to claim the golfer's mulligan and take another shot. But for the record, No to the first, I would not accept the interim position, and Maybe to the second, but with a caveat.

The first is easier to answer because emotionally, professionally, personally, and certainly financially, the price we paid was just too high.

As for the second major mistake, violating the Eleventh Commandment… this one is harder. On the one hand, it meant bypassing an ecclesiastical guardrail that separates interim ministers from the settled position for a reason.

We are learning in these perilous days with regard to our liberal democratic institutions and traditions that we ignore guardrails to our peril. In addition, I failed to distinguish the extent to which the theological compromise (essentially, the power of coercion displacing the power of persuasion) would leave a sea of winners and losers on the battlefield (Ann and me two of them). In that sense, and because it did no good, I am inclined to see my Eleventh Commandment decision as an error not to be repeated.

And yet, the theory behind the proposal was sound enough to take the chance, giving the interim process a cushion of time and space to do its work. Unfortunately, the exact nature of the interim process was poorly conceived and then prematurely cancelled, so we cannot know how it might have ended. The fact that it might have ended differently, though, is in my view justification for not closing the door on the proposal to jump over the guardrail, the inherent dangers and anticipated foolishness notwithstanding.

The thing is, sometimes we must make a decision in the moment, having neither enough information as to its wisdom nor enough control to manage its consequences. We give it our best shot and hope for a safe, if not happy, landing on the other side, and so decisions made, consequences noted, there remains only my final word on the place quoting, as did our prophet Dr. Martin Luther King, Jr., the words of the old Gospel song:

> Free at last, free at last
> I thank God, I'm free at last.

CHAPTER 8

WITH BREATH IN THE BODY, THERE'S WORK TO BE DONE

"Preach the gospel at all times. If necessary, use words."

~ST. FRANCIS OF ASSISI

Seek peace in the silence of a dawn.
Seek peace in the beauty of a song.
Gone the night of fear,
The day is breaking new.
Seek peace, God's peace.
Seek peace in the whisper of a prayer.
Seek peace in the sharing of a care.
By God's loving touch
Each morning we're renewed.
Seek peace,
Be joyful in a glorious day.

~ANN MARIE KURRASCH
American composer and songwriter (© *1984 Ann Marie Kurrasch*)

I AM NOT AN OPTIMIST, but I remain ever hopeful.

The two, of course, are not at all the same. Optimism is little more than a mental disposition, a positive outlook on tomorrow quite apart from how dour the present may appear today. Optimists ground their confidence on humankind's intellectual capacity and its creative potential. They draw heavily from the well of science and its application in technology (wedded to sufficient economic incentive) to solve problems. From feeding and providing for an anticipated nine billion people by midcentury to generating clean energy and resolving the climate crisis, everything is in place—all it needs is a mechanism, an agent, an actor to give it wings.

I do not discount any of this. Who knows, maybe somebody working somewhere will come up with something at the right time to make the necessary difference, but optimism is essentially passive because the "someone-somewhere" formula lets its practitioners off the hook by assigning agency to others. The actual development of appropriate solutions to real problems rests with "them," with experts or visionaries, for example, who with any luck also have access to seats of political and economic power for solutions that must be produced and distributed at scale, as we say.

While I am not optimistic about any of this, I do in fact remain steadfastly and ever hopeful about a successful resolution to these and a host of similar issues. The reason is that like optimism, hope begins at the same point and envisions the possibility of the same or even a better outcome, but unlike optimism, hope recognizes that the successful resolution of a problem or challenge is merely a possibility, nothing more, certainly nothing approaching a guarantee. Yes, we might feed nine billion people, *if*...; yes, we might wean ourselves from our addiction to oil, *if*...; yes, humanity might rescue itself and the planet (not that the planet needs rescuing, but it's becoming increasingly clear that humanity does), *if*....

In this case, the variable—"*if*"—acknowledges that between the problem or challenge and its resolution lies an actual response sufficient in scope to release the requisite energy to get the job done. From whom does that response come? Certainly not the amorphous someone-somewhere-sometime, but real people in real time possessed by what William Sloane Coffin calls in his memoir, *Once to Every Man*, a passion for the possible (emphasis added):

> Realism demands pessimism. But hope demands that we take a dark view of the present only because we hold a bright view of the future; and *hope arouses, as nothing else can arouse, a passion for the possible.*

Hope is active, energetic, and dynamic. A people aroused with a passion for the possible will have both hope and the energy to engage upon the work that brings it to fruition in the world. As Daniel Day Williams put it, "[hope] does not put everything at rest; it puts everything in motion." In the end, hope is very personal.

I am not an optimist, but I remain ever hopeful, and without question, a theology of hope has provided the necessary foundation whereby I could remain active within and committed to the church for a half-century. After all, since God shares power with humankind, those most interesting (if not the most vexing) of creatures, we are by definition intimately involved in the ongoing, evolutionary drama of creation. Uniquely, do we bear the image of God in our very being, Creator and co-creator working side by side, certainly not as equals but definitely in partnership, addressing problems, facing challenges, exercising our considerable gifts and directing the world's substantial resources to ends in accordance with the purposes of God? Of course we are hopeful! What choice do we have?

However, there is a flaw in this otherwise fine fabric: because God's power is persuasive and not coercive, God necessarily grants us co-creators freedom to exercise our power in the ways of God...or not. We may well hear the Ten Commandments, for example, as *Thou Shalt*, but we live them as *Thou Mayest*, which is to say we might obey an expressed order from Headquarters...or we might not. History suggests more of the latter than the former, but then—well, we never know. A dystopian shadow clearly hangs over the cultural landscape today, as if to confirm that humankind had its chance but chose instead to opt out of the divine imperative, and yet, at the same time the hopeful side of me surveys that landscape and says, "Yes, but..." and "What if...?" and gets back to work.

In a way, what choice do we have? Our relationship with God does not offer seasonal work from which we can retire when it no longer suits our fancy or even when it no longer satisfies our needs. How many times over the years have I cited the familiar mantra that our mission continues so long as there is breath in our bodies. *How* we express our commitments as co-creators with God will change as time and circumstances change; *that* we will express those commitments is a given.

I do have to say, though, that as I age the mantra gets harder and harder to express with conviction. After a half-century in the trenches, it just feels like those next in line need to pick up the mantle and do the work. When is enough quite enough indeed, freeing the servant from further service? Never, so long as there is breath in the body? Really?

A tricky landscape to navigate, aging. As Mark Twain wrote in facing his own advanced age (*Mark Twain's Letters*), "Now I am seventy. Seventy! I am old. I recognize it, but I don't realize it. I wonder if a person ever ceases to feel young? I mean for a whole day at a time?"

The venerable humorist achieved that milestone in 1905 when life expectancy in the United States was 47 for men and 50 for women. Indeed, he was old! I now look at 70 through a rearview mirror, and while I do *recognize* it, I must say that I scarcely *realize* it, perhaps for good reason, for according to the Social Security Administration, men who *reach* 65 can expect to *live* to age 84 (women who reach 65 will live on average to 87). The century mark is if not commonplace, certainly much less exceptional. Between Social Security and Medicare, along with a little help from AARP and an occasional Senior Discount, we now proclaim "70 is the new 60" (or maybe even the new 55). Maybe Mark Twain's plaintive cry no longer applies? Seventy? Old?

The Psalmist has a different view (the Bible always views everything differently), calculating that we have had our share of life in this world by age 70 (the proverbial "three score years and ten"); by reason of strength they might stretch to four score, not necessarily to be desired, apparently (Psalm 90.10). As in most all biblical matters, we discount the details. Still, taken together, I am old enough so as no longer to have to worry about dying young, but clearly not so old as to feel...old.

But age is creeping up. Early in my 71st year I was diagnosed with prostate cancer, the very disease that killed my dad when he was just 57 (I was 30). There is a genetic component to prostate cancer that greatly increases the risk of a similar diagnosis in men whose fathers, uncles, and brothers had themselves developed the disease, and I can remember feeling rather apprehensive and mildly irritable each year as my annual physical approached; that low-level, just under-the-radar irritability lasted my entire 57th year (which, I later learned, was not unusual). Having now lived "long enough" (the Psalmist, again), or more to the point, having long since relinquished child-rearing and related financial responsibilities, receiving the word was almost anticlimactic. Of course, it helped immeasurably that I had a "good pathology report" (numerical scores and tumor classification landing me in the encouraging sector on the life-expectancy chart). As my urologist put it, at the end I'll be dealing with my cardiologist, not him (gallows humor—I wonder if they teach that stuff in medical school or if it's written in the genes). Taken together, I consider myself fortunate: my markers pointed to a favorable prognosis, medical science had gained much ground on the disease since my dad's time, and excellent medical resources were available; no small matter, I had the insurance to pay for it (national health care, please—justice demands such); best of all, I had an outstanding doctor who brought the only two words that really matter: cancer free.

The body may be cancer free but the word itself, having once entered the realm of self-consciousness, tends to remain (along with its companion, mortality), and it raises the unavoidable question that having now run my lap and having dutifully passed the baton to the next in line, what's next? What does one *do* when *doing* suddenly finds itself superseded by *being*, when the focus is less on advancing the Reign of God and more on the sticky matter of aging gracefully and living maturely (the respected elder in societies that respect their elders)?

Not that the disciple ever ceases to "advance the Reign of God," but having passed the baton and all that, and now gazing upon the social and environmental landscape wherein the Reign of God seems rather in retreat, just what does this old-line liberal and sidelined Protestant have yet to do? For the follower of Jesus, where is that elusive threshold through which one passes and is then home free? I do not see myself abandoning the liberal wing of the theological spectrum and its roost in what is left of mainstream Protestantism. I was raised in a church where "thoughtful people worship," and while I try to balance the two, the religious enterprise for me continues as always to favor the head to the heart, the intellectual pondering to its experiential grounding (although I would gladly turn aside for Moses' burning bush or Elijah's still small voice). I still dwell excessively (if not obsessively) on the social, economic, and political implications of Jesus' radical new ethic for a new world struggling mightily and painfully to be born; it may be too late, but somebody has to support that voice crying in the wilderness.

Perhaps that "home-free" threshold is just a phantom of our imagination, our lap never quite completed, the nagging question about having done enough ever inescapable. We look to Jesus for some guidance here. After all, he has made these outlandish demands about loving God and neighbor alike, but rather than giving a definitive answer to a simple question, he tells a story: "There was this Samaritan, see, ..." (Luke10.29–37).

I think of that when I see a panhandler standing at the entrance to the grocery store parking lot. I have just purchased our groceries for the week; they fill several bags, paid for with a credit card backed by money in the bank; in the bags are numerous items we enjoy that have nothing to do with sustaining life (a little alcohol; a couple of choices from the long ice cream aisle, his and hers; some special coffee, our tastes having moved up the food chain from Folgers years ago). Because we can, we look for seafood sustainably harvested and eggs gathered from free-range chickens (sign of humane treatment of animals); we think about humane treatment of the labor used in the production of what we choose to eat. All this adds a bit to the cost, but it is a small matter self-righteously absorbed. Carefully stashed in my car, I choose a different driveway to leave the parking lot so as to avoid the beggar at the gate, who for all I know might be Jesus, my neighbor.

I cannot help but think of an orthodox Jew of my acquaintance who, facing the same situation, would pause long enough to give the neighbor a little cash because, as he says, his faith tells him he "cannot not respond to the person in need."

So much yet to do? Endless things yet to do. In the words of the old General Confession, "We have left undone those things which we ought to have done, and we have done those things which we ought not to have done."

I struggle with the sins of omission as applied to my generation as a whole, the Boomers. Now that we are beginning to move from center stage to the sidelines and beyond, what lingering attention we get has to do with the emerging shape of our legacy. The reviews are, predictably, mixed. On the one hand, many of us came of age during the volatile decade of the '60s and developed a strong liberal social consciousness around issues of peace and justice. It is said that as we age, we become more conservative. I question that both in my own life and in the lives of countless people I have known over the years. What I believed then took theological root in the Social Gospel and is still a core commitment of my life. So it is with many of us, not a few with far deeper roots and activism to back it up.

At the same time, the Boomers have provided three presidents and in light of the last two (#43 and #45—though technically born a very late Boomer, #44 grew up with the Gen Xers and I rather charitably assign the first Black president to that cohort), the country is perhaps best served by my generation not offering one more of its own. Admittedly, casting doubt on a whole generation by a single measurement of any kind, much less a presidential race, borders on the frivolous, if not the absurd. After all, the voters themselves cover five distinct generations, none of which brings a shared political philosophy to the table anyway, but the victor can only claim the office if the political process, meaning the voters, put him there. Whether we get the presidents we deserve, rarely do we get the leadership we need. We may complain incessantly about how the system fails the people—the machinations of the Electoral College and the manipulations of the democratic process through voter suppression, gerrymandering, Citizens United, and social media—but the fact remains that voters elect our presidents. On the *preparation* of the people to vote hangs the fate of the country.

A tall order, preparing the public to exercise their democratic prerogatives. Asked what sort of government the delegates had created, Benjamin Franklin said it well, "A Republic, if you can keep it." Keeping our Republic, though, requires constant vigilance and a steady commitment to the needs of the public square. While not ignoring racial injustice and regional and cultural differences, the public square in which I and a large swath of the Boomer generation came of age included good public schools and the availability of affordable higher education, safe neighborhoods and a middle-class standard of living, and a cultural ambiance that was, if not progressive, at least processive, looking ahead if not always moving ahead: this was their incredible gift to us, but in the words of the popular book, we (read: White, middle-class beneficiaries of the nation's largess) did not pay enough of this bounty and its enormous potential forward where it mattered the most, *in the maintenance of and improvements to the public square.*

Perhaps ours was a generation with too much money and too little character, too much Me and too little Us. What might a privileged generation in a prosperous nation have added to the public square if only its members had paid forward a somewhat larger share of the pie that they most definitely have paid to themselves? What kind of world might we have handed off to the generations poised to take our place if only our stewardship of the Republic had brought to the American experiment in democracy so much as a slightly better return on the investment America made in the post-war generation?

Instead, we arrive at a point where, as W. B. Yeats put it a century ago in "The Second Coming" (1920), "things fall apart." We take our measure of the world and conclude as did the poet that "the center cannot hold," how can it with both "mere anarchy" and its "blood-dimmed tide" set loose upon the world.

The harshest judgment of all to hear, however, is the couplet at the end of the first stanza:

> The best lack all conviction, while the worst
> Are full of passionate intensity.

Surely, some nobility can be found somewhere, those who counter a collapsing world with the strength of their convictions and a corresponding passionate intensity properly directed toward the greater good. It certainly feels like things are falling apart, but however fragile, the center does continue to hold...so far. Might not credit be given where credit is due, or does the mere appeal to "credit due" only highlight an underlying self-righteousness lurking nearby?

Or is even our alleged righteousness itself a delusion? I remember how aggrieved I felt the first time I heard some pundit suggest that had there been no draft, there might not have been an antiwar movement during the Vietnam era, that we were just too selfish to commit to a common cause and too focused on our own interests to risk dying in the jungles of a country few could find on the map at the time. How dare she question the high moral standards we had set for ourselves and our country, said I. And to what cause, exactly were we to commit? Our leaders lied; we measured the consequences in the daily body count; for *their* sins did we raise our voices.

Say what you will about the mixed motives of students and those on the cusp of adulthood, churches at the time also raised their voices to protest the war in Vietnam and they had Jesus on their side, the Jesus who practiced nonviolence and clearly taught his disciples to follow suit (the Sermon on the Mount, Matthew 5–7, offers some challenging and disturbing insights in this regard). He would have no gun tucked into the folds of his robe; imagining his name on the NRA roster is just absurd. We may dispatch our assailants to the place where such individuals go, but let us not be so naïve as to suppose that heaven rejoices.

Surely God hurts when the creation hurts, and cries tears for, if not our failures, then certainly our inadequacies. For 2,000 years, we have paid homage to the words and ways of Jesus, and yet sometimes in his name and oftentimes ignoring his name, we have visited inexplicable cruelty on our own kind, not to mention the planet and its other creatures. The foremost absurdity, if not the paramount obscenity, of the human predicament is the capacity of the nations in the Nuclear Club to destroy the planet many times over with their abundance of spears and swords. It just seems like we should be further along than we are.

Well, easy to describe—not so clear, though, is how to respond, but try we did. I remember a particularly poignant exercise in this area. The time was either near the end of the Cold War or perhaps just after the collapse of the Soviet Union. A few (precious few) gathered in the church under the social action umbrella to talk about peace. The issue before us was the number of nuclear weapons deployed worldwide and to dramatize the point, steel ball bearings were poured from a cardboard container into a metal waste basket. I have long forgotten the ratio of ball bearings to nuclear missiles, but the exercise took what felt like an interminable time (probably no more than 90 seconds) and made a horrendous racket until it blessedly ended—after which, the point made, comes the inevitable, Now what? What to do? What *can* we do: feeling powerless (David armed with his ball bearings and Goliath backed by the military-industrial complex and its propaganda machine), what was there to do?

With the actual collapse of the Soviet Union, we exchanged our ball bearings for the so-called Peace Dividend where, if not all, then at least some of the national treasure now focused on military preparedness and warfare might instead be available for peace. It never materialized, of course, never could materialize, so many jobs, so much money, such power concentrated in the military-industrial complex.

Fair enough, blame it on the military-industrial complex, but war and peace are mediated through persons, and persons have a way of talking the talk when it comes to peace but not so much walking its walk. In fact, when it comes to peace and nonviolence generally, we have to question how badly we *really* want peace in the first place. As a parishioner once described herself, we might possibly think of ourselves as *aspiring* pacifists, but somehow claiming to be an aspiring pacifist sounds a bit like being a little bit pregnant: either you're all-in or it doesn't count.

Of course, we all *say* we want peace, but what if novelist Walker Percy is right, that while we may *claim* to honor peace, we *actually* find peace boring and so sooner or later we will manage to find a reason to return to war. Will Barrett, a character in his book, *The Second Coming* (1980), notes that "[World War II] came. His father was happy. Most people seemed happy. Fifty million people were killed. People dreamed of peace. Peace came. His father became unhappy. Most people seemed unhappy." Starting at an early age, we prepare for the conflicts to come: I once watched some little boys practice football. They were so small they looked like they might collapse under the weight of their uniforms. Little warriors in training they were, their fathers cheering them on, preparing them for the conflicts to come.

Of course, even if we *say* that we want peace, well we know that we live in the kind of world where protecting ourselves from the violence of others is just part of the human condition, and so even aspiring pacifists must answer a question before a situation requiring its execution presents itself: in protecting one's own life or the lives of innocent people, is violence against another morally justifiable? The very foundation of the so-called Just War doctrine hangs on the answer.

This came home to me on a camping trip that included Ann, our daughter Debbie (then about eight), and me. We had looked at the map and picked a rather remote corner of the Sierra Nevada mountains of California as our destination. It was not exactly wilderness camping, for a gravel logging and fire road ran beside our campsite, but we saw a scant handful of vehicles use it and we were several miles from what might loosely be called civilization.

Everything went well until our last day. While hiking, we came across some other campers, and we paused long enough to chat. Before continuing on our respective ways, they warned us that thieves were working in the area. Their special target was four-wheel-drive vehicles (we had just purchased our first). Not surprisingly, I got little sleep that night! Every sound made me fully awake and alert, and I was prepared to grab the ax by my head to defend my family and myself if and when the imagined intruder burst through our camper.

I recall this isolated and perhaps not very interesting tale because it brought home a commitment most of us would only consider normal, namely, to protect our families from the evildoer, matching violence with violence if need be. I had no illusions about my prowess with an ax, but it was there, and I would have used it. That was the point, the sobering point. The intent—the initial commitment to use a weapon against another person—was all that mattered, for it brought home not only the nature of the world in which we live but also the nature of my participation in it. Ax or pistol? It scarcely matters, for once the decision is made to use it, the difference is one of degree, not kind.

Only natural, we say; perfectly understandable; legally justified; ethically justifiable. The prophets can talk all they want about the latter days when we will beat our swords into plowshares and our spears into pruning hooks and study the ways of war no more (Isaiah 2.1–4; Micah 4.1–4); they can dream wistfully of the Messiah, chosen and anointed of God, at whose advent even wolves would dwell with lambs and lions would eat straw like oxen (Isaiah 11.1–9); but in the real world and in the present day, when forced to choose between one's family or a Charles Manson…it must take almost a second to decide.

Enter the world of gray, the messy world that fills the space between promise and reality, between the kingdom (or realm) to come and the kingdom (or world) we have. We are born into the latter but some will propose, and gladly say, that Jesus was that promised Messiah who invites us to be *born* into the new world as well (John 3.1–21), this "terrible moral huntsman [who would dig us] out of the snug burrows in which [we] had lived hitherto. In the white blaze of this kingdom of his there was to be no property, no privilege, no pride and precedence; no motive indeed and no reward but love"…is this what we have signed up for? Really, to join his "resolve to revolutionize the world,…to change and fuse and enlarge all human life" (H. G. Wells one more time, resurrected from an earlier chapter)?

What went wrong that it should come to…*this*? Do we really need to review one more time the drama that followed the creation story in Genesis, how the First Pair disrupt their relationship with God and confound God's intentions; subsequent generations pit siblings against each other; the Flood deemed the original experiment was a flop and wiped the slate clean for Creation 2.0, which was no better; at the end of the collapse, not just persons but whole nations pushed God away and each other around. A four-fold separation now defines the relationships humanity had with God, the neighbor, each individual's own self, and the creation itself and sets the stage for that marvelous story of the call of Abraham (Gen. 12) and the beginning of the drama of salvation by which God calls a fragmented, broken creation to undertake the journey to the place it belongs in the perfected purposes of God.

To that end, we beat swords into plowshares and spears into pruning hooks…or in the real-world version, we engage in exercises where we pour ball bearings into a metal can and dream of Peace Dividends because we can… because we must. A fool's errand or not, the church steps in those directions because we have no choice; doing so is our call, the invitation to embark upon an impossible mission of transformation, and the creative power to bring it about. It is the oxygen to the church's soul.

Church people are a people possessed. They are possessed by an idea, call it the *Idea* of Jesus. The Idea of Jesus poses any number of questions, like who he is that we would even begin much less continue walking in his ways, ever discerning our mission individually and corporately as we go. As the Idea itself permeates our consciousness over the course of a lifetime, we come to understand not just who Jesus is but who we are in relation to him and what it means to live into God's future as his disciples.

I should note that for many, the Idea of Jesus is essentially what survived the crucifixion and rose victorious on Easter. So powerful was his imprint on the world while he lived that not even his death could extinguish it. Humankind would not and could not entertain the very...well, idea that the world *after* Jesus might return to the world *before* Jesus. Quite the contrary, possessed by the Idea of Jesus, his people go forth to embody the life of Jesus in the thoughts they entertain, the commitments and decisions they make, the values they adopt, and just the way they live day by day for a lifetime, and as the Idea permeates their lives, it continues to work its way through them into the world. Borrowing from Teilhard de Chardin, the Idea of Jesus appears in the world as the energy of love, a force more powerful than the winds, the waves, the tides, and gravity and as transformative as the discovery of fire.

Admittedly, it is an interesting, even compelling, thought, that what emerged from the tomb on Easter was not the body but the message, the words and ways, of Jesus, but I still maintain that unless one has genuinely grappled with—or more to the point, been arrested by—what happened to the atoms and molecules of his body between Good Friday and Easter Sunday, one has probably missed the Idea of Jesus as well.

Possessed by the Idea of Jesus we go forth to continue the work of Jesus. In that sense, staging mere exercises like pouring ball bearings into a waste bucket, while good in and of themselves, is not enough. As near as I could tell, we did nothing to advance the cause of peace. We were preaching to the choir, confirming commitments already in place and shoring up attitudes already appalled by, in this case, the obscene and the absurd. We more or less assumed that rational people espousing a faith informed by the Prince of Peace would "vote their conscience" and write the necessary and appropriate checks. Call it the leaven-in-the-bread approach to human progress: working in their quiet way, the words and ways of Jesus enter into our lives and our lives change accordingly (Matt. 13.33, par.).

This is all to the good, of course. These and similar programs find fertile soil and leave their imprint. Those horrible missiles do remain in the ground…so far, but it is not enough. It is never enough. Eventually, the church has to get out of itself and into the world, its people continuing along the path, as the mantra goes, so long as there is breath in their bodies, engaging not one another of the blessed community but each other in that community waiting to be born.

Undoubtedly, that accounts for my remaining in the church following my dismissal from the First Congregational Church of Los Angeles, the pain and humiliation only exacerbated by my subsequent disillusionment with friends and colleagues over the whole sordid affair. Not that the church was my only option, but I continued to choose that option personally and professionally, and it led to a very happy and satisfying resolution.

One day a colleague familiar with the church and its people from whom I had abruptly separated called and asked if I had ever thought of the Disciples of Christ—technically, the Christian Church (Disciples of Christ). At one time he was part of the National Association of Congregational Christian Churches as was I, now serving a Disciples church in Los Angeles, and my answer was immediate and short: "No." But a few days later I sat down with him and the Regional Minister of the Pacific Southwest Regional Church of the Christian Church (Disciples of Christ), and there began a 14-month journey that led to a call to serve the Downey Memorial Christian Church.

A mainline Protestant denomination, the Disciples of Christ, the DOC, began in the early 19th century on the American frontier (at the time, Appalachia marking the "frontier"), one of three branches of the Christian Church that trace their roots to the Stone-Campbell Movement (as it is sometimes called even today). That the Christian Church is indigenous to America is no minor footnote to Disciples history. Its founders may have brought their Presbyterian roots to the new world, but the Movement itself did not develop as the American "extension" of a Reformation church with British or European origins and a theological foundation built on one of the "Big Three," Luther, Calvin, and Wesley.[19] In fact, the Disciples Movement does not see itself as emerging out of the Reformation at all because from its beginning, the ecclesiastical objective was not Reformation but Restoration: specifically, the restoration of the original church as founded by the first generation of apostles, its principles adequately defined in the New Testament itself. A laudable goal, the project must nonetheless contend with the inconvenient detail that *the* New Testament church is not to be found in the New Testament—churches, yes, but not a single, monolithic, and clearly identifiable church. Again, that the Christian Church (Disciples of Christ) is but one of three branches in the broader Christian Church family further underscores the difficulty (if not impossibility) of finding the essential church *anywhere*, whether in the biblical story itself or on the pages of the many books that line seminary libraries and pastoral studies alike.

Reformation—Restoration: it sounds like the proverbial distinction without a difference, and perhaps because I grew up in and served for so many years only Reformation churches, arguing fervently for the ongoing Re-formation of the church (the hyphen intentionally inserted), I considered the Reformation and Restorationist Movements as essentially two sides of the same coin and treated them as such. That authentic Disciples of Christ historians would offer their correction to my sloppiness is duly noted.

---

19. A proper examination of the Reformation generally and the Disciples' place in American Protestantism particularly would note that many voices gave shape to the Reformation before it emerged historically and powerfully around these three major figures and as it continued to evolve during the ensuing five hundred years to the present day. Certainly, inevitably, some of those voices would find their way into the evolving journey of the Disciples of Christ as well. My only point here is to suggest that Reformation and Restoration objectives might not be so different after all. The other two branches of the Stone-Campbell/Christian Church family are the Christian Churches and Churches of Christ; in the immediate wake of Restructure (below), some 3,500 congregations (with a total membership of about 750,000) withdrew from the Disciples Year Book and clustered in these two groupings.

The Christian Church (Disciples of Christ) is noncreedal in its faith and congregational in its polity. "No creed but Christ" is the familiar affirmation of the Disciples, Scripture itself being deemed sufficient for faith in Christ. In place of a creed or other binding statement of faith, a covenant serves as the "glue" that holds Local, Regional (what other denominations might call Conferences or Synods), and General (or national, including international) manifestations of the church together over time. The "Preamble" to the *Design for the Christian Church (Disciples of Christ)*, the 1968 document that restructured the denomination, provided a way for Disciples to affirm their covenantal commitments with one another and with all who confess Christ:

> As members of the Christian Church,
> We confess that Jesus is the Christ,
> the Son of the living God,
> and proclaim him Lord and Savior of the world.
>
> In Christ's name and by his grace
> we accept our mission of witness
> and service to all people.
>
> We rejoice in God,
> maker of heaven and earth,
> and in the covenant of love
> which binds us to God and one another.
>
> Through baptism into Christ
> we enter into newness of life
> and are made one with the whole people of God.
>
> In the communion of the Holy Spirit
> we are joined together in discipleship
> and in obedience to Christ.
>
> At the table of the Lord
> we celebrate with thanksgiving
> the saving acts and presence of Christ.

Within the universal church
we receive the gift of ministry
and the light of scripture.

In the bonds of Christian faith
we yield ourselves to God
that we may serve the One
whose kingdom has no end.

Blessing, glory and honor
be to God forever. Amen.

The covenantal foundation builds interdependent and mutually supportive and accountable relationships throughout all three of the church's
manifestations. Without a controlling creed, theological diversity will inevitably follow as it did among the Disciples, itself a gift the church offers its
members. Diversity, however, carries a risk: the tendency for competing
perspectives to polarize and fracture the integrity of the ecclesiastical body.
Given that the Disciples of Christ as a whole is viewed as one of the country's
more progressive Protestant voices, the church might seem especially vulnerable to its theological diversity and the wide array of frequently competing
missional priorities that follows. WWJD—What *Would* Jesus Do? Well, it
depends…which Jesus do you have in mind: the Sermon on the Mount Jesus
or the Cosmic Christ; the Jesus of Matthew 25.40 or John 3.16; not to ignore,
of course, Micah (6.8) and Amos (5.21–24) and the whole prophetic tradition (in which Jesus himself stands).

Having seen churches fight, the robust health of the Disciples of Christ is
at once a surprise and a joy. This is not a Pollyanna observation. After all, the
three branches of the Christian Church show no signs of overcoming their
disagreements (theological and otherwise) with one another, and not to be
forgotten is the rejection of a proposed gay candidate for General Minister
and President, or better, the means for his rejection, for on the day of the
vote, conservative churches filled buses with opposition voters who drove
to the assembly where they registered and marked their ballots "No" before

returning home, their duty done. Not that their opposition to a gay candidate for that office in and of itself threatened the integrity of the body but participating in the process only long enough to prejudice the outcome clearly violates the demands of covenant—to stand together and discern together God's purposes for the denomination—and that *covenantal* failure did threaten and weaken the body.

Such instances notwithstanding, the Christian Church (Disciples of Christ) enjoys a dynamic internal life and pursues a multifaceted agenda and complex program. Certainly like all the mainline denominations, they continue to lose numerical strength, and small, fragile churches abound, but while its continuing commitment to theological diversity always carries the potential for disruption, the church does remarkably well maintaining a high level of internal integrity. Perhaps their secret lies in the church's foundation, for from its beginning, ever since Thomas Campbell delivered his *Declaration and Address* in 1809, Disciples have held "that the church of Christ upon earth is essentially, intentionally, and constitutionally one." "In essentials, Unity," they say; "in non-essentials, Liberty; and in all things, Charity." In other words, perhaps because they so believe *in* Christian unity, the Disciples are blessed with a remarkable underlying spirit *of* unity, a sign that freedom and diversity can exist side by side and thrive in so doing.

Significantly, covenantal *principle* firmly embedded, the *Design for the Christian Church* proceeds to establish a supportive organizational structure the purpose of which is, first, to encourage the local, regional, and national churches in covenantal *practice* and, second, to balance the ancient polarities—freedom and community, unity and diversity, congregationalism and catholicity. The less sanguine might observe that what covenant demands in theory, the denomination advances in practice by channeling the people's work into a preordained mold that may—but also may not—serve the spirit of covenant, if not the Spirit otherwise animating this covenant. In other words, pragmatically speaking, does the day-to-day life of the church revolve (much) less around a covenant written upon the heart (Jeremiah 31.33) and (much) more on established rules of the road (defined by those who create and refine the rules of the road)? The tension duly noted, I'll simply repeat the mantra that as with any covenantal relationship, constant vigilance applied in love nourishes the participants and the health of the ties that bind.

It may not be perfect, and in fact the creators of the *Design for the Christian Church (Disciples of Christ)* attest that it is by no means a finished document, but it does serve a good end. Conceptually inspired, brilliantly executed, it stands a half-century later as a prototypical model for non-creedal, congregationally governed churches.

Ecclesiastically orphaned at the time, I found within the Disciples of Christ not just a compatible denomination in which to land late in my professional career but more especially an unexpectedly vibrant and spiritually enriching faith community personally. A happy landing.

That landing took shape at Downey Memorial Christian Church (Disciples of Christ), located some 15 miles southeast of what passes for downtown Los Angeles. It was formed in 1958 during that nostalgic Golden Age of mainline Protestantism, a mid-century response to a growing theological divide that had taken root among the Disciples (and Protestants generally) decades earlier. On one side of this divide, the advocates of a traditional and certainly more orthodox biblicism lined up, what we associate today with Evangelical or Fundamentalist expressions of Christianity (the terms somewhat loosely—some might say carelessly—applied when not carefully defined, as here). On the other side of the divide were the so-called "New Liberals." They supported a burgeoning style of scholarship that appreciated both the tools of historical and biblical criticism in understanding the nature and message of the Scriptures and an intellectual awareness of the social-cultural context in which they were applied. This became the standard model of academic scholarship typical of the seminaries of mainline denominations through the balance of the 20th century.

The two competing schools of thought—traditional and orthodox for some, liberal and (as we say today) progressive for others—had profound consequences for the future development of the Stone-Campbell movement, for the theological tensions that began in the face of 20th century modernism and, as noted above, continued through Restructuring resulted in the departure by the middle decades of the 20th century of some 750,000 members in 3,500 congregations; as always in these matters, the question was who had forsaken the heritage that gave the movement its birth, or put differently, in which body does the heritage continue? Either way, a half-century later, the church committed to correcting the scandal of church division itself would remain scandalized by division, a common heritage expressed in its three branches.

Locally, the Downey First Christian Church had joined the orthodox migration. This left a void subsequently filled by the Downey Memorial Christian Church (Disciples of Christ)—DMCC, for short. In recognition of those who had carried the Disciples banner in a previous time and to provide continuity between the two churches, Downey Memorial Christian Church included the word "Memorial" in its name.

With the aerospace industry at its peak and good-paying manufacturing jobs readily available (GM and Ford were still building cars nearby), bedroom communities like Downey developed all across the Los Angeles area to accommodate the growing population. Supported by the robust socioeconomic climate and an expanding pool of families interested in a church home, Downey Memorial grew and prospered in its early years.

Perhaps because of its origins on the no-frills frontier, Disciples churches bear a rather utilitarian and architectural simplicity in their design. Large or small, no one would ever accuse the Disciples of suffering from an "edifice complex." So with the Downey Disciples. The church purchased a two-acre site with rather narrow frontage on a very busy thoroughfare and constructed a strictly utilitarian social hall and an uninspiring, two-story educational building. (When first I saw this latter edifice, I wondered if the congregation had built a modest, four-unit apartment complex, perhaps thinking of something affordable for retired clergy.)

While still combining Disciples simplicity with frontier meeting house utility, the sanctuary was clearly the exception, for instead of commonplace stucco, the walls were made of a concrete and rock aggregate and replacing the forgettable flat roof was a vaulted ceiling which complemented the stark and otherwise cold interior with the warmth of darkly stained wood beams. Most remarkable of all, though, was the chancel, which included a baptistery that emulated the Jordan River. This was a remarkable departure from the concrete cavities commonly (if not awkwardly) placed within most chancel settings. Truth be told, the elongated pool elicited thoughts of a Jacuzzi or patio spa, and it required the same filtering, heating, and water treatment of any backyard pool. Appropriate planting, supported by natural light, completed the ambiance. It was truly sacred space and I loved it!

The story commonly told of the mainline churches in postwar America was the DMCC story. Like most of its kind, it reached its numerical peak in the mid-1960s with a membership somewhat in excess of 350 and a Sunday school enrollment of 160, not a large church at the time but large enough to support a full-time minister and a program typical of the time. Over the next 40 years, two generations grew up and moved away, not to be replaced, Sunday school enrollment declining to the single digits at the turn of the century. Adult membership decline lagged behind, but by the end of the century a combination of age, retirement, and the lure of a less-urban environment had taken its toll, all exacerbated by a changing demographic, formal membership dipping below 100 (itself an inflated number).

These, of course, are quantitative measures of congregational growth and decline and they ignore the more subjective qualitative assessment of the church's spiritual life and witness. Numerically, trends at the local church level find their counterpart at the synod or conference (what the Disciples call the Regional Church) levels and for the denomination (the National or General Church) as a whole. In other words, each level or manifestation (Local, Regional, General) of the church struggles with a declining and aging membership, reduced financial means, and a decreased vitality as measured by the lay and professional leadership pool and program offerings.

To be sure, there are regional differences, the West Coast hedonists enjoying tendencies still latent (though maybe not by much) in the South and mid-section of the country, but the numbers reflect the cultural marginalization of institutional Christianity (a shift from mainline to sideline for cultural Protestantism in particular). Some might want to separate *liberal* Protestantism from *conservative* Evangelicalism and Fundamentalism, suggesting that having lost its soul, liberal theology just ran out of steam and good riddance, but even there, a once-robust—or at least numerically, a *seemingly* robust—expression of conservative Christian faith itself appears to have plateaued, its energy spent, its own soul lost.

Along with its cultural marginalization, a second challenge landed on the doorstep of the Downey congregation: profound demographic change. A single statistic puts that shift in perspective, namely, that at the turn of the century, 58% of Downey was Hispanic. Said differently, in just ten years, from 1990 to 2000, the White (non-Hispanic) population had declined from 54% to 29% and the Hispanic population jumped from 32% to 58%. In round numbers, as the 21st century got under way, one-third of the population was White and two-thirds was Hispanic.

In an earlier chapter but similar context, I had cited the parishioner who in his setting had remarked, somewhat crassly but no less accurately, that there were not enough White people left in town to prop up all the White churches—he was a longstanding and key lay leader of the Downey church, and his remark captured perfectly the dilemma for the Disciples. The question, of course, was what to do.

Essentially, the church had two options. One, close the church and sell the property, had already claimed several Disciples churches in nearby communities. While often a legitimate option in and of itself, the church still had enough people, time, and resources to consider a second avenue, the objective of which is not to close the church but to transform its ministry. We call it Congregational Transformation or Congregational Revitalization.

How far we had come—or more to the point, how much the situation had changed with regard to the marginalization of the Mainline Church!—since the early days of church renewal in the 1970s and 80s. At that time, we thought we needed only to tinker around the edges to keep participating members from leaving and to get people who had drifted away to return. Adjust the schedule (to accommodate busy families), add an early service (so busy families could still get out and about, the day not "lost" in church), introduce an electronic keyboard (for those who did not grow up listening to pipe organs), supplement old hymnody with praise music (for those who wanted a beat—never mind the generally contradictory theology), maintain visual appeal (at least look prosperous), and above all, do everything with professionalism (to compete with the performance and entertainment expectations shaped by television). Do that and they—the churched and unchurched alike—will find ample reason to take their place in the worshipping community.

In other words, build it and they will come, but for all our effort, in the end, they did not come. As I mentioned in an earlier chapter, the Alban Institute did pioneering work in helping us understand the cultural marginalization of mainline Protestantism (if not institutional religion generally). Looking back, instead of "trying smarter," we had all just "worked harder," and only after they still did not come, we finally "got smart," whereupon we saw the birth of missional church and the dawn of Congregational Transformation.

Unlike Church Renewal, which started with the local church in its current institutional incarnation and offered a smorgasbord of programmatic and other improvements to counter emerging vulnerabilities, Congregational Transformation took a step back from the church-as-institution and began instead with the Jesus Movement as the lens through which the question of the church-in-mission would take shape. From that profoundly different perspective, a profoundly different question follows: how might our local Mission Station, a visible expression of the Jesus Movement in its time and place, connect with the community in which we find ourselves? What does it mean to *be* church and *do* ministry in this time and place? Given our gifts and passions, what do we discern as God's will for this faith community? If the ministries through which we have connected with the community in the past no longer are effective vehicles to do so in the present, then what ministries need to emerge so as to prepare us as a people of faith to fulfill our understanding of the mission to which God has called us?

This shift in perspective giving priority to mission over form can only have been inspired by the Holy Spirit.

In practice, Congregational Transformation is a variation of the Turkish proverb, "if the mountain won't come to Muhammad, then Muhammad must go to the mountain." In this case, if people had lost both interest and confidence in traditional religion in America by the turn of the century and were by and large ignoring the church on Sunday (and every other day as well), then the church would have to go to the people.

At first glance, it sounds like the traditional model of the church-in-mission where the church responds to the Great Commission (Matthew 28.16–20) by sending its missionaries into the world to convert the lost. In the 19th century, the great century for Christian mission, the "sending" churches of England, Europe, and America formed Missionary Societies under whose umbrellas missionaries traveled to foreign lands. Their excesses are well documented, cultural imperialism and economic exploitation being perhaps the most egregious (we recall the reputation of the Congregational missionaries to Hawaii, that they went out to do good and did very well indeed), but while not ignoring their excesses, let us not overlook their commitment and sacrifice and phenomenal success as well, for by that century's end the missionary movement had reached the ends of the earth, planting churches throughout the entire world and eventually placing them under indigenous leadership.

Like its 19th century predecessor, missional church orients itself to the other, to those outside the faith community. Unlike the earlier model, however, missional church does not send specifically designated individuals called missionaries to a "mission field," typically foreign and decidedly non-Christian; rather, having discerned God's purpose for their local church in light of its gifts and passions, a missional church sends itself, or better, extends itself into its "neighborhood" (perhaps the literal neighborhood, the area within a radius of a few blocks from the church's meeting site, though more likely the "wider community," a town or suburb or region defined by a shared socioeconomic identity). Either way, missional church embodies the Second of the Great Commandments, to love the neighbor for the sake of the neighbor alone; it has no hidden agenda (identifying prospective members, say, who will pay the bills to keep the church afloat).

Most notable of all is the means of communicating or bearing witness to the Gospel message. This is, after all, the mission of the church, to bring the words and ways of Jesus to bear upon the life of the community, but how? Traditional models followed a big-jug-poured-into-little-mugs approach: what the sending church already knows, the receiving people need to learn. Missional church, though, makes a strategic shift away from this top-down to a relational model. Instead of a vertical, I-know-you-have-yet-to-learn, one-up and one-down relationship, the church engages the world horizontally where neither participant knows fully (Paul, again, in the Love Chapter, 1 Cor. 13) and so has much to learn, each from the other. Such relationships are mutual and respectful.

Certainly, having embraced the words and ways of Jesus, the Gospel becomes part of the relationships the church and the wider community establish together. Because some already live the faith, its story inevitably emerges within the life of the community (the neighborhood) itself. At one time, the proclamation was largely verbal; it took place in church and during that hour of worship on Sunday morning where the words of professionals reign supreme. Unfortunately, people stopped coming to that place for that hour to hear such persons, and so the proclamation moved outside, to the neighborhood and the wider community and within relationships born and nurtured in an atmosphere of love. In place of a preacher and a pulpit, the proclamation came through any and all whose lives bore the fruit of the transforming power of the words and ways of Jesus. It was as if missional church took seriously that old saw about people rather seeing a sermon than hearing one anytime. The church finally took St. Francis seriously, "Preach the Gospel at all times; if necessary, use words."

So, what sermon might the wider community of Downey want to see? My brief and sad sojourn among the Los Angeles Congregationalists had largely cured me of a lifelong desire to create cross-cultural, multi-ethnic bodies of worshiping and serving Christians. We may live in a cultural melting pot but we do not welcome such in our religious communities. Everyone says differently, of course, and as long as minority representation remains small, a mere token (I read somewhere that the tipping point is around 14%), we can hide our segregationist impulses behind the façade of an "Everyone Welcome" message on the church marque and conversations about "Radical Hospitality" in the board minutes.

I still did harbor, however, the vision of the church as an outpost of progressive theology and witness. Like a city on a hill, its beacon shining upon all manner of humanity whatever its ethnic and cultural composition (Matthew 5.14ff), as the Downey congregation prepared to embrace the challenge of a transformative agenda, might the question of God's purpose lead them in such a direction? A progressive church in the wilds of the Los Angeles melting pot: there was a vision to stir the soul.

But alas, whatever stirred my soul was quite beside the point because in the transformational process the members themselves do the heavy lifting. They will weigh options having merit, but the congregation was not of a progressive bent, and failing to make the case myself for establishing such an outpost in their backyard, I could hardly expect the members to express much enthusiasm for it. In addition, having sufficient time and financing to transform the theory into something concrete, giving it visibility and building support in the community, was dubious at best. One day, the core leadership told me they had another plan and that was the end of the matter.

The plan was called New Beginnings. A ministry of the Disciples of Christ, New Beginnings brings the resources of a team of church consultants to local congregations struggling with issues of mission and purpose amidst the perplexities of the ever-shifting sands of a church's unique cultural context. The initial phase involved an onsite visit to the church and a detailed assessment of its history and present circumstances as measured numerically by membership, participation, and financial trends (typically all downward). Complementing the data was an analysis of what the figures suggested when it came to the matter of the church's engagement with the community and the effectiveness of its outreach. The final report to the church also included exhaustive sociological data highlighting the socioeconomic characteristics of the wider community and the people living within the sphere of the church's neighborhood. At this point the first phase of the New Beginnings process offers the members a pretty clear snapshot of their church and its place in the community at this particular moment.

The genius of New Beginnings, though, lies not in this first phase, the snapshot itself, but in what the members then do with it, for strictly speaking New Beginnings is not a program with prescribed (or even recommended) solutions to identified problems (top-down) but a ministry that guides the members in a structured conversation out of which solutions (or direction) to identified problems begin to emerge (bottom-up). In short, the congregation assumes responsibility for discerning the nature of its present and the possible contours of its future ministries.

The Downey members engaged this process, followed the steps in the guided conversation, and adopted a perfectly reasonable direction for an Anglo church in a largely Hispanic community: to start a new ministry directed to second- and third-generation Latinos under a Latino pastor. Initially, the pastor would join the existing staff as an Associate Minister, and the new ministry would develop under the umbrella of the church itself, not as a separate church sharing facilities and resources. Eventually it would supplant the Anglo church, the Associate Minister simultaneously succeeding the then-Senior Minister. That, of course, would be...Me!

A strange feeling, indeed, actively working to put yourself out of a job, and not to miss the immediate implication of the church's decision, my immediate priority was to facilitate the search process that would bring my replacement to the church.

I had one advantage not always available to those who were in my position: I could (and subsequently would) retire. Had I been younger at this time, with fewer career prospects, I might have been less enthusiastic about even introducing congregational transformation to the church's leadership, and I suspect that the perceived economic threat of subsequent unemployment may explain why very few mainline Protestant churches take advantage of the transformational agenda even though most would benefit greatly from it. That threat could come from two quarters: for one, ethnic-demographic change (as in Downey's case) might require corresponding ethnic leadership; not quite as obvious, another threat might come in the form of a new ministry or changes to an existing ministry requiring interest in and skills for the new work that the minister does not have and is not likely to acquire. Professional pride might be operating as well, an outside assessor poking around in the closets and coming up with ideas doubling as a challenge to the competence of Lone Ranger clergy-types to deal with things at home themselves.

The process leading to the adoption of its new ministry had taken the Downey church months, but with the favorable vote to proceed with its implementation, the "former" Anglo church effectively ceased to exist. Obviously, the people did not hand the keys over to a new group and walk away, but with attention *and* resources largely directed to the new ministry (guidelines called for a 70-30 split of time and treasure in favor of the new beginning), the Anglo church's agenda and significantly its related pastoral responsibilities ceased to exist as well. *That* church had no future and so its people no longer needed to think about setting goals, developing appropriate programs, and building and equipping the membership for new ministries (or any ministries, for that matter—what was the point?). All that would fall to new leadership and the new congregation that would develop in and take *their* place. It was like presiding over a long funeral before the body had breathed its last.

On the surface, it might appear as if nothing had immediately changed for the members and me, but at least for me the psychological adjustment was enormous. Not only was I to facilitate the search process that would bring my successor to the church but also in the meantime I effectively gained a new title: no longer pastor of the church, I became instead the chaplain of its remaining members. Granted, the de facto change in the job description was not entirely unexpected on my part, an unintended consequence of a necessary decision—I could see it coming—but its arrival brought with it two troubling matters: for one, as chaplain, I had too little to do and was bored. I kept myself busy, but pastoral ministry had always presented me with a smorgasbord of duties and responsibilities requiring the attention of a generalist and now I had just one, interim caretaker of a vanishing church. I was a horse put out to pasture with some races yet to run.

Then, having time on my hands for which I continued to be paid left me with an ethical dilemma: how could I justify taking full-time compensation for part-time work? I had seen too many instances where ministers hung onto their full-time positions long after the church and its members needed—and could afford—full-time attention, and I had vowed never to cross that line. Because the cost of an employee and the demands of keeping a building open in those situations would likely exceed current giving, churches in transitional situations typically kept themselves afloat by drawing down its reserves (endowments, protected or otherwise, and other savings). In a variation of the theme, I learned soon after starting at Downey that its own operating budget, including salary support for a full-time pastor, depended on the generosity of a single donor without whom the church would have closed years earlier. I justified it at the time by engaging a transformational agenda and the full range of pastoral responsibilities. I told myself we were not looking inward to the interests of the remaining members but honestly exploring the question of how the church might continue locally or whether the time had come to channel its legacy in other ministries (essentially, converting its property and other assets into endowed investments). Now, with that work completed and time on my hands, I could no longer justify full-time compensation from a congregation that had not really supported its own operating budget for years (I often wondered if the members knew they had a patron).

I shared my dilemma with the church's leadership and to their credit (I think?) they did not share my ethical quandary—nor to my knowledge did the members themselves complain about the misapplication of their financial treasures to my upkeep. I had made a commitment to myself to remain in place until the search committee had selected the new minister—after that, no promises. The new minister did arrive, a young woman with a deep and abiding faith, a solid education, pastoral competence, and an engaging enthusiasm for the new work, and I quickly discerned that there was little I had to offer her as she assumed her responsibilities. She was in effect starting a new church (albeit under the umbrella of the "former" one). If I could have started such a church, we would not have needed to call her in the first place. So, my work now apparently finished, the ethical quandary resurfaced. Along with it, came the R-word…retirement.

A mixed blessing, retirement. It presents three problems. The first two are practical, having the finances to get through it and sufficient discretionary funds and the health to enjoy it. (There is nothing like a Medicare card to reduce one's stress in this regard…which also has a way of increasing one's longevity.) The third is more subjective—what in the world to do with it once you have it? After all, living in retirement for 20 or 25 years has become commonplace, and retirements lasting as long as one's working years are not exactly unknown.

Clergy standing in the Disciples of Christ is renewed annually, and my status for nearly a decade had been "Retired Active." An apt description, it means I intend to continue the practice of ministry, if only occasionally or on a part-time basis, which I did after leaving Downey and relocating to the San Luis Obispo area on the Central Coast. I served as Interim Minister for 18 months at a nearby UCC church and a year after that I was invited to serve the Disciples Church in Morro Bay indefinitely. Like so many of our churches, the Morro Bay congregation had reached that point where its own survival was in doubt. We introduced a version of New Beginnings which resulted in a new mission, Earth Care Ministries, but it was a case of too little, too late, and after nearly three years we closed the church.

I noted above that I would later serve as a New Beginnings Contract Assessor, and during my early retirement I had that opportunity, visiting nearly a score of churches in the western part of the country. I also served first as the Executive Director of and later, when the funding ran out, as a member of the Board of Directors of People of Faith for Justice, an interfaith voice for social and environmental justice on the Central Coast, in which role I still continue.

I also surprised myself (shocked is more like it) by joining a local Rotary Club. I was not a good service club member when it was expected I join one and then once free of all expectations, I joined one anyway. At one time, churches wanted their ministers connected to a service club badly enough to pay the expense, but as church membership started to fall off and budgets became harder to fund, service club fees were easy line items to remove and clergy participation declined accordingly. Such was true for any number of otherwise potential service club members who might have the interest but who were either unwilling or unable to cover the expense from the family budget. Along with the need to balance the increasing complexity of home and family life and the demands in the workplace, as well as the changing shape of community service and the growth of trade and professional associations, service club membership began to decline dramatically.

Rotary looked at its own decline and began to experiment with ways to accommodate the changing social, cultural, and financial landscape without compromising its mission and purpose. The result was the creation of non-traditional clubs that typically met less frequently (reducing time commitments), did not include a meal (saving considerable expense), and had a more focused, if not singular, program emphasis (planting trees, for example, or a similar eco-application). Rotary's global work, particularly in polio eradication, and its highly regarded Foundation are two reasons for my interest as well, and of course club membership also provides something of an entry point by which I can give something back to the community, but without a willingness to introduce new organizational structures, I would not be a Rotarian today. Churches would do well to take note.

In more recent years, I have retired my "Active Retired" status in favor of "Retired Inactive." Self-descriptive, the title simply means what it says: I am now Retired. Period. As a never-say-never kind of person, I suppose I must leave the door open just a crack, just in case. (And just recently, I did have a dream where a search committee came knocking, inquiring about my interest…I thankfully awoke before facing the prospect of telling my good wife of "our" good fortune, but she would only have repeated what she said when I first proposed living on and sailing around the world in a boat, "You'll be lonely," so there's that.) Anyway, and speaking realistically, at this point I harbor no realistic intention of revisiting my "Retired Inactive" status. Having observed the 50th anniversary of my ordination, it just seems right.

That said, there still remains the nagging matter of continuing purpose and usefulness. Maybe I have (gratefully) passed the mantle to a new generation and I relish the freedom it brings, but one cannot just exist aimlessly, wandering freely from day to day as if in a bubble, and so now do I hear my own mantra coming back to haunt me, something about our mission as co-creators with God continuing so long as there is breath in our bodies. A lifetime in the trenches and no time off for good behavior, especially when the world's problems feel so intractable? Not so long as there is breath in the body!

About the time I start looking for the off ramp, I hear another of Ann's songs echoing in the recesses of my mind. Built on the musings of Ecclesiastes (himself a Preacher), she calls it "Speak Up for Justice Now." It opens with the chorus and then asks a series of questions:

Chorus:

To everything there is a season.
Is this the time for Peace?
To everything there is a reason.
Is this the time to speak?

Verses:

Who is left to gather the stones
from those who have scattered them here and afar?

Who is left to mend and restore
for those who have only torn down?

Who is left to plant the good crops
for those whose fields have gone fallow and brown?

Who is left to treasure the good
from all that has now been tossed out?

Who is left to show love and care
for those who often hated and scorned?

Who is left to sing and to dance
for those who can now only mourn?

Ending:

Now is the time to not be quiet,
A time to heal and vow.
It's up to us, for we are chosen.
Speak up for Justice now!

© 2014 Ann Marie Kurrasch

"Retired Inactive"…an oxymoron.

CHAPTER 9

THE VIEW
FROM THE FRONT

"I want to know God's thoughts...the rest are details."

~ALBERT EINSTEIN
theoretical physicist

"Possible things are easy to believe.
The Glorious Impossibles are what bring joy to our hearts,
hope to our lives, songs to our lips."

~MADELEINE L'ENGLE
American writer

WHEN I WAS A KID sitting in the pew, I sometimes wondered what the minister, sitting in the chancel, was thinking about when he wasn't (shall we say) otherwise occupied. Hopefully, it had something to do with the subject at hand, but then being human.... Actually, the view from the pulpit gives those who stand there week after week plenty to think about, some of it rather humorous: the suppressed, or not-so suppressed, yawn (it's the air, not the droning); a quick, or not-so-quick, glance at the watch (yes, it's still ticking, referring to a time when watches actually ticked); a whispered comment (what are they smiling about?).

Wonder and appreciation fill some of the time, along with gratitude for faithfulness and commitments measured in decades (the church clearly making a difference in its people).

Jesus says we're not supposed to worry, so instead of worrying I find myself ruminating, like, does this hymn work, or was that thought lost? After all, we hear a lot these days about how words and language no longer signify the same thing they did when most people read from the same playbook. Creeds and formulas, hymns and Scripture, sermons and prayers: how do we put it together these days? This was a constant question, inevitable and unavoidable as I took in my view from the front.

The awareness of new and continuing challenges, realized and frustrated hopes, the joys and disappointments of everyday life: this was a constant, too (church people not so different from everyone else in so many ways).

Creatures of habit, we do have "our" pews, so when a pew was empty, I took note of a member's absence. Maybe it was nothing: a nice day for golf, a planned weekend away...or maybe it was something more, something wrong: another fall, one more trip to the ER, an allusion in last week's sermon, a comment really not appreciated.

Nothing captures the view from the front, though, and exemplifies the privilege that pastors enjoy by virtue of their position, like baptisms, weddings, and funerals (the Alpha and the Omega of ministry, the beginning and the end and, for good measure, everything that comes in between). Most of my pastorates occurred in churches that practiced infant baptism. In adult baptism, the baptismal candidates take responsibility for their spiritual decision and the direction it sets; for infants and children, primary responsibility rests on parents to acknowledge and nurture the spiritual component of the young child until such time as the child reaches the so-called age of accountability. As we will see, the church has a role as well, though it really falls to the parents to nurture the seeds planted in baptism.

The baptismal liturgy begins with appropriate words to that effect, directed primarily to the parents, and then, unless they have voiced their discontent, otherwise known as howling, I take and hold the infant or toddler. (So dependent, ever trusting, I think to myself.)

I glance at the parents, look at the first pew where a family member or relative is operating a camera, and check the body language of the sponsors—are they all up to this, I ask myself? (I think of my own children and some random synapse flashes on the soccer ball that had bounced off my daughter's face ages ago—so vulnerable. I'm reminded of the squeaky hinge on the front door I never oiled, the better to hear it when she and her brother come home, safe.)

A word of admonition is addressed to the sponsors: "Your standing here is more than honorary," I tell them; "you are to be involved in this child's life; as a sign and symbol of your commitment, will you sit in the rain and watch this child play soccer?" They say yes. I believe them. (If they don't, they'll have to take it up with God.)

I move to the font that holds a small bowl of water, turning so the camera can get a good picture. Church renewal over the years has also included attention to how the faith community worships, that is, how its doctrinal affirmations take shape in its liturgy and hymnody. The idea is that the language by which the church expresses its doctrine, shapes its rituals, and encourages its disciplines has a direct bearing on whether its own people can connect their faith and its application to a secular society in which they live day to day... or not. In my experience, liturgical renewal, the newer hymnals published by mainline denominations, and a contemporary setting generally serve the purpose quite well—generally though not always—and when it comes to the two sacraments (Baptism and the Lord's Supper), rather than leave things to chance, I become quite traditional, citing the conventional formulary: "I baptize you in the name of the Father, and of the Son, and of the Holy Spirit." Hand in the water three times, and three times water drips on the child's forehead. The Unitarians in our midst squirm at the Trinitarian affirmation. (Let them, I think. We are deep in mystery now and need all the help we can get. The mystery of life, of a self, of becoming a person, of watching the whole drama unfold, of touching the holy... Father, Son, and Holy Spirit, indeed. Whatever helps.)

I wipe the excess water away and ask God to bless this child. (A silly request, I say to myself, God blesses this child quite apart from my feeble words.)

"And may God's Spirit dwell with you forever." (Forever? How casually do we think of time, as if it goes on forever, and maybe it does, somewhere. But here it passes all too quickly. One day they ask to be carried, the next they want the keys to the car. Then they're off, living lives in distant places.)

Theologically, baptism is the entry point into the body of Christ, represented by the congregation. I note that they, the members, have a role in this child's life, something akin to an extended family of aunts and uncles, grandmothers and grandfathers, brothers and sisters, and to symbolize the adoption of this new child into a wider family, I place him or her in the arms of one of the new aunts or uncles or whatever, sign and seal of the pledge to care for and nurture the child and so one another. (Being selected to hold the child by virtue of selecting the correct pew that morning is like winning the lottery.) Although not asked to sit in the rain at sports events, everyone affirms they are part of the family. I offer a final prayer and return the child to the parents.

Certificates and a rose—a symbol of all that is precious in life—and it is over. Seeds planted—seeds nourished: who knows how they will take root, what fruit they will bear, how this child and its family will be different? In any event, as of this moment, off to the nursery they go, a flying away of sorts, a preview of things to come. Life is a pilgrimage, a journey, as we say. A family has invited the church to be part of their journey, inviting the members to make a difference in how that journey unfolds, and the church agreed. Of course, the church agreed—it's what churches do, its transformative language making a difference in a common journey for everyone. The choir gets ready to sing, and I get ready to read the biblical lesson for the day, watching Mom or Dad carry their child down the hall.

Funerals (or the more popular Memorial Services) are also points of privilege. Like baptism and other rites of passage, they offer their own access to the sacred and holy. Indeed, in that moment when life bows to death and we confront what someone has termed life's finest form of adventure, the sacred and the holy take center stage. In this secular age, such language sounds increasingly quaint, if not altogether foreign, but unless we conclude that oblivion is the fate of "all things bright and beautiful, all creatures great and small," death pushes two questions to the forefront of human consciousness: why is there something instead of nothing and what, if anything, awaits on the other side of the final passage when the "something" that is my life ends here?

Channeling the Bard, is our hour on the stage a tale told by an idiot, all sound and fury, signifying nothing, or does Another infuse not just this momentary life but the whole of creation with meaning and purpose and might that wider purpose (*must* that wider purpose) include our participation, the alleged crown of creation, we who stand just a little less than God in the order of things, crowned with glory and honor (Psalm 8)?

Many people, church people included, do not ask (or largely ignore) the life-and-death, existential questions religion routinely addresses, but unless one has decided that nothing and no one awaits on the other side, some response, some assurance, some hint of things to come will often feel necessary, certainly something more than a gathering at the club and a toast to the memory of the now-departed. Like many of my Protestant colleagues, I had no ecclesiastical restrictions limiting my pastoral services to church members alone, and so funeral directors frequently called me on behalf of a family that did not have a church relationship but still wanted a clergyperson to officiate at a service.

I always honored the inner strength it must take for the unchurched to open the door to me, the church's representative, and I took the opportunity and its responsibility very seriously. I recognized that for many people, weddings and funerals and maybe key holidays are the rare exceptions to a more general practice of keeping the church at arm's length, and so maybe little more than social convention drove the decision to bring religion more directly into their lives at that moment, but I still gave the family more credit than that. To the uninitiated (and sometimes to the fully initiated), churches are a strange world unto themselves, their leading representatives a peculiar breed, and it took real resolve to invite both into the family in the midst of its grief.

I must say I normally felt some trepidation myself knocking on the door. In the immediate wake of their loss, the family history would be on full display, both that which they would naturally want to celebrate and the pieces they might wish to hide, like unresolved conflict, guilt, perhaps relief (and guilt for feeling relieved). Already vulnerable, how would they react to me, an intruder treading upon their sacred space? I reminded myself why I was there, to listen and to help them plan a service that would meet their needs, and because they had invited the church to share the moment, I was also there to affirm the "something more" that otherwise may remain unsaid in a celebration-of-life gathering.

Certainly at so serious a time as the intrusion of death, something must be said. Something significant, something worthy of the moment, but what? What to say—and how to say it: admittedly, this poses something of a dilemma at services for those you've never met. Of course, in such moments we affirm what we loosely call the "promises of faith," but the promises of faith, here centering on the prospects of heaven, seem to come with a catch and apply only to those who have entered into what is often called a "saving" relationship with God through Christ. As per the testimony of family and friends, the deceased may indeed have lived a good life, even a religious life as measured by the Ten Commandments or the Golden Rule, but a good life even when guided by religious constructs says little about the actual nature of one's relationships with God and neighbor and one's own self, the network and its connections where salvation lives, stagnates, or dies. Not that those with a church relationship are necessarily "saved" and that those without a church stand in mortal jeopardy, but what to say about the promises of faith regarding eternity in relation to someone they never met gives parish ministers reason to pause. (The same hesitation may apply to parishioners they know only too well.)

One way out of the dilemma is not to say anything at all, perhaps to the relief of both the pastor and the congregation, and just celebrate the life of the person now gone. For so many, the whole Story just lands with a dull thud anyway, "the Scandalous Thing, the Wrinkle in Time, the Jew-Christ-Church business, God's alleged intervention in history," as Sutter puts it in Walker Percy's *The Last Gentleman*. Among the reasons for rejecting the Scandalous Thing: having to spend eternity with Southern Baptists (with apologies to Southern Baptists...I might say the same of Congregationalists I have known). I attended a Charismatic praise service once just to see what had caused so many to (pardon my bias) jettison their respectable Protestant moorings, and after a particularly lengthy and rapturous profession of a love for Jesus in song, the preacher suggested that this is what we would be doing for all eternity, at which point I decided I was not going (not that I needed to worry, as they might have said).

But do we not miss the point? How arrogant we are, we who see in a mirror dimly (1 Cor. 13.12), outlining the contours of eternity! Having neither seen nor heard the definitive word on the matter (1 Cor. 2.9), might we not rather want to serve ourselves a generous measure of humility before returning to our task…where we find ourselves pondering the contours of eternity! Call it the inescapable challenge because, after all, in worship generally and certainly at so serious a time as the intrusion of death specifically, something must be said, something significant, something worthy of the moment. I have attended memorial services where even to me the words sounded silly and the pastor saying them looked foolish, but that is no reason to pretend such words do not exist. I have also attended services where the pastor, having nothing to say, said nothing…and looked pathetic. Maybe it's less a question of what is said and more a matter of how? That is to say, if the words no longer signify (Walker Percy again), perhaps the deficiency lies less with the words themselves, the language as such, and more with those who have yet to master sufficiently the language that will signify?

For myself, as a Christian universalist, I hold to the view that like it or not, the great adventure—life succumbing to death and opening unto life— embraces all of us. Such is the nature of God's love, that God does not (even that God *cannot*) lose anything or forget anyone. The "something" we call our lives is not extinguished by the transition we call death. Even more, the life to come does not begin at the moment of death; quite the contrary, to enter upon the "saving" relationship with God through Christ is to taste in this moment and in this place the promise of faith and with it the hint of comfort in the short-term, healing in the long-term, and hope that in time we will indeed pick up our lives and walk again.

A harbinger of things to come, my first funeral came as a request from the funeral director in a neighboring town. We had not been in Chadron too long, and I knew it would happen sooner or later, but at that point I had not even attended a funeral service much less organized and conducted one, although I had a Book of Worship and some notes from a class where such things were discussed. What could go wrong?

Customs and conventions for funeral services vary with geography—little things, important things, like getting the family in and out and standing and sitting and passing responsibilities back and forth between the minister and the funeral director and moving the casket from the church to the hearse— and by and large, some awkwardness aside, things went pretty well until an elderly lady collapsed in the pew in the middle of the sanctuary. This was summer and it was hot, really hot, and the small church was really full and suddenly the ushers had something to do—which they did, gently guiding this dear old lady, now the center of attention, to the door. (At least she had not, you know, gone over to the other side, for which I was grateful). Or so it seemed, for when next we see her, she is stretched out full-length on the lawn, with no hint as to whether she was in recovery or next in line for the minister's second funeral service. (What struck me was the sense of calm that prevailed as the pall-bearers placed the casket in the hearse for the drive to the cemetery, others quietly waiting, their friend and neighbor slowly recovering before they took her home.)

In between the call to the undertaker and the benediction at the cemetery, there is lots of laughter...and food. I called on families at their homes following a death and frequently found people standing almost shoulder to shoulder, family and friends talking, laughing, and telling stories. Standing face-to-face with death, we find terra firma, solid earth, in the things that constitute life, eating and drinking and family and friends—the solid community, now disrupted by the loss of one of its members.

For some reason, this was especially true of unchurched families, a house crowded with people, lots of boisterous conversation, lots of kids, enough activity to take the edge off the reason that had brought them together. Maybe our more staid and reserved church families just put on a different face when the minister called. (Heaven knows there was plenty of eating and drinking and laughter in the staid churches I served.) Not familiar with the protocols of church life, the unchurched lived the only life they knew, in this particular moment a genuinely supportive community rallying around both a family and the rest of its members now confronted with the ultimate of mysteries.

Just getting to the cemetery from the church or funeral home for the committal service can be precarious, especially if it involves a long procession, and I was always glad to ride with the funeral director in the hearse. The drivers were told to keep their cars close together and not to pay attention to the color of the light when going through intersections, but inevitably gaps would appear, and one funeral director told about the time a car darted into the midst of a long procession from the adjacent lane on a busy street and then turned into a McDonalds parking lot at the next driveway access, followed by most of the rest of the procession behind him.

In the same way that I could and always did accept requests for funerals, so could I do the same for weddings, and truth be told, many churches—and their clergy—found a significant source of income from the wedding business, but I never went that far in my churches. We welcomed those who came to us but did not otherwise encourage wedding traffic to wander our way.

Especially in more recent years, weddings came to represent the growing disconnect between the church and the wider community, at least with regard to younger generations from whose ranks most wedding couples emerged. They served as a stark reminder that many of us with declining attendance and increasingly unused educational wings in the Mainline churches had just lost contact with the two generations that followed the Boomers, Gen X (roughly, those born between 1965 and 1980) and Millennials or Gen Y (born 1981-1994. The bookend years for the generations seem to shift somewhat with time.) Gen Z is now fully launched as well and includes those born between 1995 and 2015 (the older members were sometimes counted as Millennials). These younger adults gradually (and then increasingly as Gen Y came along) grew up outside the church and so had no exposure to the church's language. Little wonder that when the time comes to plan a church wedding, suggesting along the way that married life might have a spiritual component, Gen-X and -Y and undoubtedly -Z would present a much different, and pastorally a much more difficult, challenge!

A more difficult challenge, indeed…for everybody. Just picture a young couple wanting to get married in a church. Having no connection to one of their own, they somehow find their way to us. Maybe for an occasional holiday, quite possibly for a friend's wedding, or very likely a family funeral, they would have experienced "church," but this was different. This was personal. This meant walking down the hallway to the church offices and the minister's study where they would talk about, you know, their relationship…and stuff. It must have been terrifying for them.

Ever so much easier to profess their mutual love and let it go at that, skipping the church and going right to married part, all without the benefit of clergy (as we used to say). And if not terrifying, perhaps merely annoying, Evelyn Underhill's quip comparing the clergy to the irritating clerks in the post office one must endure. Acting as the Gatekeeper to the altar, the church's rules and my expectations standing in the way, who knows what hoops I may impose on them? Annoying indeed.

Not that it was any easier on my side, not exactly terrifying but certainly troublesome and problematic, listening to their approaching footsteps, for how do we even begin talking with two, typically young people about something as profound as marriage—that is to say, *their* marriage—in a church setting when the church itself and its words and ways are likely so foreign.

Not infrequently, they would bring children from previous relationships, if not the current relationship, the children having arrived before the nuptials were performed (indeed, some offspring served in the wedding party and witnessed the creation of the marital bond of which they were already its fruit). With rare exceptions, the people with whom I met were healthy, hopeful, responsible, capable men and women; they had plans and jobs and addresses; when the time came, family and friends would sit in the pews, wishing them well. As would I.

We get acquainted and when it seems appropriate, the conversation takes a more focused turn: about the spiritual side of your life together, I say. The matter at hand is covenant. A great word, covenant, and the answer to the most fundamental question: what is it about a marriage ceremony that makes your relationship different from not having a ceremony at all?

Weddings and funerals are the exceptions to what passes as just another, otherwise normal Wednesday. Introduce a wedding into the mix and a veritable roller coaster of emotions begins to stir, stimulated by the revived history (and the accompanying baggage) of past relationships and the anticipation (and accompanying uncertainty) of new and expanding ones. Joyful—of course; painful—probably; bittersweet—naturally.

Surviving the wedding, the couple rushes off to their new adventure, the family goes home, and things return to something approaching normal. Though it takes more time, years in fact, the aftermath of a funeral follows a similar pattern: the community of family and friends that gathered in the face of loss returns to the demands of jobs and kids and settled routines and a new normal begins to take tentative root. Life goes on, maybe not in quite the same way, but it goes on nonetheless.

So in the church. It's one thing to be with the church in its intense moments, when feelings run deep and emotions cover the map, but what is the church like on just another Wednesday? How are the pilgrims and how goes the pilgrimage when the prevailing winds are fairly calm? To find out, the minister would probably want to make the proverbial pastoral call.

At one time, it would have been the proverbial *routine* pastoral call, and in smaller churches even today, pastoral visitation undoubtedly receives more of a minister's time than I ever could (or wanted) to give it—and perhaps more than many church members care to receive it, the demands on our time pulling families in so many directions all the time.

Sometimes our distractions compete with the demands, their combined force diluting time and energy. Not that distractions are of recent origin for church members and their spiritual leaders. I can remember, for example, older ministers describing how they would leave their cars running in parishioners' driveways when television sets first started appearing in homes. The idea was to park the car as close to the living room where the TV was likely sitting because the car's electrical generator (today's cars have alternators) interfered with the signal. As a result, the parishioner, the beneficiary of the pastor's time and attention, would not be distracted by the program because there was nothing to watch.

You can imagine the conflict: do I open the door for the pastor or do I pretend I am not home so I don't miss "Queen for a Day" (the NBC television show that ran from 1956 to 1964)—tough call.

The view from the front has primary reference to those special places where ministers meet their people, in the pulpit and at the altar, graveside and bedside, where they work and how they live. The occasions range from the mundane and banal to the exotic and exceptional, from just another Wednesday to the unexpected crisis. Seemingly invincible one day and inescapably vulnerable the next, as saint and sinner and pilgrim to the end, the view from the front catches it all, and whatever the guise, wherever they meet, the pastor knocks on a door and is almost always welcomed and invited to enter another person's life. There is but one word to describe it: privilege. Mine has been a privileged calling.

But not without its complications and frustrations, chief among them (and the common thread weaving its way throughout these pages): that we gather not just in faith but also for faithfulness, a people of faith gathered in the church of Christ and called to a shared mission, a mission as central to the church as fire is to burning (as Emil Brunner reminds us: no burning, no fire—no mission, no church). If ever (or more accurately, whenever) tensions developed between me and my parishioners, I could find their roots here, in how we differently understood our missional calling. It taught an early lesson: that church work requires the long look, what Old Ben called "perspective," what I came to call a tolerance for ambiguity, what God calls grace, and what normal folks call a sense of humor.

Whether I actually see her or not, whether she is even there or not, my view from the front will momentarily pause at the pew where the First Lady sits. Not that anyone other than me ever graced Ann with the honorary title, but I have always so honored her myself. Until the tension became too much to bear at Los Angeles, she was almost always in her pew on a Sunday. I never asked (because I never wanted to know?) if she would have joined "my" church had she not been favored (saddled?) with her position as First Lady. In the early years, when our children were young, they sat with her, both very well behaved (she saw to that…and they knew it). Our generation of parish clergy was carefully coached on not developing close personal relationships with parishioners or showing favoritism and so once our children's world expanded beyond the Sunday morning pew, their mother sat, if not entirely alone, then suitably distant, as befitted her status, a commentary on her role.

We never know what goes on behind closed doors where families navigate the challenges of daily life, and in that respect, there is nothing unique about the Parsonage Family either, except for the expectations that attach to the members of the family who live there. In my case, it comes with the territory, just part of the job, but unlike most jobs, parish ministry puts the pastor's whole family in a common fishbowl, the scrutiny not generally welcomed and potentially the source of some resentment. Maybe I just project on others feelings I imagine I would feel were the circumstances reversed. Without question, *ours* (not just mine) has been a privileged life, enormously so, but still, it does come with a certain cost.

Perhaps nowhere is this more evident than when controversial, potentially disruptive issues come before the church, the kind that push the congregation's cultural boundaries and at a certain point threaten the financial security of the family. Elsewhere, I have described how the Câmara Conundrum serves as a reminder that carrying the proclamation of Jesus' Gospel to its intended conclusion could render one unemployed. Try keeping its associated stress out of the family dynamics. Disruptions writ large! Even more disruptive, however, is uprooting the family and moving to a new position. Church politics fuels the former, but generally the decision to begin a new ministry in a different location is of a different order altogether.

So much as even entertaining the notion of a new ministry was a big decision for Ann and me, and as with all our decisions big and small, it would begin with lots of conversation and finally resolve itself in a shared conclusion. We may not always agree during the discussion stage or feel quite the same about the results once we get there, but are not the give-and-take decisions and commitments of everyday life and the inevitable compromises along the way the stuff of marriage?

But there is one category of decision-making where that may not be entirely accurate, where we are not just two voices sharing our views on a critically important issue and arriving at a resolution because a third Party hovers over the two of us, an ostensibly holy Presence taking shape as the church. Three voices in a single conversation about the church and my (our?) ministry and what it could look like and where it might take us and, for heaven's sake, why? Three voices, but hardly three *equal* voices, more like two against one, the one that amorphous thing, the church (like a mistress, unreachable, impervious, the other woman none of us is supposed to have). Against *that* voice, how can mere humans compete? We both felt that, but in different ways. For me, at issue was the notion of call, like the call of Abraham (Gen.12.1–4a), but Ann heard the same word and thought first of the humans in her immediate orbit…what about the family, she said, what are *we* asking of them? And later when it was just we two, what about me, your wife, what are *you* asking of me? At times, many times, all the time it just loomed so large over the conversation, three voices, three *unequal* voices.

It looms no more, and in looking back at the key moments when we made our "joint decisions" about that third Party, I have to wonder how many wives would put up with, if not exactly an itinerant and somewhat nomadic life, then at least its inherent disruptions, the next one always possible even if it never comes. Of course, the question could be asked of any clergy couple and family structure in their several and various forms, but I am thinking specifically of wives married to men who are ministers—or to be perfectly blunt, the wife married to me for more than half a century.

At no time was this three-part conversation more demanding, more challenging, and (in retrospect) more perilous than when we were trying to make sense of the dynamics at Royal Oak following the unhappy conclusion to the experiment in multiple-staff ministry. The church was in a sour mood generally, and Ann and I were struggling with what, if anything, the largely invisible undercurrents might portend for our immediate future. Complicating our deliberations was something we called our Pacific Pivot. The idea had started out innocently enough. As originally conceived, Ann and I thought of our Pacific

Pivot as a simple return to California *someday*, maybe when we retired (at the time a good ten years in the future), but as it turned out, quite unexpectedly, our Pivot came much more quickly and would include three components. The first was my term as Moderator of the International Congregational Fellowship (1997-2001) and its invitation to host the 2001 Quadrennial Meeting in Seoul. A delightful and complex story, its telling will come at a later date. Suffice to say here that several planning trips and the meeting itself introduced me to South Korea and its people and provided me a connection to Southeast Asia that seems inordinately strong for having only visited there—call it a feeling of kinship. A pivot to the Pacific, call it, only on the *far* side.

The third component was the fateful decision to accept the interim position at Los Angeles, a move that brought the Pacific Pivot to its original, intended completion on the *near* side. Taken together, we seem to have overshot our original idea of stopping at the Pacific Ocean where it touched California, but the Universe heard it differently (perhaps the Universe has a sense of humor?), for in between these bookend components was the stunningly unexpected second piece, our move to Lahaina, Maui, Hawaii.

At the time, though, the idea of a Pacific Pivot really was nothing more than an idea. Still firmly ensconced in Royal Oak and with no intention of moving anywhere in particular in the immediate future, one of those seemingly random, mostly disconnected events came zooming in from left field. A friend from California who knew of our interest in returning home *someday* let us know that the 2000 General Conference of the United Methodist Church would be held in Cleveland, a short three-hour drive from Detroit, and that the District Superintendents of the California-Pacific Annual Conference of the United Methodist Church would be in attendance. Perhaps we might find time to meet together and get acquainted, she suggested. It seemed a little bizarre, but stranger things have happened, so we jumped in the car and met them for dinner where we talked about the possibility of serving one of their California churches: was the Conference open to someone like me; where might we go; would I (could I) adjust to a Methodist system with Bishops and the like? Little things. The discussion was cordial and everyone was friendly and eventually one of the District Superintendents asked, "Have you thought about Hawaii?"

In a word, no. In fact, not only had I not thought about it, but we had never even visited the island paradise. That the invitation to do so came from the United Methodists made it all the more astounding, but in the fall of 2000, the Universe called my bluff and neither of us ever having visited Hawaii, I stepped off the plane and into a new life as the minister of the Lahaina United Methodist Church. Ann would follow a few weeks later as planned…until suddenly a phone call suggested otherwise.

We had seemingly navigated the three-party conversation that found me in Hawaii, and so I neither expected nor at the time truly appreciated my son's call to tell me his mother was not coming after all. Obviously, this was not a tenable position to take and could I do anything to help. Of course she was tired, exhausted, really; yes, it was a long flight; understandably, she would have some misgivings about the strange world that awaited; the distance from the family was problematical but airplanes and the internet covered some of that and everybody agreed to gather on the distant shore for Christmas. So, one more hurdle and, well, one more hurdle….

But she said she wasn't coming. This time was one time too many. We had a home, we had a life, in Royal Oak. We may have grown up in California but we had lived two-thirds of our married life in the Midwest. We liked it; we liked the people; we were comfortable…it was home—what more needs to be said— and then once again, the third Party intervened.

I do not want to treat the decision to move to Hawaii cavalierly. The fact is we agonized over it for weeks. The denominational shift itself was a major issue. Selling the house, dealing with its contents, and uprooting ourselves had not surprisingly proved emotionally exhausting. We sent an embarrassingly large shipment of stuff ahead of us, held a garage sale for as much of the rest as we could sell or give away, and asked our son to take the leftovers to his home in Chicago until we "figured something out" (twenty years later, we've yet to figure it out).

Even before we left town, some people had warned us about "island fever" (the anxiety of finding yourself on a little speck of land surrounded by a lot of water). Did I hear about the bride who had to cut her honeymoon short because of island fever, one asked? (No, I had not, but thanks for sharing.) We had read the books that described what awaited people from the mainland who moved to the islands, the gist of which was that it's not the mainland. As we would soon discover, the books were right: at times it did feel a little foreign, which apparently explains a favorite tale the locals liked to tell about the occasional American tourist who would walk into the post office to inquire how much it costs to mail a postcard "back to the States?" Nevertheless, foreign or not, when the moment to decide finally arrived, we decided together to take this surprising step.

For all the reasons that made this a joint decision, there was one aspect of the venture that made it a somewhat easier decision for me: I would have a job. For Ann, employment was a tad more nebulous. Possibly the local schools would have music positions…or not ("not" being the case). In the end, she had a lot more to give up than I did and considerably more uncertainty to live with before discerning if we—if *she*—had chosen wisely…no wonder she told our son to call and tell me she was not coming.

I wonder if the same thought had occurred to Sarah, Abraham's wife, upon learning that her husband and a third Party, God, had been talking, the upshot of which was that he was to pack up the family and move to some undisclosed location where he would found a nation. Abraham, of course, would need some help in the form of progeny, presumably with Sarah his wife, although at this point they had no children and at 75 Sarah's participation in addressing the shortfall was questionable. When God finally did inform her that the next generation was coming, Sarah laughed (though whether she laughed at God or with God is open to interpretation). Unfortunately, the text does not otherwise record her thoughts on the new venture. All we know is that in the end, Abraham went as directed and that he took Sarah with him (whether a choice on her part or a matter of expectations—perhaps some of each—also a matter of conjecture).

Not that any of our decisions are ever entirely devoid of expectations, both those imposed by others and those we impose on ourselves, but history does record that the next day Ann got on the plane and flew to Maui, and I trust that all things considered, this was her choice. Concluding otherwise, saying in effect that she flew to Maui "as expected," would imply that I take her for granted, and I take nothing for granted, least of all those closest to me. Surely, aging and those inevitable reminders of our mortality teach us that much, to take nothing for granted, each day and those with whom we share it a gift, so instead I will say it like this: that the next day Ann got on the plane and flew to Maui to continue together the life that we had shared together at that point for more than thirty years. I was grateful then and I remain grateful today, more than two decades later. I am the first to say that ministry is a wonderful calling, but at least in my case, that vocation requires not just a good partner to take the journey as well but a rare partner who will put up with the third Party and the inevitable disruptions that accompany the journey, including the ones that never come to pass.

From Detroit to Maui was a major disruption, and not just because of the distance and the logistics but more especially because of what finally became so inescapably real, the scope of the community and its network of relationships we were leaving behind. Familial and social, personal and professional, social and ecclesiastical, comfortable and predictable...in other words, home: we were leaving home. I don't think we appreciated, could not possibly appreciate, a disruption of that magnitude until, facing a flight the next day, its scope became unavoidably and maybe irrevocably clear. What put it in perfect relief was the somewhat unnatural reversal of things, that even though our children were well established elsewhere, this time it was the parents leaving home for a little speck of land surrounded by a lot of water.

Well, not to belabor the point, but about that impending flight the next day, a not insignificant detail. Ever hovering nearby, the third Party may have an outsize influence on the outcome, but the outcome finally depends on two people saying Yes to what is until that moment only a suggestion, not a command. In that respect, Ann's Yes was always pivotal because it might have been No. Just imagine, she might have said No, but instead she said Yes and got on the plane, and I like to think that I would have done the same in her position. At least, that's what I tell myself. All I know for sure is that she said Yes.

And having said Yes and then having arrived, what did we find? To the casual visitor, like most who come as tourists, Maui and Hawaii generally are nearly synonymous with Paradise. How can it be otherwise? With their natural beauty and their richly textured and exotic culture, the Islands so awaken and so over-whelm all the senses that flaws in the tapestry cease to exist. A Paradise it is.

Live there for awhile, though, and the tapestry's flaws begin to emerge, especially for transplants with white skin. Modern Hawaii is a land of immigrants, some newly arrived and others long-established. Pacific Islander, Japanese, Filipino, Mexican, and Central American peoples arrived in distinct and successive waves to work in the pineapple and sugar cane fields and later the hotel and resort industry. Long before any of them, of course, Polynesian people had settled Hawaii only to have their land stolen in an 1893 coup orchestrated by Western business (read "White") interests and backed by the United States Marines, and ever since, though a minority of the population (about 25% today), to have white skin is to belong to the continuing economic and political power structure, the privileged class.

The currency of the privileged class has little to do with the traditional measures of economic advantage like property, investments, or even money in the bank but rather opportunity. Lots of young people just graduating from college, for example, come to the islands for a year or two on a lark. They might work two or three jobs in the service industry that caters to tourism just to support themselves at a rather primitive level, but eventually most of them return to the mainland and get on with their lives. In their own eyes, they are anything but wealthy monetarily, but they typically have choices and opportunities in the short run and with an education they have a future in the long run. This constitutes "wealth" of another kind, a "currency" well beyond the reach of many an immigrant and native islander alike.

Understandably, native and immigrant populations harbor some resentment toward those who enjoy such privileges. Biblically, the sins of the fathers and mothers, the guilt of the elders, transfers to the beneficiaries for all generations generally (Exodus 20.5, 34.7, et al.) and so here specifically: the 19th century land grab may as well have happened yesterday in the sense that the economic and political power of the elders and its inherent privileges adheres now to the children, the injustice then felt just as keenly today.

That resentment actually surfaced as a form of not-so-subtle reverse discrimination that I experienced soon after arriving on the island. Hawaii requires an annual vehicle inspection that must be satisfactorily completed before receiving a license renewal. Having brought our car with us from Michigan I took it to the nearby service station for its inspection so I could license it in our new home. No big deal, I thought, until I got out of the car. No words were spoken, no words were necessary, but I got the message (later confirmed by my parishioners to whom I relayed my experience) that between my white skin and the imported car (twelve years old at the time, but an obvious signal I intended to stay), I was welcome neither at that station nor on the island. The attendant, native Hawaiian, completed the inspection and I quickly left, never to return, but the encounter taught me to be sensitive to the reaction my presence created, not just among the native Hawaiian population but among the many island residents who stood outside the circle of the wealthy and the privileged, not necessarily hostile toward but clearly separated from those of my class and color. The peoples and cultures comprising the Hawaiian landscape did indeed weave a richly textured tapestry that I miss to this day, but the fabric records historical injustices that must not and, for those who live there, cannot be ignored.

Injustice unaddressed may account for the T-shirt featured in one of the many Lahaina shops catering to tourists. It pictures a man—a *White* man—on a spit being slowly roasted over an open fire. Luaus featuring roasted pig were especially popular with the tourists and the Tongan members of my church frequently, seemingly spontaneously, held *genuine* luaus on the church grounds with full Hawaiian fare and entertainment to which Ann and I were always invited. Anyway, beneath the image of this White man on a spit were these words: *HAOLE*—the Other White Meat. "Haole" is the Hawaiian word for any non-Polynesian, or foreigner, with special emphasis on Caucasians. One of my lingering regrets is that I never purchased such a social commentary, so succinctly stated.

Haole or not, one ever-lingering interest I looked forward to exploring in Hawaii was its ethnic and cultural melting pot. If a people could be found someplace in the world, we would find them in Hawaii, I reasoned. It followed, I decided, that if they could exist side by side in relative peace on the island outposts, there might be hope for the rest of the world. This first test, getting the car inspected, was not terribly encouraging...but then that test was not to claim the last word on the subject as the Lahaina church, a microcosm of the surrounding village, would one day demonstrate.

As for that microcosm, the church began as the Lahaina Methodist Mission in 1896, the mission focusing on the workers and families employed by the sugar and pineapple industries. The congregation was mostly Japanese in those early days with a Sunday school, a Japanese Language School, and English Classes. Its ministers were Japanese until the 1939 appointment of the first English-speaking minister, although Japanese services continued for the first-generation Japanese.

In 1924, a Filipino congregation was established as the Mala Village Camp, later renamed the Filipino Methodist Church; it merged with the Lahaina Methodist Church in 1958. The Methodist Church and the United Brethren Church themselves merged in 1968 to create the United Methodist Church.

With deep Japanese and Filipino roots, LUMC had begun to develop a Tongan congregation as well near the end of the last century. Tonga, officially the Kingdom of Tonga, is a Polynesian nation of some 170 South Pacific islands, 36 of which are inhabited; in 2020, its population was about 106,000. Like their Japanese and Filipino predecessors, Tongan immigrants had come to the Hawaiian Islands to work in the sugar and pineapple industries and, as sugarcane and pineapple production itself migrated to countries where labor costing $100 on Maui could be found for as little as $5, Tongans began working in the resorts and tourist support services generally.

By the time I arrived in Lahaina, the church was numerically divided between what were essentially two congregations, one Tongan and the other English (that is, English-speaking, culturally Western peoples of European and Asian heritage). Claiming the entire Sunday school and the larger share of the total worship attendance, the Tongans were actually the stronger of the two numerically, but the English congregation had the much longer tenure and provided most of the financial support and so predictably, its members exercised a disproportionate share of power that might otherwise have been more equitably distributed across the entire membership were the church working together as a single body. Officially, both were members of the single Lahaina United Methodist Church, but between language and the tendency of any immigrant population to seek both refuge and safety in the comfort of its familiar culture, in practice the Tongan congregation was *functionally* (and nearly structurally) independent, essentially tenants in another congregation's building.

The English congregation reflected the island's diversity in peoples and cultures and included second-, third-, and later-generation Japanese and Filipino members, relatively newcomer Caucasians (mostly retired plus a smattering of professional people), and a few other Polynesian peoples (Samoan, Hawaiian, Maori, and Marshallese). It was an interesting assembly that greeted me on a Sunday morning, and I enjoyed it and them immensely.

In addition, the English congregation included another category of "member," one that significantly changed the dynamics of the worship services: tourist. In fact, at times, we actually thought of LUMC as three congregations, Tongan, English, and tourist. In the second half of the last century, and manifestly by its end, Maui had become a tourist destination and West Maui especially had the look and feel of a resort community. Tourists did not come to worship services in large numbers, but I was surprised to find that tourists came at all! Ann and I have returned to Lahaina as tourists ourselves and we managed very nicely to enjoy a leisurely Sunday morning that did not include three hymns and a sermon. Our own decadence notwithstanding, almost every week I gladly welcomed visitors from the mainland, and not infrequently we were an international body as well and, truth be told, our attendance numbers would have looked pretty dismal without them.

Technically speaking, I was only "on loan" to the Annual Conference, appointed by the Bishop and subject to the denomination's Book of Discipline but not recognized as an ordained United Methodist pastor with standing in the denomination. I was also not the first choice for the post. Two other proper Methodists had been flown from the mainland to Lahaina to look around and upon their return home, both had come up with good reasons why they could not accept the offer. The Bishop and District Superintendent were not about to waste their funds on Ann and me, a most improper Methodist, and I went anyway. What that says about both sides of the equation, wayward Congregationalist and the ecclesiastical keepers of the Methodist kingdom on distant Maui, I leave to the psychoanalysts. The more interesting question, though, is had we visited, would we have followed suit, crafting a perfectly acceptable rationale for turning down the invitation? How often have I asked myself that very question.

My assignment (clearly expressed to me but not to the congregation at large) was to reestablish LUMC as a church, the assumption being that the church had wandered off course by becoming another stop on the entertainment circuit (the focus, accordingly, falling on the so-called *third*—that is to say, the tourist—congregation). It should be noted that scarcely any of the resident members of the English church voiced any discontent with the state of the church and its practices prior to my arrival. Quite the contrary, they would have taken great exception to hearing their church described as an artifact for the tourist trade, its institutional health bearing the marks of considerable neglect, its people needing to…change.

Well, the die cast, the assignment in place for the one United Methodist Church in Lahaina, its two constituencies existing in essentially parallel universes, the question was how to proceed. For starters, my oft-cited Pauline text (Gal. 3.28) firmly in mind, I took the "one-church" designation seriously and tried to build bridges where and as I could.

The fact is, I thoroughly enjoyed the Tongan people. With my complete lack of Tongan and a rudimentary but passable English scattered among just a few of their leaders, we could scarcely communicate at all with each other, but occasionally, I would slip into the back of the church on a Sunday evening to extend to them the courtesy and respect of the English congregation, if not their titular pastor, and to listen to their singing, a captivating six-part harmony that offered a foretaste of worlds to come. Not that they only sang in the church and on a Sunday evening, for they gathered during the week as a community and whenever their community gathered, they sang, not infrequently for hours on end and late into the night (to the chagrin of neighbors trying to sleep). Theirs was a basic evangelical faith that found expression in the old Gospel songs they had learned from the Methodist missionaries. Largely foreign to my upbringing and training, I must still say that my heart was warmed as I sat in the back of a Pacific Island, plantation-style church, the spirit of John Wesley hovering nearby, and sang the Gospel songs anyway, me in English, my people in Tongan.

The one-church designation, English *and* Tongan together in a common enterprise, suggested another goal, equal representation in the church's governing structure. In the Methodist system, the pastor chairs the Nominating Committee which meant that finding people to serve on the church's various committees was my responsibility. Since acculturation is a huge challenge for an immigrant people and since churches have overcome cultural barriers through their oneness in Christ (Gal. 3.28…again), a 50-50 balance between the two groupings of members provided a ready-made, obvious avenue to a greater end.

Or not. The project made some of the English people irate: they (the Tongans) are taking over…do I want this to be a Tongan church, they ask. (Déjà vu all over again.) The fact of the matter was that *numerically*, it already was a Tongan church. That most of the income and so all the expenditures were in the hands of the English was merely a technicality, but it was sufficient to carry the day and so the experiment in balanced leadership never materialized.

At best, the experiment was premature, our respective English and Tongan worlds were just too different to meld into a shared undertaking, but then in seemingly random moments, glimmers of light. One day, Ann and I were swimming at a beach frequented mostly by locals. Given its location across the highway from the Post Office, the locals called it Post Office Beach. I was approaching the beach on the return leg of a long swim when I noticed a line from a fishing pole in the water just ahead. It was not in my way and posed no threat but my course would disturb the calm waters and scare away any nearby fish, reducing the fisherman's chance of catching something. Not wanting to interfere with his late afternoon enjoyment of the beach, not to mention his Catch of the Day, I altered my course and swam outside his line, allowing enough space so as not to disturb the immediate area.

It was really a small gesture on my part. It extended my swim by a small amount but posed no hardship and I did not give it a second thought...until I got out of the water and the fisherman came to shake my hand and thank me. A *true* local and a Filipino, he had made a point of leaving his fishing spot, climbing over some rocks, and walking a short way down the beach to thank *me*, a haole, for what to me was a common courtesy. His was a sacrifice, not just because of the effort it took to meet me but because the color of my skin placed me squarely among the privileged and within the power structure, an intruder in sacred space where I had not been invited and was not particularly welcome.

We chatted for a moment and he returned to his fishing and Ann and I returned to our spacious parsonage, how different the universes we inhabited. But the experience obviously left its mark on me, and it drove home the point that we begin to address our differences by acknowledging one another and the simple truth of our existence, human beings in shared space on the planet we each call home. A simple gesture on my part (not even a gesture, just common courtesy—in other words, no gold star for me) and he returns the favor and for one brief moment a Filipino fisherman and a haole swimmer were just two guys on a beach in Maui.

Two guys on a beach in Maui....

What about two peoples in a church on Maui? Two very different peoples, Tongans and English, but also brothers and sisters on a common journey following the Way of the Christ? How different? The Methodists from Honolulu must have wrestled with the same question because an English member of the Oahu church commented on the lack of Tongan participation in the life and work of their shared congregation, and a Tongan member responded. Focusing on cultural differences between the two peoples, he pointed out:

- You are future-oriented; we are present-oriented.
- You are time-conscious; we lack time consciousness, as we do things when we feel like doing it.
- You emphasize self-actualization; we emphasize sharing and generosity.
- You emphasize competition; we emphasize cooperation.
- You put great importance on youth; we give respect to the aged.
- You are open with your thoughts and feelings; we are not, we are shy.
- You are sometimes aggressive; we are sometimes submissive.
- You emphasize the thinking process; we emphasize the feeling process.

We and you…us and them. Two peoples, brothers and sisters, on a shared journey following in the Way of the Christ…who have little, if anything, to do with each other. Not exactly like two guys on a beach in Maui.

And then one day a large grant unexpectedly landed on my desk.

It came with no conditions or expectations and it did not take me long to draw up a list of options which the grant might fund. Worthy and necessary, but not particularly inspiring, I hoped we could get a little shot in the arm while avoiding the ecclesiastical version of a family squabbling over the inheritance. I assembled our Administrative Council to make some decisions, and still thinking of the English and Tongan congregations as a single church, I invited the Tongan leadership to join us and they responded with four of their key leaders.

Interestingly enough, the Tongan leaders did not want to talk about building needs or even program development and related projects but about their children. Even more, they wanted to talk about their place in the church, a perilous subject that took great courage on their part even to raise because it was fraught with much misunderstanding and miscommunication and because they knew that their place took a back seat to the English. I had asked them and they willingly agreed to participate twice monthly in the English service. Their beautiful harmonies added immeasurably to the service though I feared that visitors might see them more as a Polynesian curiosity than worship leaders, a subtle form of, if not racism, then certainly cultural imperialism (which amounts to the same thing). Their gift notwithstanding, and members for a decade, they may as well have been an outside group renting space all those years for all the difference it made.

They persisted, however, and along the way one of the Tongan members said that their children were already losing the Tongan language. Even more alarming, simply by virtue of attending the public schools, the traditional locus of assimilation of immigrant populations into the dominant American culture (a foreign and dangerous culture from the Pacific Island viewpoint), the next generation was slipping away from traditional Tongan family and community structures. Key problems they named included boredom and anger (itself born of feelings of powerlessness and hopelessness) leading in turn to such destructive behaviors as drug and alcohol abuse. For the faithful, with public schools increasingly secularized, the church assumed a pivotal role in the enculturation of new populations, especially as in this case, with the first generation of American born.

A familiar pattern with immigrant peoples, but what to do? Interestingly enough, as the Tongans voiced their story, the English story began to fade into the background, away from the lackluster (even if necessary) building projects and program initiatives, in favor of Tongan concerns. Some later described the meeting as a "historic" shift in the church's axis so that it faced in a new and different direction; maybe not for the first time, but at least this time, the English and Tongan congregations had actually seen one another.

The upshot was that we put most of the grant into staff and program and hired a Tongan woman to serve as Associate Pastor of the church. She would have primary responsibility for youth and youth outreach to Tongan and other Pacific Island people in the vicinity of the church but in addition, her very presence would help address the gap between Polynesian and Western cultures. At that time, she was only the second Tongan woman pastor with a full undergraduate and seminary education in the California-Pacific Annual Conference.

This was all rather remarkable. Upon arriving, I had found a largely dysfunctional, rudderless church plagued by organizational chaos, rent by divided loyalties (Paul's Corinthians had nothing on Lahaina, 1 Cor. 1.10-17), and beset with financial instability. At least with the English side of the church (and island life generally perhaps), a feeling of impermanence always hovered nearby. Even among those who had lived on the island for years, jobs, medical concerns, and family considerations often required people to return to the mainland or move to other islands. The effects of age and attrition were only too apparent given the handful of faithful souls who kept things going. True, the resort community provided a steady number of visitors, which helped bolster Sunday attendance figures, but visitors do not share in conversations and decisions about mission and purpose or participate in a church's ministries and so cannot be expected to bring or add stability to the ongoing life of the *established* congregation.

But in a very short time we had raised the question of a mission pertinent to the island setting and had made significant progress in shared worship and increased levels of interaction and cooperation between the English-speaking and Tongan congregations. In effect, we had provided the groundwork out of which would spring a very significant conversation once the grant appeared and its use was directed to support cross-cultural staffing. Funding would prove to be a formidable barrier in the successful execution of this experiment long-term, but there in our little corner of the vineyard in Lahaina, a handful of United Methodist wayfarers from two very different cultural contexts actually joined hands and took the leap into a very different future.

Two peoples in a church on Maui...two very different peoples, Tongans and English, but also brothers and sisters on a common journey following the Way of the Christ. Two peoples...one church.

Having said so much about the Maui sojourn—and having left so much more on the cutting room floor—I find it mildly curious that I have yet to say much at all about the spirituality of the islands. Curious indeed, since I had long anticipated exploring whether and how Eastern and Western philosophical foundations and religious traditions might draw from and so benefit each other. I cannot say I made much progress on that question, neither at the time nor in the years since, but I have little doubt that in advancing civilization in the course of the 21st century, perhaps even saving civilization in the face of climate change, Eastern and Western spirituality will need to become conversant with each other.

How we even begin to have that conversation may require a reassessment of the labels we use to identify who needs to talk with whom, as if East and West are themselves the significant and presumably monolithic entities around which whole continents and Polynesian and Pacific Island perspectives in the Southern Hemisphere will find their respective places around that table.

What I will continue to call for convenience sake the East-West conversation will be a terrifically high mountain to climb. Quite inadvertently, a visitor cast light on why I look back on this period as not particularly productive as far as that exchange is concerned…because it takes hard work!

I routinely included what I called thought-pieces at the top of the Sunday bulletin. These were short, one- or two-sentence insights from notable thinkers that (to me) helped focus the worshiping congregation on the day's overall theme. On this particular Sunday, Alfred North Whitehead was featured, and after the service, the visitor introduced herself as a student working on a PhD at Claremont; her subject: Alfred North Whitehead. Her comment: "I didn't expect to find Whitehead 'out here'" (my emphasis).

"Out here"—as if a mismatch clearly existed between the tools (Whitehead and process thought) and their geographical implementation—but why not out here? Too primitive? (Insult duly noted.) Or too soon, that is, not that the sensual, sun-loving island folks are incapable of grasping Whitehead, but has anyone prepared the soil? As I have come to learn in more recent years, Whitehead's process thought has found far more fertile soil "over there," in the East (in China, specifically), than "back there," in the West (thinking of my comfortable middle-class, very Western, suburban congregations where his process thought informed my sermons for years).

In other words, why not expect to find Whitehead "out here," but as Paul said of the Gospel, how will they hear without a preacher to till the soil (Rom. 10.14)?

And just what will the preacher face "out here," as well as "back there," if not just everywhere? Quite inadvertently, another visitor brought the point home one day with a knock on the parsonage door.

My visitor spoke poor English, but I eventually grasped that he wanted me to come to the back of his car, parked in the driveway, and bless the several plastic containers of water he had gathered from someplace or another. His daughter was ill, he said, and as the Holy One, I could surely transform what was merely tap water into a life-giving, healing spring, Yes? Imagine my awkwardness, in his eyes the local shaman, staring into the truck of his car, blessing the water he expected to deliver his daughter of her serious illness. This at the dawn of the 21st century! He came back a second time (new water calling for more prayer), but not a third. Perhaps his daughter recovered, the healing spring having done its job...or not, hers a sickness unto death, impervious to waters of any kind, the shaman a mere mortal with feet of clay and a faith to match.

On the one hand, I was on solid ground. After all, Jesus turned water into wine (John 2.1–12) and hinted his followers would do that and more (John 14.12). On the other hand, doing as Jesus did in the real world and actually quieting life's storms, healing the sick, and otherwise administering the transformative power of Love, greater than the power of wind and tide (quoting yet again Teilhard de Chardin), has from the beginning plagued hapless disciples (Matt. 14.31 and, distressingly, elsewhere).

I wonder what he actually expected—that I would perhaps (naturally?) change the chemistry of the water or otherwise infuse it with healing powers (echoes of John 5.2–9a, although Jesus bypasses the water and heals the paralytic verbally)? I have laid hands on and prayed for the healing of countless parishioners in hospitals, nursing homes, and living rooms over the years, but in that setting, we understood healing less miraculously—less, that is, as pick-up-your-bed-and-walk (John 5.8), which is rather more the exception than the rule—and more holistically, where mind, body, and spirit together find their fullness and completeness in relation to God.

With our language barrier, explaining such a theological construct to my visitor was simply not possible, leaving each of us in very different universes, but as I thought about my universe, I realized that our separate worlds did not reduce to language alone. I call myself a Christocentric, process oriented, Christian universalist; at that particular moment, I was living in a Polynesian world and serving a Protestant church in the Reformed (read: Western) tradition; my Liberal Arts education and religious upbringing favored the head over the heart and an appreciation for good literature and the broad smorgasbord of ideas that have used me; I felt comfortable navigating where the Bible led and what science said; these were my tools, but in that environment, were they up to the job, in this case, responding to the request to turn bottles of water into a healing spring for the benefit of a sick child and her parents?

More generally, of course, we might wonder if, outside of the particular environment from which they have sprung, our tools are up to the job no matter where we find ourselves geographically, whether on a Pacific Island, in suburban Royal Oak, or (these days) beside the California version of the Pacific coast. Ideas and the systems by which we organize our thinking, the language with which we express them: borrowing again from Walker Percy, do they signify anything; does their communication build bridges of understanding between people and communities; or are we just locked within our own little worlds, our truth—our reality?

Our stay on Maui was a scant two years. I cannot say that a particular issue or major problem drove the decision, more like a confluence of several lesser concerns coming together at about the same time that together caused us to question a long-term commitment to the Island. I would feel an occasional twinge of island fever, nothing debilitating but still lurking in the shadows, and the 9/11 terrorist attack brought home the personal matter of just how far away from home we really were. We had visited all the islands by that time and had Maui had more the feel of the Big Island (Hawaii) we might have felt differently about a longer tenure. Having been such ourselves from time to time, we had no issue with the tourists, and as I mentioned they made a big difference in our Sunday attendance and the general ambiance of the sanctuary, but because it was concentrated in such a small area, we did grow weary of the resort atmosphere after awhile. Not insignificant but in and of themselves, certainly these constituted lesser concerns.

More significant was the church's pivot point. We did add a Tongan pastor to the staff and not only was she doing very good work but as far as the church was concerned, she had most of the work to do. I surveyed the situation and came to the one conclusion available: that whether the church had gotten off track, focusing on tourism at the expense of the community, was a debate never to be settled in the present day, but my assignment was to take what we might call a "different approach," and so I had.

Instinctively, the culmination of my theological conviction and decades of experience working in culturally diverse communities, I focused on the neighborhood and the people who lived there generally, the immigrant and first-generation Tongan community specifically. That community needed trained, indigenous leadership...which just happened to be on site. Between the surprise gift of the grant and the meeting where English and Tongan together committed a major portion of the grant to salary support for Tongan leadership, had not God and the people of God, Creator and co-creator, come together. With the grant support about to run out, was it not rather obvious what the Bishop needed to do...and so what I needed to do? With neither the need for nor sufficient funding to support two ministers at the Lahaina church, why would the Bishop not recognize the priority of the Tongans given their numbers and the challenges facing an immigrant people and its succeeding generations for well-trained, Tongan spiritual leadership?

Unfortunately, but predictably, appointing the Associate Pastor as Pastor of the church did not occur. Perhaps it was just a step too far, creating what certainly would have become a Tongan congregation in the midst of a resort environment. No one asked for my opinion on the subject, so this is only my conjecture, but as it turned out, the English congregation retained leadership and control, my successor would be Filipino, and when the Associate's position ran out of funds, she was moved to another island.

About the same time, I received a phone call from my District Superintendent in which she informed me that I had become her problem. Specifically, given my assessment of the situation at Lahaina and (in my view) the positive developments in Tongan pastoral leadership, I had requested a new appointment whereupon I was informed that my appointment to Lahaina was for Lahaina only and that there was none other in the offing. This was surprising, indeed, because it contradicted assurances given to us at the start that the Conference needed pastoral leadership for this church now and if after two years we wanted a change, the Conference would gladly move us back to the mainland. Nothing in writing, just assurances. Now, two years later, I could go through the process of having my ordination recognized by the Conference or I could stay at Lahaina, those were my two choices.

I chose option three: completing the Pacific Pivot.

CHAPTER 10

EPILOGUE:
A PENULTIMATE WORD

"Finally, beloved…."

~APOSTLE PAUL
to the Church at Philippi

MY GENERATION IS NOW ENGAGED in that time-driven, if not
time-honored, practice of passing the mantle of responsibility to a new generation. Such is the journey of life in this world: in each generation, the children
grow up and take their place and eventually they take over their elders' place
as well. So be it. There is freedom in setting aside the daily routine and its tasks
and concerns both mundane and momentous that have consumed one's time
and attention decade after decade, but that does not necessarily mean we no
longer engage with the questions that now fall to others to answer. In my case,
of course, that includes the question of the church and where it goes from here.
That there will be a church in the near and distant future I have no doubt, but
what will it look like—or more to the point, in the near and distant future, what
shape will its disciples give to the beloved community entrusted to their care?

Of course, merely asking the question almost brings to mind a plethora of
answers and with them the suggestion of what just might be a lingering curse,
the desire to be of use, to have an outsized sense of purpose when diminished
duties and responsibilities no longer require such. Still, before fully exiting
the stage, what about any enduring words, parting thoughts, looming intimations of ultimate truths? At journey's end, do we not look back and take stock

of our record, those countless decisions good and bad, judgments right and wrong, and moments glorious and otherwise? Think of the lessons learned, the wisdom gained, the gems yet to share with the next generation!

Or not. For one thing, good, bad, and indifferent, the record will one day speak for itself, its wisdom rising to the top like cream (should the fickle judgment of history find any). Besides, for some peculiar reason, wisdom does not easily (if ever) transfer from person to person, much less generation to generation. Humankind had to invent the wheel but once, but each generation seemingly needs to learn anew how best to use that technological marvel. Don't-do-as-I-did might be excellent advice, but often we take it to heart only when, having fumbled the ball ourselves, it then becomes…well, a "lesson learned," so I resolve to resist these temptations and let the record speak for itself, and conclude this saga with a simple affirmation and a penultimate word.

Not that any of us gets a rerun in this life, but when the time comes to look back, we cannot help but ponder the question; if given the chance, would we do the same thing again? At the time of his retirement, I asked my good friend and mentor Ben if he would do it again—would he take up the life of pastoral ministry if he had it to do over? He answered to the effect that he would if he could do it during a time that resembled the time he was now wrapping up, and nearly four decades later I ask myself the same question and come to much the same conclusion.

The church takes many forms, and I would be the last to pretend that the Mainline Protestant version was the quintessential embodiment of the Jesus Movement, but front and center in American culture for much of the 20th century and to a lesser extent even into the 21st century, this was the church of my childhood and youth, the church I served for more than 50 years, the church I loved, and now the church for which I grieve. This is not to say it no longer exists anywhere, but most everywhere it is either greatly diminished, a mere image of its former self, or gone altogether. One of my last decisions in the ministry was to lead the remaining handful of members of the First Christian Church (Disciples of Christ) of Morro Bay in closing their beloved church—it broke everyone's heart, including mine, not least because for me it marked the end of that era and my church, but given a chance to serve such a church again?

Yes, I would.

Of course, nothing stops the onward march of the Jesus Movement taking shape in any number of expressions called church. Already we see the emerging church beginning to dot the landscape, sign and seal of the New Reformation clearly underway, a new generation of lay and professional leaders giving it birth. I think of you, the people who will embody the Jesus Movement as this century and its horrific challenges unfold. I feel envy of you, lament for you, and also feel a measure of remorse for me for not having done better by you. But then you may as well remember that you are called, and so you might as well get to work, for really, what choice do you have?

And when the journey brings you to the point where you prepare to pass the mantle to your successors, you will perhaps register the same curious blend of wonder and relief that I feel—wonder that comes with the summons even to have begun the race, and relief that from some deep inner well you found the resources to finish—a further hint, perhaps, of the gracious and generous Love propelling the Universe to its intended fulfillment. I marvel at the challenges Ann and I readily accepted and the hurdles thrust in the path along the way. We enjoyed incredibly good fortune in the journey overall and good people generally with whom to live and work, and underpinning and sustaining my work and our lives were three foundational gifts. Two have primary reference to my vocation: a strong and continuing belief in my calling to do this work and good theology to give it shape. The third is more encompassing: my good lady and our family.

Along the Way, a penultimate word, the simple prescription Paul offered to the Philippians:

> Finally, beloved, whatever is true, whatever is honorable, whatever is just, whatever is pure, whatever is pleasing, whatever is commendable, if there is any excellence and if there is anything worthy of praise, think about these things...and the God of peace will be with you.

In other words, just the basics: truth, goodness, honor; that which is worthy of human being; that which brings beauty to human experience; food for thought, that in turn feeds the thoughts that shape who and what we become and, perhaps, what becomes of the world.

May the God of peace be with you.

To which the heavenly court said, Amen.

ABOUT THE AUTHOR

Though born in South Dakota, Dr. Richard (Rich) Kurrasch's time spent in Los Angeles during the '50s and '60s were among the most formative of his life. In 1971, he and wife Ann Marie relocated to the Nebraska Panhandle to begin serving their first church. Over the next fifty years, their journey included pastorates in California and the Upper Midwest, with an unexpected detour to Maui.

Kurrasch holds a Bachelor of Arts from the University of California at Riverside, a Master of Divinity from Bethany Theological Seminary, Richmond, Indiana, and a Doctor of Ministry from the School of Theology at Claremont, California.

He has always placed great importance on the role of the church in building cross-cultural relationships and so especially enjoyed a four-year term as Moderator of the International Congregational Fellowship that ended with a quadrennial meeting in Seoul, South Korea. Since retiring and moving to the Central Coast of California, Kurrasch has been a member of the Board of Directors of People of Faith for Justice, an interfaith voice for social and environmental justice and an advocate for Ecological Civilization in the San Luis Obispo area.

Rich and Ann Marie are outdoor enthusiasts and have traveled and camped throughout much of the United States. The time on Maui revived his interest in surfing although in recent years, the cold Pacific has given way to kayaking on the quieter waters of a nearby lake. They both continue to enjoy creative outlets: Ann Marie in music, and Rich in writing. His website is www.RichardRKurrasch.com. They have two children and two grandchildren.

www.ingramcontent.com/pod-product-compliance
Lightning Source LLC
LaVergne TN
LVHW011321080426
835513LV00006B/152